Latin American Economic Outlook 2012

TRANSFORMING THE STATE FOR DEVELOPMENT

OECD
UNITED NATIONS
ECLAC

This work is published on the responsibility of the Secretary-General of the OECD. The opinions expressed and arguments employed in this publication do not necessarily reflect those of the OECD, its Development Centre or of the governments of their member countries or those of the United Nations Economic Commission for Latin America and the Caribbean (UN-ECLAC).

This document and any map included herein are without prejudice to the status of or sovereignty over any territory, to the delimitation of international frontiers and boundaries and to the name of any territory, city or area.

Please cite this publication as:
OECD/ECLAC (2011), *Latin American Economic Outlook 2012: Transforming the State for Development*, OECD Publishing.
http://dx.doi.org/10.1787/leo-2012-en

ISBN 978-92-64-12170-6 (print)
ISBN 978-92-64-12171-3 (PDF)

Annual: Latin American Economic Outlook
ISSN 2072-5159 (print)
ISSN 2072-5140 (online)

ECLAC Reference Number: LC/G.2501

Preface

The current international context of Latin America and the Caribbean opens a window of opportunity that countries in the region should use to design long-term development strategies. In addition to the gradual consolidation and strengthening of its democratic systems, most of the region has withstood the economic and financial crisis well, in great part thanks to the responsible macroeconomic management over the last years.

The state can and must play a fundamental role in building on these advantages and in confronting the many challenges that still remain, in particular with regard to improving the quality of life and reducing poverty and inequality. This can be achieved by: creating good-quality jobs; consolidating fiscal systems that are solid, transparent and fair; investing in education and training; increasing the efficiency of infrastructure investment; and supporting innovation and productive development.

This publication is the product of a joint effort by the Development Centre of the Organisation for Economic Co-operation and Development (OECD) and the Economic Commission for Latin America and the Caribbean (ECLAC), undertaken in order to analyse the role of the state in the economic growth and development of Latin American and Caribbean countries. We ask: What should be the main elements of the reform of the state in Latin America and the Caribbean? What lessons can be drawn from previous reform efforts in the region and beyond?

The main message of our work is that the social policies of the last years alone are not enough to create more equitable and inclusive societies. The state must strengthen the quality and effectiveness of fiscal and monetary policy, as well as actively promote education, investment and productive development.

Latin American Economic Outlook 2012 tackles these questions in light of best practices in public policy both within Latin America the Caribbean and outside the region. We hope these insights will contribute to the efforts of Heads of State and Government at the 21st Ibero-American Summit in Asunción in strengthening the capacity of states to promote economic development that improves the opportunities and the quality of life of the region's citizens.

Alicia Bárcena
Executive Secretary
Economic Commission for
Latin America and the Caribbean
(ECLAC)

Angel Gurría
Secretary-General
Organisation for Economic
Co-operation and Development
(OECD)

Acknowledgements

This publication was jointly elaborated by the Economic Commission for Latin America and the Caribbean (ECLAC) and the Development Centre of the Organisation for Economic Co-operation and Development (OECD).

On the side of the OECD Development Centre, Rolando Avendaño, Alberto Amurgo Pacheco, Nallely Carro, Bárbara Castelletti, Christian Daude, Jeff Dayton-Johnson, Ana González, Hamlet Gutiérrez, Anna Jankowska, Ángel Melguizo, Sebastián Nieto Parra, José Ramón Perea, Anna Pietikäinen, Annalisa Primi and Annalisa Prizzon contributed to the drafting and revision of the report. Hugo Ñopo, of the Inter-American Development Bank, and Eduardo Bitrán, a lecturer at Adolfo Ibáñez University, contributed to the preparation of the Education and Infrastructure chapters, respectively. Eduardo Levy Yeyati, a professor at Torcuato Di Tella University, contributed with the box on capital controls in the Macroeconomic Overview chapter.

This team was led by Jeff Dayton-Johnson and Christian Daude. The authors would like to thank Mario Pezzini, Director of the Development Centre, and Carlos Álvarez, Deputy Director of the Centre, for their input and direction. The Development Centre particularly recognises the contribution made by Mario Marcel, Deputy Director, and by Stéphane Jacobzone, Counsellor for the Reform of the Public Sector, of the Directorate of Public Governance and Territorial Development, to the Public Administration chapter.

The team would like to extend its sincere thanks to colleagues in other OECD departments for their valuable comments to different versions of the report, in particular the Centre for Tax Policy and Administration; the Directorate for Education; the Directorate for Employment, Labour and Social Affairs; the Economics Department; the Statistics Directorate; the Public Governance and Territorial Development Directorate; and the Office of the Secretary-General. With regard to the production of the report, we would like to acknowledge the support of the Development Centre's Publications and New Media team, the OECD's Public Affairs and Communications Directorate, and the team of translators and proofreaders who worked with us on this edition of LEO.

The OECD Development Centre is particularly grateful to the Spanish and Chilean finance and foreign affairs ministries, the Swiss Agency for Development and Co-operation, Endesa, and BBVA Pensiones y Seguros for their continued financial support to *Latin American Economic Outlook*.

Finally, we would like to thank the Latin American and Caribbean member countries of the Development Centre: Argentina, Brazil, Chile, Colombia, Costa Rica, the Dominican Republic, Mexico and Peru.

For the Economic Commission for Latin American and the Caribbean, the following staff members were responsible for drafting and editing the text: Elisa Calza, María Victoria Espada, Juan Pablo Jiménez, Andrea Laplane, Isabel López, Ricardo Martner, Wilson Péres, Fernando Rojas and Sebastián Rovira.

The ECLAC team was co-ordinated by Sebastián Rovira, the Economic Affairs Officer of the Division of Production, Productivity and Management (DDPM), under the guidance of Mario Cimoli, Director of the DDPM. In addition, we would like to thank staff in the Division for Economic Development, the Division for Social Development (Daniela Trucco) and the Division for Natural Resources and Infrastructure (Gabriel Pérez, Daniel Perrotti, Ricardo J. Sánchez and Gordon Wilmsmeir), as well as staff at the Institute for Economic and Social Planning (ILPES), for their collaboration and contributions.

Finally, we would like to thank ECLAC's Documents and Publications Division for its invaluable work in copy-editing and typesetting the chapters that make up *Latin American Economic Outlook 2012*.

Table of contents

Boxes

Tables

Figures

Diagrams

Acronyms and abbreviations

BNDES	Brazilian Development Bank
CIAT	Inter-American Center of Tax Administration
COMTRADE	United Nations Commodity Trade Statistics Database
EAP	Economically Active Population
ECLAC	Economic Commission for Latin America
FDI	Foreign Direct Investment
IDB	Inter-American Development Bank
IMF	International Monetary Fund
IT	Information Technology
ILPES	Latin-American and Caribbean Institute of Economic and Social Planning
GDP	Gross Domestic Product
NPM	New Public Management
OECD	Organisation for Economic Co-operation and Development
PISA	Programme for International Student Assessment
R+D	Research and development
RICYT	Ibero-American and Inter-American Network of Sciences and Technology Index
SEBIG	Ibero-American General Secretariat
UNESCO	United Nations Educational, Scientific and Cultural Organization
VAT	Value Added Tax

Executive summary

Latin America's solid economic performance since 2003 has created the opportunity for transforming the state, enabling the adoption of ambitious public policies that lock in the prospect of long-term development and mitigate short-term risks. Despite important differences in current economic conditions within the region —with South America outperforming Central America, Mexico and the Caribbean— strong external demand (especially from emerging economies like China), in combination with vigorous internal demand, resulted in an average annual GDP growth rate of almost 5% during 2003-08.[1] Part of this performance was also due to good macroeconomic management that created sufficient fiscal space to manage the effects of the global financial crisis without jeopardising fiscal sustainability (Figure 0.1). Between 2000 and 2007, public debt in the region shrank on average by 15 percentage points of GDP, while fiscal balances moved from an overall deficit of 2.4% of GDP to a surplus of 0.4% of GDP. Macroeconomic policies and higher primary export prices strengthened macroeconomic stability and provided resources for implementing anti-poverty programmes and increasing access to basic public services. This led to less pronounced recessions and swift recoveries compared to OECD economies. While real GDP growth in the advanced economies is expected to remain sluggish, Latin America is expected to grow 4.4% in 2011 and 4% in 2012.[2] In this context, Latin American countries have the opportunity to design and implement public policies with long-term development goals and also reduce some medium and short-term risks.

The region should strengthen its macroeconomic policy space to guard against uncertainties in the global economic outlook and volatility in international capital markets. The global economy continues to be the main source of uncertainty for Latin America and the Caribbean. Large capital inflows, due to significant interest rate differentials between the region and the developed economies, and the subsequent exchange rate and inflationary pressures were defining features of the first semester of 2011 and still deserve special attention. Fiscal problems in the euro zone could have serious repercussions in international financial markets, including emerging markets, where capital flow reversals could trigger large swings in the real exchange rate with disruptive effects on economic activity. The region's trade with China —which more than tripled during the 2000s— was one of the factors that facilitated the region's quick recovery. Nevertheless, today this makes the region more exposed to a potential growth slowdown in China, which would affect the region through lower export demand and commodity prices. Both would have a strong impact on fiscal accounts in many countries of the region. As a result of significant national fiscal and monetary stimuli, several countries are currently in an expansionary phase of the business cycle, in which a countercyclical fiscal policy helps strengthen the response capacity and mitigates against the risks associated with a reversal in the business cycle. Instruments such as stabilisation funds and credible fiscal rules (sufficiently flexible to adapt to extraordinary economic circumstances) can be effective tools for rebuilding fiscal space.

Figure 0.1. Latin American economies won fiscal space, which they used to confront the financial crisis and reduce poverty, but they are still vulnerable to further shocks
(Variation in percentage points of GDP)

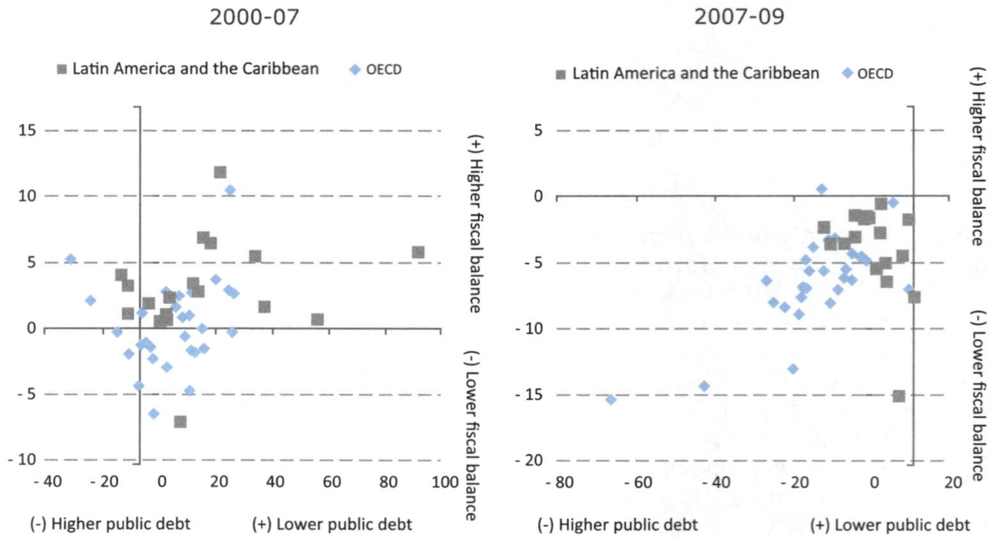

Note: each point represents one country. The panels include OECD countries and 19 countries from Latin America and the Caribbean.

Source: CEPALSTAT Statistics on public finances for Latin America and the Caribbean and OECD (2011) for the other countries.
http://dx.doi.org/10.1787/888932522208

Macroeconomic policies should also be consistent with long-term requirements linked to economic and demographic changes. Although the main objective in the short-run is to rebuild fiscal space, which was diminished due to the policy response to the crisis, governments should at the same time address macroeconomic and structural restrictions and problems that limit the region's opportunities to achieve its development goals. In this sense, while larger inflows of foreign investment are in principle good news for the Latin American economies, they come with several challenges: greater exchange-rate volatility, "Dutch disease" (an appreciation of the national currency that harms the international competitiveness of exports except commodities), and potentially unsustainable credit expansions. Governments should use available instruments to contain excessive volatility, inflation and appreciation pressures on the exchange rate which are not the result of economic fundamentals. Under extraordinary circumstances, capital controls and taxes on short-term financial transactions can be an effective tool to contain currency appreciations, especially when prudential financial regulations are not sufficient to guarantee financial stability. These measures do not just reduce the volatility of economic fluctuations, but also remove obstacles to economic diversification and provide predictability to foster investment in new technologies and stability in public finances, which enable the adoption of long-term policies for more and better growth. This occurs in a context in which demographic growth and other structural changes —such as the aspirations of the incipient middle classes— mean that countries in Latin America will require more fiscal room for manoeuvre in order to provide the required services.

Latin American countries should take advantage of current opportunities to remove development barriers and take a quantitative and qualitative leap ahead in the provision of public services. Despite important progress in reducing poverty during the boom —from 44% of the population in 2002 to 33% in 2008— and to a lesser extent in decreasing inequality, there are still important gaps to be closed and challenges to be faced. In particular, the region must increase its efforts to reduce social inequalities. One in three Latin Americans (180 million people) still lives below the poverty line and 10 Latin American economies rank among the 15 most unequal economies in the world. Conditional cash transfer programmes have been successful in reducing poverty, but the lack of broader social safety nets is a severe problem for the majority of Latin America's citizens. Another key challenge is creating mechanisms and incentives for a knowledge- and innovation-based economy that would achieve higher productivity levels and a more diversified economy in an environment where incentives and signals —like the exchange rate— often strengthen profitability and the expansion of natural resource–based sectors. Latin American countries should create the bases for development to be sustainable even when external conditions are less favourable. In this sense, governments in the region's resource-rich economies should consider using part of the windfall rents of higher commodity prices to promote diversification and competitiveness in the rest of the economy by investing in education, infrastructure and innovation. If governments do not act now, exports will continue to be concentrated in low-added-value primary products with oligopolistic markets that hinder the entry of new firms and do not facilitate income redistribution and social inclusion. In such a situation, more households would be vulnerable to adverse shocks like illness or natural disasters, including those that are not living in poverty (e.g. the nascent middle classes[3]). The stakes are high in the policy debate about transforming the state for development, because insufficient development results could exacerbate social conflicts and weaken institutions.

Fiscal reforms to reduce the enormous gap between the requirements and the available resources are needed to build states that are able to respond to the development challenges. In the last two decades, including the recent crisis, the strength of public finances in the region has been remarkable. Debt levels have been reduced (from around 80% of GDP at the beginning of the 1990s to around 30% today) in part thanks to an increase in fiscal revenues. Furthermore, public expenditure has become more effective at promoting growth, reducing poverty and redistributing income, through increased social expenditure and public investment. In addition, budget rigidities have been reduced and fiscal space increased. However, the majority of Latin American countries have fewer resources per capita to fulfil the expectations of their citizens than developed and even many emerging economies. This is the true constraint facing countries in the region that are striving to meet the demands of their societies.

Not only is fiscal revenue in Latin America low, but tax bases tend to be narrow and are biased towards non-progressive taxes. With the exception of some countries in the Southern Cone, like Argentina, Brazil and Uruguay, which have revenues similar to the OECD average at around 30% of GDP, overall fiscal revenue in the region is low (Figure 0.2). In addition, personal income tax levels are lower, there are more deductions and exemptions than in other countries, and tax structures are concentrated in indirect taxes. The low fiscal revenue is due to high levels of tax fraud and avoidance, high degrees of informality and the limited capacity of the tax administration. Therefore, tax administrations' institutional capacity should be strengthened, income tax bases should be broadened, and other types of taxes should be explored. These reforms should be accompanied by efforts to raise the quality of public services and initiatives to educate citizens about fiscal matters to increase tax morale. Low levels of fiscal revenue in Latin America impede states from making the necessary investment in education, infrastructure and productive development, which, together with health and social protection, are key levers to increase productivity, competitiveness and social inclusion.

Figure 0.2. Tax revenue in Latin America is low
(Public tax revenue as a percentage of GDP, 2008)

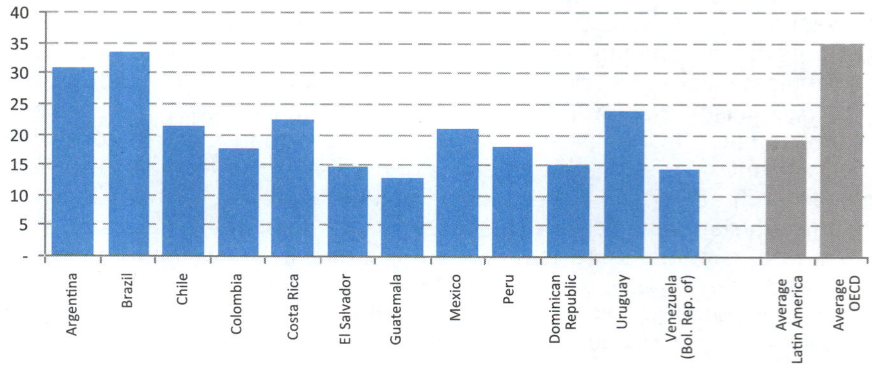

Notes: a) The statistics refer to the non-financial public sector in the case of Argentina, Colombia, Costa Rica, El Salvador, Mexico and the Bolivarian Republic of Venezuela; the central government in Brazil, Chile and Peru, and central government in Guatemala, Dominican Republic and Uruguay; b) the levying of taxes in Mexico includes certain items of income from oil production.

Source: Compiled using data from CEPELSTAT and Revenue Statistics in Latin America, ECLAC-CIAT-OECD.
http://dx.doi.org/10.1787/888932522227

Tax bases are also limited by the extensive use of tax expenditure: deductions and exemptions. Governments should consider eliminating several of these types of tax expenditure, particularly those that are most regressive and distortionary. They should also provide more information, be more transparent and carry out studies on the effects of their tax expenditure. In particular, based on technical evaluations on the effectiveness of the items of tax expenditure currently in place, governments should consider transforming those items of expenditure with redistributive and social objectives into more transparent transfers and expenditure policies. When evaluating the effectiveness of different instruments (tax expenditure versus direct subsidies) the relative institutional capacity of tax administrations in comparison to the capacity of agencies responsible for expenditure must be considered.

Fiscal policy does little to reduce inequality in Latin America, due to low levels of direct personal taxes and public social expenditure, as well as inadequate targeting of expenditure. This explains the significant differences in the effectiveness of fiscal policy at reducing inequalities compared with in OECD economies (Figure 0.3). These difference are most significant for cash transfers, rather than for in-kind transfers such as expenditure on education and health. To revert this situation, governments must reinforce income transfer programmes for low-income households and the solidarity pillars of social protection systems, in particular the pension system, while taking care not to create incentives that would favour the informal economy or encourage people not to work.The large differences in the level of social expenditure between countries in the region (ranging from 7% of GDP in Guatemala to around 25% of GDP in Brazil) reflect major differences in the design of social protection systems, especially in pensions and healthcare, as well as in the proportion of the population covered by health, education and unemployment benefits.

Figure 0.3. Fiscal policy does little to reduce inequality in Latin America
(Gini indices)

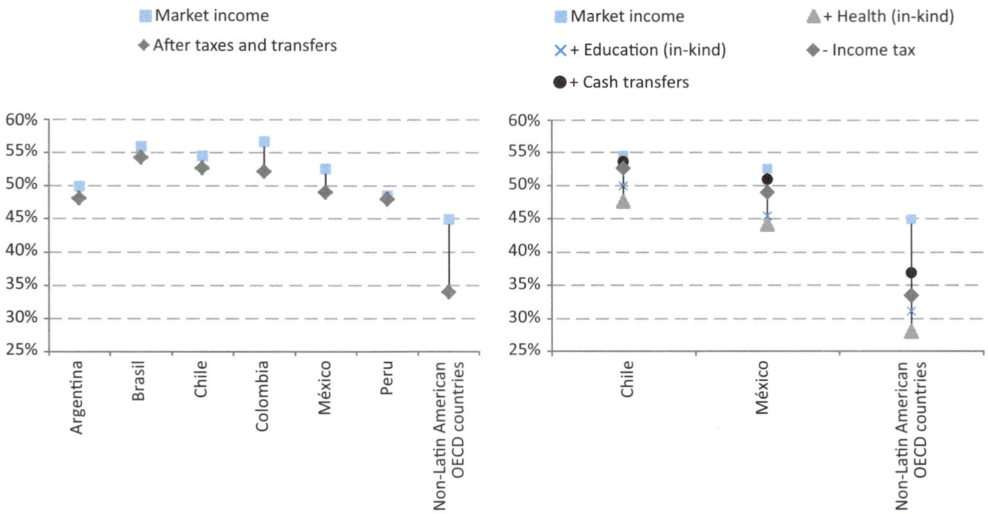

Source: OECD (2008a) for non-Latin American OECD countries, OECD (2008b) for Argentina, Brazil, Colombia and Peru, and estimations based on household surveys for Chile and Mexico.
http://dx.doi.org/10.1787/888932522246

Therefore, the creation of a fiscal pact that reinforces the social contract between the citizens and the state can be fundamental.[4] The success of fiscal reforms depends on there being a link between taxes and expenditure and people realising that taxes enable the provision of public services from which they can benefit. Fiscal reforms move forward when: *i)* they are solidly backed by previous analyses and ex post evaluations, which are transparent and take all relevant factors into account; *ii)* they have been adapted to the country, in particular regarding transition periods needed for their implementation; *iii)* there is clear leadership and support by large sectors of the population. Fiscal pacts —agreements between the relevant social, economic and political actors— can be general or focused on a particular sector such as education, employment, social protection or infrastructure, or they can be structured around a common principle like equality, public security or the fight against poverty. The legislature has a key role in building such agreements, supporting them within the budget and negotiating the reforms needed to improve the tax system.

Beyond more financial resources, the state should also transform itself to respond better to the needs of its citizens and manage resources in a more effective, efficient and transparent way. The state is a fundamental actor in modern society and Latin America is not an exception. Democratic consolidation, economic growth, the development of social protection systems, urbanisation and globalisation have led to a constant expansion in the functions of the state and the resources needed to sustain them. Despite recent increases in public expenditure as a percentage of GDP —an indicator of the size of the state— in some countries of the region it is still significantly lower than in the OECD (Figure 0.4). Many Latin American governments do not have the necessary tools to identify development opportunities and implement policies.

States should therefore increase their management capacities and strengthen their human resources: The professionalisation of public services is one of the main challenges for reforming public sector management in Latin

Figure 0.4. Public expenditure is lower in Latin America than in the OECD
(Public expenditure as a percentage of GDP)

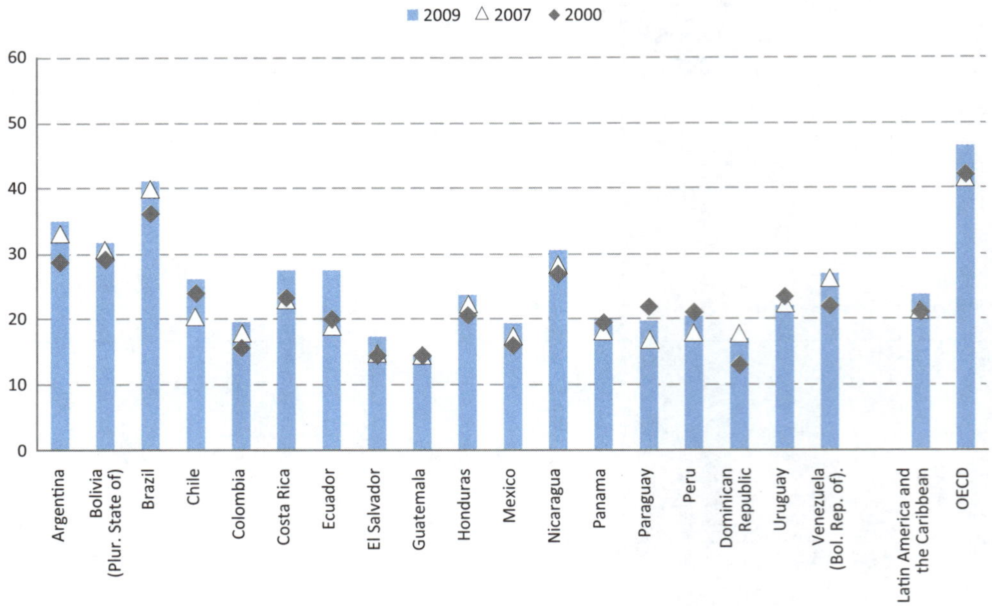

Note: The statistics refer to general government in the case of Argentina, Plurinational State of Bolivia, Brazil, Chile, Costa Rica, Nicaragua and Peru and central government in the case of Colombia, Ecuador, El Salvador, Guatemala, Honduras, Mexico, Panama, Paraguay, Dominican Republic, Uruguay and the Bolivarian Republic of Venezuela.

Source: Based on data from CEPALSTAT and OECD Government at a Glance (OECD, 2011d).
http://dx.doi.org/10.1787/888932522265

America. At the same time, states need effective tools for planning and coordinating policies, programmes and projects to fulfil their transformational role. Institutions such as fiscal rules and medium-term fiscal frameworks should be strengthened. More transparency and accountability should be introduced in the budgetary process. States should also introduce evaluation mechanisms for policies and programmes, as well as national public investment systems.

Efficiency and effectiveness are crucial to meeting the development challenges. Doing more with the same resources, or using fewer resources to do the same, would free up resources that could be allocated to other priorities. Improved efficiency would also help gain public support for the necessary reforms: when citizens see that the state is using its resources efficiently and that they benefit from the services it provides, the state gains legitimacy and citizens become more willing to pay taxes. The public sector can achieve greater effectiveness through the definition of planning instruments by policy makers, along with an effective co-ordination of policies, programmes and projects.

Finally, more transparency in public management reinforces the efficiency and effectiveness of public interventions. Policies and actions to reduce corruption should be based on greater access to information and civic participation in public policies. New technologies (e.g. the use of the Internet for e-government or the more recent development of open government) can help, but public sector institutions have to change the way they operate and adapt to fully take advantage of the potential opportunities.

Beyond improving the delivery and transparency of policies and programmes, the transformation of the state should also help identify new strategies to define and achieve its primary development objectives. Sustainable and inclusive growth can be supported by three key areas: education, infrastructure, and productive development and innovation. To overcome the structural barriers to the region's development and achieve equitable development, states must identify strategies. Governments must use more resources, greater effectiveness and greater transparency in the use of public resources and efficiency in the implementation of policies. But these measures are not sufficient: they must also identify priority areas for action and create the necessary governance structures to carry out the different programmes. Broadening the coverage and quality of the education system, increasing the density of and access to infrastructure, and increasing investment in productive development and innovation are crucial to the transformation and diversification of the region's productive structure. This will boost the technological content of the region's exports and improve its standing in global value chains. All these elements will be crucial to increase the region's productivity, generate good-quality jobs and develop more equitable economic systems.

The coverage of and spending on the region's education systems has improved consistently over the last few decades. However, the quality of education remains low and access is unequal. In primary education, countries in the region have reached levels of coverage comparable to those of OECD economies, but the coverage of secondary and tertiary education are lagging behind: 82% compared to 99% for secondary education, and 43% compared to 76% for tertiary education, respectively. While the quality of education has improved, significant gaps remain. Internationally comparable evidence on the quality of schooling, such as the OECD's PISA study, shows that Latin American students perform worse than their counterparts in OECD economies. For example, in reading tests, almost 50% of Latin American students fail to reach the minimum acceptable level; in OECD economies this figure is less than 20% on average. At the same time, differences in performance by geographic area (urban vs. rural), by gender, by type of school (public vs. private) and by socio-economic status remain high and have even increased (Figure 0.5). For example, in Argentina, Mexico and Panama the performance gap between urban and rural schools is more than 45 points, after correcting for socio-economic status. This means that rural students are effectively lagging more than a school year behind their urban counterparts.

There are two main trends in the management of education services: increasing decentralisation in its provision and higher private-sector provision of tertiary education. Although responsibilities have been transferred to regional, state and municipal levels, in many countries this process has not been accompanied by adequate investment in capacity building for the different levels of government or by adequate funding. In tertiary education —which has experienced the highest increase in demand due to demographic transition— more than 50% of students are enrolled in private institutions. This explains the increase in private spending in education, which has more than doubled between 2003 and 2009 from 1% to 2% of GDP.

Lack of infrastructure is a significant bottleneck for the sustainability of growth, competitiveness and even equity in Latin America. The region has large infrastructure gaps (some of which have increased over the past years, such as broadband Internet access) when compared to the OECD economies and emerging economies in Asia and other regions of the world. These gaps can be closed through more and better investment in infrastructure. In the first semester of 2000, Latin America showed a deficit in transport infrastructure (kilometres of paved road per square kilometre) of 85%

Figure 0.5. 15-year-old Latin Americans score below their OECD peers in reading tests, but socioeconomic differences have a greater impact on performance among students in Latin America
(In percentages)

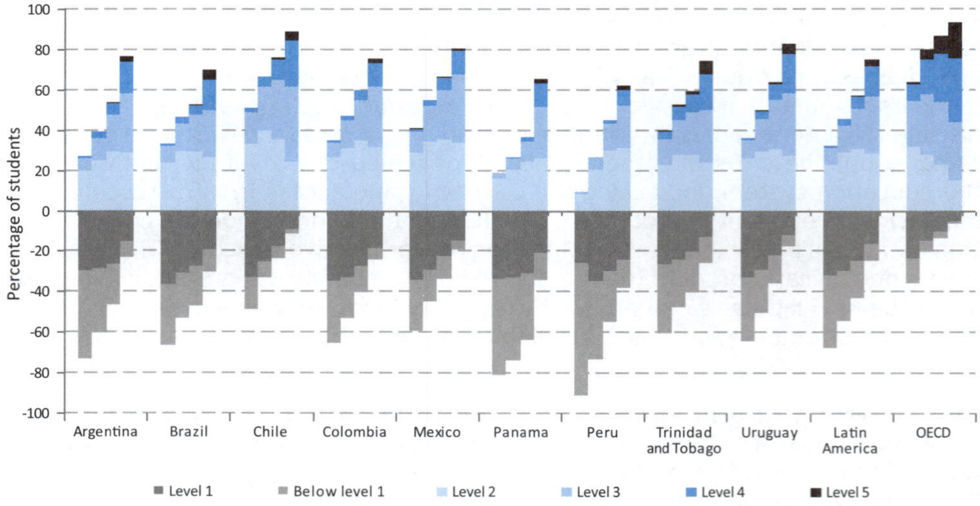

Note: The distribution of performance levels in Latin America and the OECD refers to the simple average of the weighted average levels of achievement at national level in countries participating in PISA 2009.

Source: Based on data from PISA 2009.
http://dx.doi.org/10.1787/888932522284

when compared with South-East Asia, and a gap of almost 60% in the energy sector (megawatts per 1 000 inhabitants). In the telecommunications sector, while there have been important advances, the gap in access to broadband Internet services has increased considerably, due to a lower rate of growth in the number of subscribers in Latin America compared to in OECD economies. The gap in access to fixed broadband between Latin American and the OECD economies rose from 1% in 2000 to 17% in 2009, and from 5% in 2005 to 44% in 2009 for mobile broadband (Figure 0.6).

Latin America needs an improved framework with long-term vision that can strengthen the processes of planning and managing investment in infrastructure. In the transport sector, prioritisation and project planning must maximise social returns based on an appropriate pre-feasibility process, which requires a balance between new projects and the maintenance of existing ones. Public action in the transport sector should be guided by the principle of co-modality —that is, the use of one mode or an intermodal combination for a journey or a series of journeys of persons or merchandise, maximising the efficiency of the overall journey. In the telecommunications sector, the regulatory framework needs to be adapted to accommodate convergence to common technological platforms. Regulation should be oriented toward improving the management of state-controlled resources, such as the electromagnetic spectrum, domain names and numbering.

Moreover, the incentives and norms that regulate private-sector participation in infrastructure investment, management and provision need to be improved. In the transport sector, it is especially important to establish and follow an appropriate selection process for deciding on private participation. Additionally, well-designed contracts minimise renegotiations of concessions,

Figure 0.6. The broadband gap in Latin America is large and increasing
(Percentage of broadband subscribers in the total population)

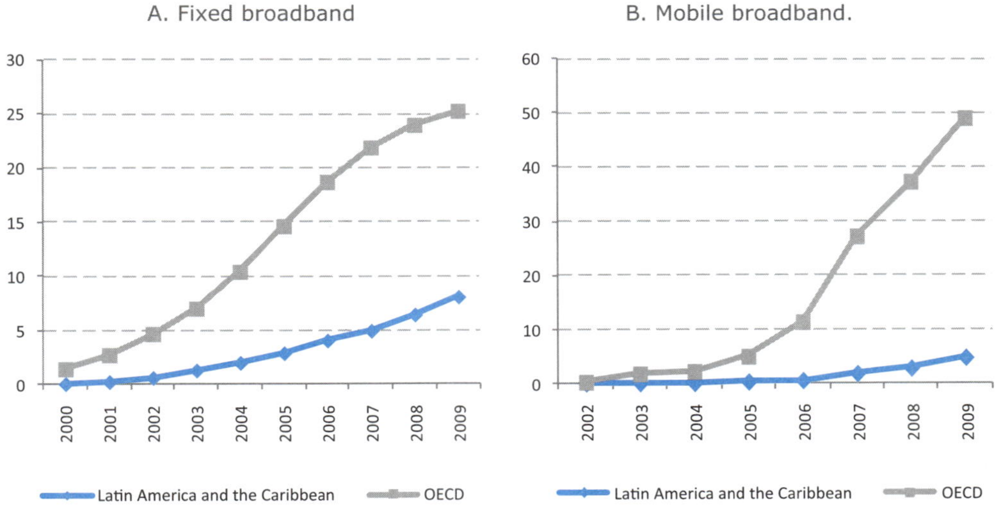

Note: Simple regional averages.

Source: Regional Broadband Observatory (ORBA) based on International Telecommunications Union (ITU) data
http://dx.doi.org/10.1787/888932522303

considerably reducing contingent fiscal liabilities. In Peru, Colombia and Chile, 50 out of 60 road concessions signed up to 2010 were renegotiated, generating costs of USD 7 billion. In the telecommunications sector, especially for broadband Internet access, governments must establish mechanisms and incentives to encourage investment (whether public or private) in socially desirable infrastructure to serve communities in regions which are not profitable for the private sector. For these measures to take effect, the role of the regulatory agencies and of consultation mechanisms between decision-making bodies are fundamental.

The productivity gap is a persistent problem for Latin America and the Caribbean. This reflects the limited diversification of the region's economies, their specialisation in non-technology-intensive sectors, and scant investment in research and development (R&D) and in innovation. The labour productivity gap between Latin America and the United States persists and has even increased in certain sectors. Labour productivity in technology-intensive sectors in Latin America was just 18% of the productivity in the same sectors in the United States in 1990, and 12% in 2007, reflecting little structural change in the region.[5] Natural resource-intensive sectors make up 60% of manufacturing value added in Latin America, whereas in the United States 60% of manufacturing value added is concentrated in knowledge-intensive sectors. At the same time, primary goods and manufactures based on natural resources represent up to 50% of Latin America's exports. As a result, the region invests few resources in R&D; the level of investment in R&D with respect to GDP rose from 0.5% in 2004 to 0.6% in 2008, while in the OECD economies the figures were 2.2% to 2.3% for the same period. Contrary to the experience of developed countries, Latin America's private sector invests little in R&D and the scientific and technological activities of its firms are concentrated in the acquisition of machinery and equipment (Figure 0.7).

Figure 0.7. The challenge in Latin America: mobilise private-sector R&D
(R&D investment as a percentage of GDP)

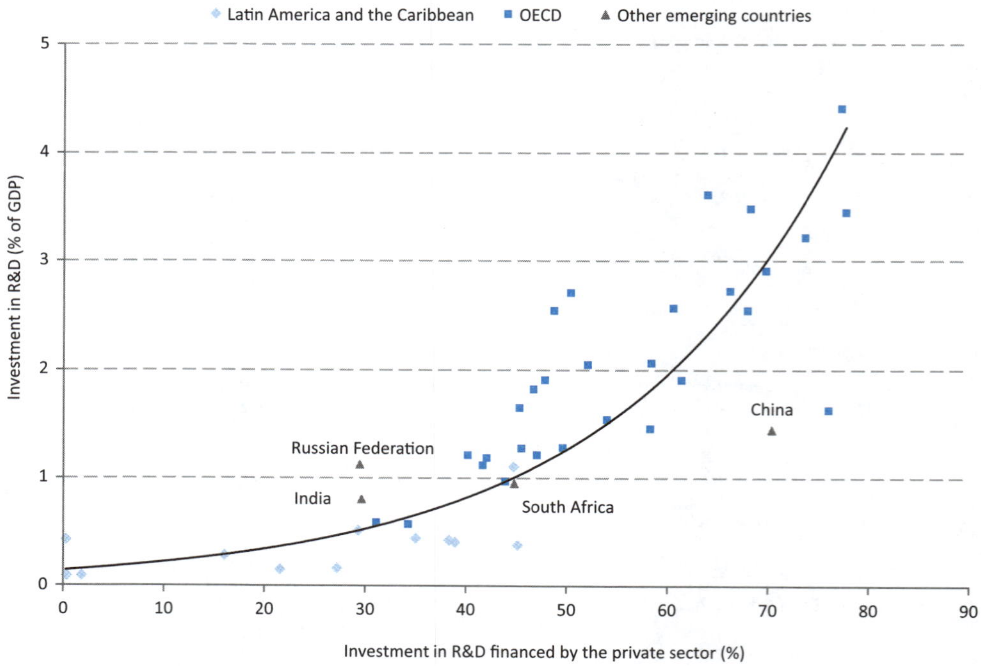

Note: The figures refer to 2002 for the Plurinational State of Bolivia, 2004 for Switzerland, 2005 for Panama and Paraguay and 2006 for Australia, China, Israel and South Africa.

Source: Based on data from the United Nations Educational, Scientific and Cultural Organization (UNESCO), see [http://www.uis.unesco.org/pages/default.aspx] Ibero-American/Inter-American Network of Science and Technology Indicators (RICYT), see [http://ricyt.org] and Main Science and Technology Indicators (MSTI) Database of the Organization of Economic Cooperation and Development (OECD).
http://dx.doi.org/10.1787/888932522322

In the past decade, institutions responsible for designing innovation policy have been strengthened, but the region still lacks policies focused on national innovation systems and adequate financial support for implementing innovation strategies. The creation of ministries and agencies dedicated to innovation strategies illustrates the growing interest for this area in several countries. For example, Argentina created the Ministry of Science, Technology and Productive Innovation in 2007; Chile established the National Innovation Council for Competitiveness (2005) and the Governmental (ministerial) Committee for Innovation for Competitiveness (2007). Since 2008, Brazil has implemented a productive development policy with strong participation from the Brazilian Development Bank (BNDES) (this strategy was updated in August 2011). Nonetheless, it remains necessary to synchronise productive development strategy and innovation policy (for example through sectoral funds, as in Argentina, Brazil and Mexico), improve planning capacity and overcome the tendency of assigning resources based on short-term assessments, and design results-oriented policies (e.g. more exporting firms, more PhD graduates employed in the production sector, new productive processes and/or market services, etc.) rather than input-oriented policies (R&D spending, enrolment in PhD courses, etc.).

Education, infrastructure and productive development and innovation are three crucial areas for achieving competitiveness, economic development

and social inclusion in a given economy. Each of these policy areas requires active public policies, strategic planning and more efficient and effective management by the state. The fiscal pact —designed to meet specific development goals— must be complemented by the modernisation of public policy management systems in five priority areas, bearing in mind that the region has institutional models of varying complexity and with different intensities of interaction between the relevant actors:

1) **Adopt management systems and results-oriented planning mechanisms.** Institutional capacity for the management of resources needs to be increased and multi-year planning for better resource efficiency should be adopted to facilitate investment in medium- and long-term projects. It is also important to seek synergies with the private sector to boost the viability and implementation of national development strategies. Designing policies based on a long-term vision and prioritising between the various reforms are fundamental in this effort. For example, it is important to balance the objectives of coverage of schooling (for instance, through investment in infrastructure) with the objectives of quality and inclusion (for instance, the capacity of the education system to reduce disparities between rural and urban regions) and the objectives of competitiveness (for instance, supporting the professional insertion of qualified human resources). An approach that focuses on *results* rather than on *inputs* also facilitates the evaluation of policies, making it possible to learn lessons from the implementation of those policies and consequently adjust them to make them more effective and efficient.

2) **Create incentives and mechanisms for vertical and horizontal coordination between different levels of government and between the public and private sectors.** This requires investment in strategic intelligence —specialised and trained human resources— in public administration and dialogue mechanisms to boost confidence between the public and private sectors. Likewise, state capacity for control and regulation needs to be increased. For example, the lack of coordination between different actors is the principal weakness of infrastructure policy in Latin America and undermines productivity, competitiveness and access. The main obstacles to effective coordination are the lack of institutional incentives for co-operation and the absence of an appropriate institutional architecture. Incentives need to be designed that favour coordination between agencies at the same level of government, between agencies at different levels of government and between public and private actors. The designation of responsibilities between different levels of government is also fundamental. In the area of education, for example, central governments must retain the power to set standards, design the basic curriculum and control the teaching statutes that define the employment conditions and professional development of teachers. Meanwhile, the professionalisation of teaching careers, linking it more closely to performance and better training facilities within schools, should involve school heads and various levels of public administration. In other policy areas, it is essential to develop hiring schemes that foster professionalisation, specialisation and the development of a civil career that is not connected to the political cycle and is capable of using advanced planning, monitoring and evaluation tools.

3) **Establish clear standards and regulation mechanisms that enable the implementation of the agreements reached.** A clear regulatory framework that facilitates the relationship between public and private sectors is essential for investment in both infrastructure and innovation. For example, in the telecommunications sector, the legal regimes in most of the region's countries are still oriented towards a service-based regulation, which is not in line with technological convergence. The regulation of telecommunications services must be reformed to avoid segmented measures which create asymmetries and regulatory distortions that are detrimental to the end consumer. Tertiary education needs to operate within a regulatory framework that includes clear evaluation and accreditation mechanisms which guarantee and improve standards.

4) **Invest in institutional strengthening and training for public management.** Devolving responsibilities to regions, states and municipalities must be accompanied by adequate fiscal resources and management capacities at the local level. The provision of education services and transport infrastructure requires precise linkages between different levels of government, making it essential to invest in training for sub-national public-policy managers. Likewise, while new instruments and criteria are defined for budgetary allocations, governments need to provide training to public managers and direct funds to facilitate local, national and regional co-operation.

5) **Generate information, indicators and institutions for public policy decision-making.** Information systems should be designed and created to provide tools with which to evaluate government action. Many countries have invested in units dedicated to the compilation and circulation of indicators in the fields of education and innovation. Much effort has gone into modernising computer systems in ministries and public agencies, increasing transparency and access to data, as seen in larger economies such as Argentina and Brazil and smaller ones like Costa Rica and Panama. At the same time, incentives to use this data in the evaluation and redesign of policy must be put in place. Unlike OECD economies, Latin America is still in the early stages of creating national institutions that analyse policy. In the area of innovation, Brazil is the most advanced country, where the Institute for Applied Economic Research (IPEA), affiliated to the Secretariat of Strategic Affairs of the Presidency of the Republic, as well as the Centre for Management of Strategic Studies (CGEE), affiliated to the Ministry of Science and Technology, carry out impact evaluation and feedback on public policies.

Summing up, despite the global financial crisis, the situation of Latin American economies has improved substantially in recent years. The governments of the region should take advantage of this opportunity to design and implement better public policies that take a more inclusive and sustainable long-term development path. While the main objective in the short-run is to rebuild fiscal space —diminished due to the policy response to the crisis— at the same time, governments should also address macroeconomic and structural obstacles that limit the region's chances of achieving its longer-term development goals. The most relevant objectives are to reduce inequality in income distribution, improve the provision of public services, create more opportunities and promote economic diversification. More efficient public management is crucial, as it would free up resources for additional development policies and increase public support for managing and implementing the required reforms. But efficiency alone is not enough: states also have to become more effective in achieving their objectives. This can only be accomplished by implementing a fiscal reform that raises the required resources to meet the development goals. Many governments in the region have identified three priority areas for investment, given their potential contribution to increasing competitiveness and social inclusion: education, infrastructure and innovation. In each one of them, a more efficient management and more effective strategic action by the state is needed.

Notes

1. ECLAC (2010a) discusses the relative importance of both factors.
2. ECLAC (2011).
3. OECD (2010a).
4. ECLAC (1998) was the first to consider the need for a new agreement regarding taxes and expenditure.
5. ECLAC (2010b)

References

ECLAC (Economic Commission for Latin America and the Caribbean) (CEPAL) (1998), *The Fiscal Covenant. Strengths, Weaknesses, Challenges*, ECLAC books, No. 47 (LC/G.1997/Rev.1-P), Santiago, Chile.

ECLAC (CEPAL) (2010a), *Preliminary Overview of the Economies of Latin America and the Caribbean 2010*, (LC/G.2480-P), ECLAC, Santiago, Chile.

ECLAC (CEPAL) (2010b), *Time for Equality: Closing Gaps, Opening Trails*. Thirty-third period of ECLAC sessions. Brasilia, 30 May – 1 June 2010, (LC/G.2432 (SES.33/3)), ECLAC, Santiago, Chile.

ECLAC (CEPAL) (2011), *Economic Survey of Latin America and the Caribbean 2010-2011*, Economic Development Division, Informative Document, ECLAC, Santiago, Chile.

OECD (Organisation for Economic Co-operation and Development) (2008), *Growing Unequal? Income Distribution and Poverty in OECD economies*, OECD, Paris.

OECD (2010a), *Latin American Economic Outlook 2011, How middle-class is Latin America?*, OECD Development Centre, Paris.

OECD (2010b), *"Pisa 2009 Results: Overcoming Social Background: Equity in Learning Opportunities and Outcomes"*. Vol. 2. OECD, Paris.

OECD (2011a), *Economic Outlook*, No. 89, OECD, Paris.

OECD (2011b), *Government at a Glance*, OECD, Paris.

OECD (2011c), *Main Science and Technology Indicators*, OECD, Paris.

CHAPTER ONE

Macroeconomic overview

Abstract

Latin American economies weathered the 2008-09 financial crisis better than those in other regions of the world —including in OECD outside Latin America— and their recovery has also been faster. The main challenge for the region is to manage this favourable environment with prudence in order to rebuild fiscal space to face potential risks, such as disruptions in capital markets due to problems in the euro zone.

Greater ties with China —which were important for the recovery— mean the region's economies are now more sensitive to a potential slowdown in Chinese growth, in particular because of its potential impact on the prices of raw materials and consequently, the fiscal accounts of many of the region's economies. The present chapter argues that it is essential to rebuild the defences of macroeconomic policy and increase predictability in public finances in order to implement policies that enable more and better growth.

1.1. Introduction

Latin American economies weathered the 2008-09 financial crisis well, and their recovery has been faster than in other regions of the world, including OECD economies. The region is growing rapidly, although there are significant differences among countries. This macroeconomic stability is the background for any discussion of the transformation of the state for development for three reasons: first, because stability provides a favourable context for designing and implementing reforms; and second, because there are factors in the macroeconomic panorama that threaten the current stability if governments do not take appropriate measures to avoid them. But the most important connection between the macroeconomic panorama and the transformation of the state is that the current favourable conditions are at least in part due to good practices in fiscal and monetary policies. In many cases, these good macroeconomic practices may be institutionalised, as was the case with the establishment of independent central banks or fiscal rules in various countries of the region.

This chapter analyses recent macroeconomic performance. Latin America is expected to grow at 4.4% in 2011[1] thanks to strong domestic demand and the continuing robust demand in Asia for its exports (section 1.2). Nevertheless, this increase in demand puts pressure on the international prices for raw materials, which, among other factors, could lead to increased inflationary pressures. This scenario poses a challenge for the region's central banks, which have to contain rising inflation without accelerating capital inflows or sacrificing growth (section 1.3). In addition, increased capital inflows – in principle good news for the region's economies —also bring challenges in terms of exchange rate volatility, with consequences for countries' external competitiveness and the potential for unsustainable credit expansion (section 1.4).

Good macroeconomic policies during the period of strong growth from 2003 to 2008 led, in many cases, to the generation and expansion of policy space (Figure 1.1, left panel). In this way, monetary and especially fiscal policies were used in a counter-cyclical manner during the 2008-09 financial crisis, which help to avoid deep recessions and cushion the impact on society's most vulnerable sectors.

The main challenge for many economies in the region is to manage this favourable but volatile environment prudently in order to rebuild policy space and the ability for macroeconomic policy response. In addition, policies should aim to increase the stability and predictability of public finances so that gaps can be closed in infrastructure, education and innovation, which will permit more and better growth in the long term. This higher growth potential is necessary so that strong growth in domestic demand does not generate price instability. In the short term, the international economy continues to be the main source of potential shocks for Latin America. The current problems in the euro zone could cause serious problems in the international financial system, including emerging markets. Reversals of capital flows can lead to large fluctuations in exchange rates with disruptive effects on the real economy. The growing influence of China in Latin American trade relations was one of the factors that contributed to the rapid recovery of the region's economies. However, greater ties with China mean that the region's economies are now more sensitive to a potential slowdown in China's growth. A fall in demand for Latin American products and in the prices of raw materials would affect the fiscal accounts of many of the region's economies.

Figure 1.1. Fiscal space before and after the crisis: 2000-07 and 2007-09

(Variation in percentage points of GDP)

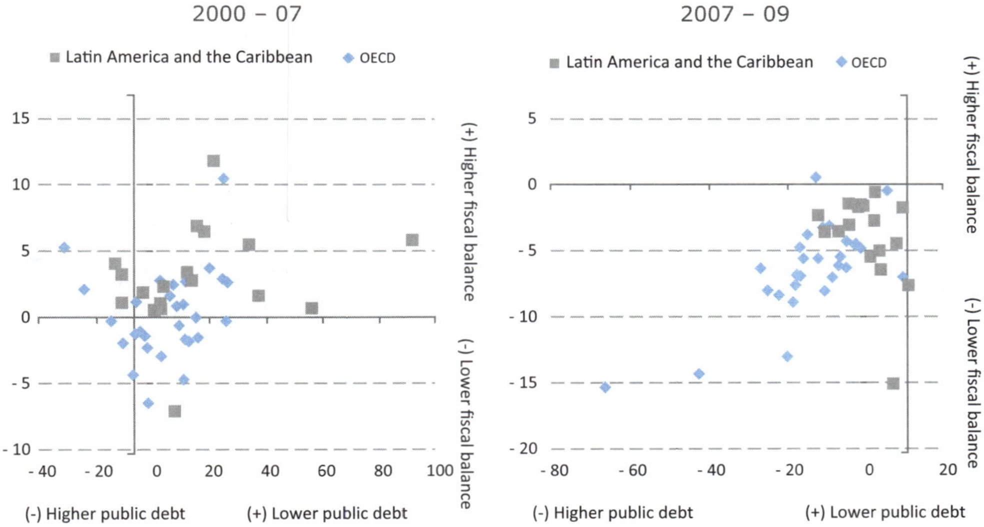

Note: each point represents one country. The panels include OECD countries and 19 countries from Latin America and the Caribbean.

Source: CEPALSTAT Statistics on public finances for Latin America and the Caribbean and OECD (2011) for the other countries.
http://dx.doi.org/10.1787/888932522341

1.2. From recovery to expansion

The recessionary effects of the international crisis on the region's economies in 2009 were only transitory. The economic growth seen in 2010 reflects the consolidation of the recovery that the majority of the region's economies began to experience in the second half of 2009. This recovery was accelerated by the impact of the counter-cyclical measures that many of the countries applied. The implementation of fiscal packages aimed at countering the effects of the international crisis was complemented by the rapid recovery of the international economy —led by the emerging economies— in the first half of 2010. As a consequence, levels of economic activity in general are now higher than before the crisis. During the first few months of 2011, economic activity for the majority of Latin American and Caribbean countries has remained buoyant, and ECLAC forecasts that growth in regional GDP in 2011 will approach 4.4%. South America will grow at a higher rate than Mexico and Central America, but the difference in performance between the two sub-regions is expected to decline in comparison with 2010.

Figure 1.2. Latin America (13 countries): variation rates of the components of expenditure in relation to the same figure in the trimester of the previous year, 2009-2010

(In percentages and USD at constant 2005 prices)

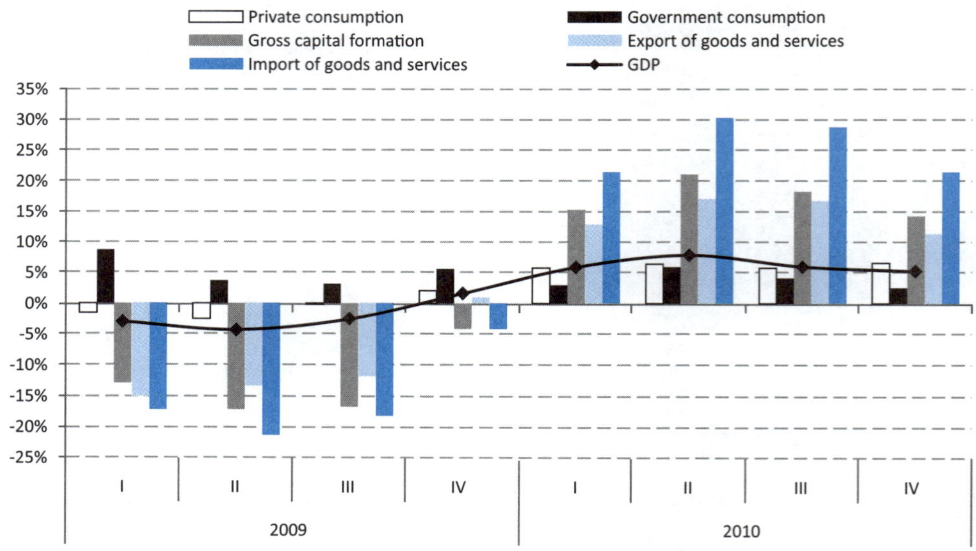

Note: The countries from Latin America covered are Argentina, Bolivia (Plur. State of), Brazil, Chile, Colombia, Costa Rica, Ecuador, Mexico, Paraguay, Peru, Dominican Republic, Uruguay, and Venezuela (Bol. Rep. of).

Source: Based on official figures.
http://dx.doi.org/10.1787/888932522360

The expansion of macroeconomic room for manoeuvre during 2003-08 in many countries of the region led to an unprecedented capacity for carrying out policies to combat the crisis. The strong macroeconomic showing of the majority of Latin American and Caribbean countries in the years leading up to the international crisis marked a significant difference from the usual financial difficulties faced by the region in difficult times. Between 2003 and 2008, these countries took advantage of the boom in the economy and in international finances, consolidating public accounts, increasing their international reserves and reducing and improving their debt profiles. The reduction observed in recent years of non-financial public-sector debt expressed as a percentage of GDP was the result of increased government revenue and economic growth, as well as changes in relative prices. In several countries, the composition of public debt changed significantly, with a higher prevalence of longer-term and fixed-interest debt and a larger share of debt held by residents and denominated in local currency.[2] All of this created more space for implementing counter-cyclical public policies, enabling unprecedented activism aimed at countering the negative effects of the deteriorating international scenario. It also made the initiation of the recovery in the second half of 2009 possible.[3]

A significant expansion of several components of GDP accounted for the high growth rate of the region in 2010 and enabled a balanced and strong recovery. The sustained dynamism of domestic demand, both from private consumption and from investment (Figure 1.2), was due to the relatively strong performance of labour markets, growth in real wages, the increase of credit to the private sector, as well as economic agents' improved expectations regarding the impact of the crisis. Low real interest rates also stimulated both consumption and investment. For countries with large volumes of remittances, their gradual recovery has also contributed to increasing levels of private consumption. Along with buoyant demand, rapid economic recovery was also facilitated by high levels of idle installed capacity, which made it possible to step up production levels quickly.[4] Gross capital formation expanded to 12.9% in 2010 due to the increase in gross fixed capital investment (9.9%) and inventory restocking. The growth of fixed investment was primarily in machinery and equipment (mostly imported) and was driven by national currency appreciation, widely available credit and lower idle capacity amid burgeoning domestic demand.[5] As a result, the rate of gross fixed investment, measured in constant dollars as a percentage of GDP, increased to 21.4%, above the 20.5% recorded in 2009 but below the 22.1% in 2008 and the maximum levels recorded in the 1970s.[6]

Strong domestic demand led to a significant upturn in the volume of imported goods and services (20.9%), in particular of consumer durables and capital goods. Given the behaviour of exports and imports of goods and services, the contribution of net exports to growth was negative in 2010. In fact, even though the value of exported goods is growing at high rates, in metal- and mineral-exporting countries (and in some hydrocarbon-exporting countries), this growth is mainly due to better export prices, rather than an increase in the volume of exports. For the region as a whole, the favourable external scenario led to an increase in the volume and prices of exports, although growth in imports was even greater, leading to a deterioration in the current account balance from -0.4% of GDP in 2009 to -1.2% in 2010.[7]

Increasing trade with China is another important factor to understand the recent dynamics of Latin American economies. The change in the world economy's centre of gravity towards the east and the south (above all China and India, but also other emerging economies) has led to a significant increase in trade with these countries.[8] In the last decade, trade with China has increased substantially in South America. For example, its share in total exports increased in Brazil (from 2% to 13%), Chile (from 5% to 23%) and Peru (from 6% to 15%) during this period. However, China continues to represent a minor proportion of trade, accounting for less than 2% of total exports for most countries in Central America and Mexico, while it has become the leading market for exports from Brazil and Chile (up from 12th and 5th in 2000, respectively) and is now the second most important market for Argentina and Peru. At the same time, imports from China have increased considerably in all of the countries of the region (Figure 1.3). Various South American countries, such as the Plurinational State of Bolivia, Chile, Ecuador, Paraguay, Peru and the Bolivarian Republic of Venezuela, do not face much competition from China because of their high specialisation in raw materials. Brazil, Colombia, Argentina and Uruguay face more competition from China, but the economies most exposed are those of Central America and Mexico, as they have very similar export structures.[9] The greater importance of emerging economies in trade relations —in particular China— is an important factor in explaining Latin American resilience during the crisis. It is also a factor in explaining differences within the region in regard to the pace of growth and policy space. This phenomenon, which has been developing since the end of the 1990s, manifests in a higher correlation between economic cycles in South America and China, while the correlation in cycles is lower for Central America and Mexico and has even been declining.[10] Therefore, economies with greater commercial ties to China suffered less during the crisis and grew more.[11]

Trade relations with China also explain the differential evolution of the terms of trade in the region. The greater demand for primary goods tied to Chinese growth is reflected in an increase in the terms of trade in the majority of countries exporting these types of goods —mainly in South America. In the rest of the region, meanwhile, the terms of trade show a declining trend, given that these are oil-importing economies, and some countries, such as in Central America, do not produce commodities demanded by the emerging Asian economies (e.g. minerals and soybeans).[12] The terms of trade in South America have been on a growth path since the beginning of the past decade —interrupted only in 2009— and in 2010 reached 60% above the 2000 level, while for Central America we see the reverse trend (14% below the 2000 level) (Figure 1.4).

Figure 1.3. Latin America: China's shares of total exports and imports, by country 2000 and 2009

(In percentage of total exports and imports by country)

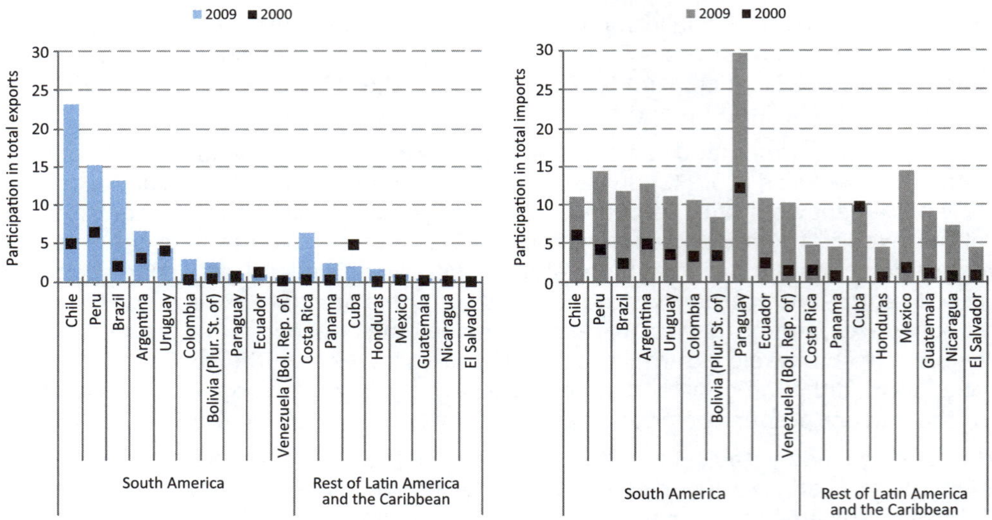

Source: Based on the United Nations Commodity Trade Statistics Database (COMTRADE).
http://dx.doi.org/10.1787/888932522379

Figure 1.4. South America and Central America: terms of trade indices, 2000-2010

(Year 2005 = 100)

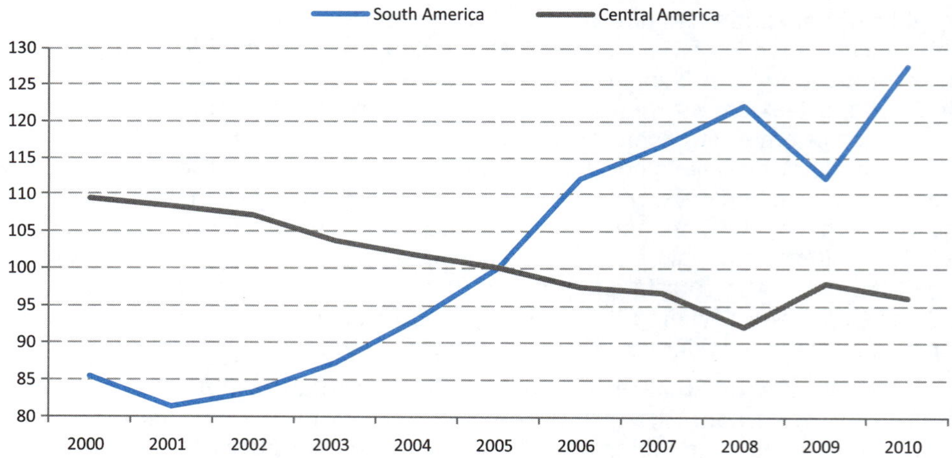

Note: The countries covered from South America and Central America are Argentina, Bolivia (Plur. State of), Brazil, Chile, Colombia, Ecuador, Paraguay, Peru, Uruguay, Venezuela (Bol. Rep. of) and Costa Rica, El Salvador, Guatemala, Honduras, Nicaragua, Panama, respectively.

Source: Based on official figures.
http://dx.doi.org/10.1787/888932522398

The new opportunities that open up with the trade dynamism of China and other emerging Asian economies also bring new challenges in terms of inflation and external vulnerability. Increases in food and fuel prices often affect the most vulnerable, particularly in urban areas of Central American and Caribbean countries that are not exporters of these goods. In addition, they create inflationary pressures and can have effects on general price levels if they translate into wage increases in a context of strong growth in domestic demand. Finally, economies that now trade more with China are more exposed to the cycles and shocks of its economy. Although it is expected that the Chinese economy will continue to be an important engine for world growth, a slowdown in Chinese growth could potentially have significant effects on the prices and volume of exports, as well as on public finances.

1.3. Inflationary pressures and price increases of primary products and fuels

Since the second half of 2010 and during the first two quarters of 2011, international prices for primary products have rebounded, while the inflation rate has begun to increase in most of the region's countries. The prices for various commodities have now gone beyond the levels reached during the 2008 crisis (Figure 1.5).[13] One of the most important structural factors is the strong growth of China and India. The process of urbanisation and industrialisation in these countries has led to enormous demands for raw materials and fuel, as has the emergence of a middle class with considerable purchasing power and a shift towards a more Western diet.[14] The increase in consumer prices went from an average 4.7% in 2009 to 6.5% in 2010, above all due to the increase in international prices for food and fuel. To this must be added the end of subsidies on certain food items and on fuel prices, particularly in Central America and Mexico. The rise in consumer price indices has been greater in Latin American countries with lower incomes, as the proportion of food in overall consumption is higher, even when the appreciation of national currencies observed in most countries in the region has mitigated the impact of the increase in prices of imported products on domestic prices.

Figure 1.5. Monthly evolution of primary international commodity prices, during the period January 2003-August 2011
(In current US dollars)

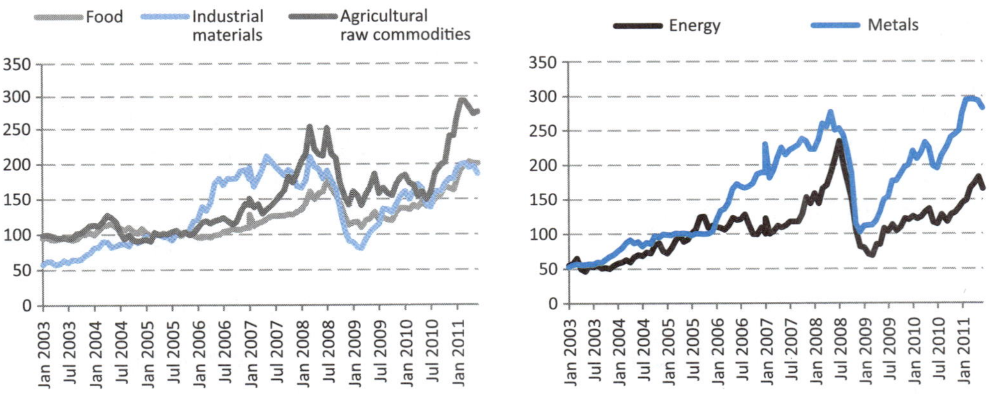

Note: Corresponds to the S&P aggregate GSCI index.

Source: Thomson Reuters Datastream.
http://dx.doi.org/10.1787/888932522417

In recent years, commodity price volatility has increased significantly. In fact, 2008 was the year with the greatest volatility since the first half of the 1970s. Volatility is affected by temporary factors impacting in the short term, such as supply shocks (for example, a poor harvest in an important producing country), variations in the effective exchange rates of the dollar and expectations in financial markets. Therefore, the forces that can lead to an increase in the volatility of agricultural markets are of at least two types: those factors that make supply and demand of these products less elastic, and those that increase the frequency and intensity of shocks. According to several studies, integration with other markets seems to be one of the main sources of increased volatility in the agricultural sector. These studies address not only integration in physical markets, such as the fuels market, or between different types of agricultural products, but above all, the closer links between commodities markets (among them, agricultural products) and financial markets.[15]

The impact of rises in food and energy prices is not the same in all countries. Apart from having a greater impact on lower income groups, these price increases create greater challenges for those countries with a high dependence on food imports. For example, in most Caribbean and Central American countries, food imports represent more than the equivalent of 5% of GDP, in comparison to an average of 4.3% for Latin America overall. Other Central American countries also have a relatively high dependence on food imports, with percentages varying between 2% and 5% of GDP. Mexico and South America have a lower dependence, which is the counterpart to the improvement in their terms of trade.[16]

Do these increases in consumer price indices warrant a response in monetary policy? The answer depends on whether inflationary pressures are more widespread than the increase of volatile components such as food and fuel. In this respect, there are differences across the region, even among countries that follow inflation-targeting policies. For example, core inflation —a measure that excludes the more volatile prices of food, drinks and transport (energy goods)— was negative in Chile and decreasing in Mexico during the first half of 2011. In Brazil, Colombia and Peru both the variation in price indices and core inflation show a rising trend. Therefore, there are indications in these economies that inflationary pressures are more intensive than the pressures generated by *commodity* prices. In these cases, especially when core inflation is near or above the upper limit of inflation targets, a more contractionary monetary policy can be effective, as in fact was observed during the second quarter of 2011.[17]

Beginning in the first quarter of 2010, as economic recovery was consolidating, some countries in the region began to implement a tighter monetary policy due to increased concern over inflation trends. Four of the countries with inflation targets —Brazil, Colombia, Chile and Peru— raised their monetary policy rates, a move that was joined by other countries such as the Dominican Republic and Uruguay, which also raised their reference rates. However, despite these increases, reference rates are still below 2008 levels, before the financial crisis spread to the region. Other countries in the region that have continued to focus on promoting economic growth have not increased their rates (such as Mexico) and have even tended towards a more expansionary monetary policy (Argentina and Costa Rica).

Actions taken by monetary policy makers seem designed to prevent increases in food and energy prices from producing changes in general price levels that could worsen inflationary expectations in the region. External pressures on the dynamics of inflation in the region, caused by rising food and energy prices, pose a new dilemma for policy makers. It is therefore necessary to balance the objectives of sustaining domestic economic recovery with avoiding monetary-financial conditions that might encourage a resurgence of inflationary expectations and the generation of bubbles in the price of domestic assets, particularly in a context of high international liquidity.

In this regard, the challenge for fiscal and monetary policy makers is three-fold: *i)* to determine to what extent external inflationary shock should be "accommodated", while managing aggregate demand (and reducing economic momentum); *ii)* to design fiscal and monetary policies that will minimise the economic cost of containing inflation and more importantly will not sharpen the risks associated with strong capital inflows and, consequently, associated with upward pressure on domestic currencies; and *iii)* adopt policies to reduce the social consequences from inflation as well as stabilisation policies.

1.4. Capital inflows: challenges to stability

Improved macroeconomic fundamentals in Latin America coupled with high liquidity and uncertainty in the capital markets of developed countries and historically low interest rates have led to large capital flows into several countries in the region. Although capital inflows, depending on their characteristics, may in principle represent greater opportunities for increasing investment rates and economic growth, the region's experience and emerging markets in general during the 1990s reveals that the volatility of these flows can generate severe macroeconomic problems and financial disruptions. Despite evidence that international investors today differentiate more among the countries of the region based on their fundamentals than they did in the past, the high synchronisation of flows towards emerging markets demonstrates the importance of global factors.[18]

These capital inflows, as well as the increase in prices for basic products, contributed to the appreciation of nominal and real exchange rates in the region. This appreciation had a particularly marked impact on the currencies of countries with inflation-targeting schemes and flexible exchange rates. As a result, 11 countries recorded nominal currency appreciations during the first 10 months of 2010 in comparison with the same period in 2009, notably the Brazilian real (13.6%), the Colombian peso (13.2%), the Uruguayan peso (13.1%), the Chilean peso (9.4%) and the Costa Rican colón (8%). In contrast, only five countries recorded a nominal depreciation of their currencies, Argentina and the Bolivarian Republic of Venezuela standing out in this regard. In real terms the situations are diverse. On the one hand, the currencies of Brazil and Colombia have appreciated with respect to the average exchange rate for the 2000s (38% and 24% respectively), while the currencies of Chile and the Bolivarian Republic of Venezuela also seem to have appreciated slightly over the same period (around 10%).[19] On the other hand, the currencies of Peru and Mexico seem to be near their historical average, while Argentina's has slightly depreciated (15% above the average for the 2000s) (Figure 1.6).[20]

Volatility and excessive appreciations of real exchange rates —above that explained by changes in fundamentals— can reduce competitiveness in the tradable sector of the economy or in tradable activities that do not benefit from increases in export prices. Short-term fluctuations in real exchange rates can have permanent negative effects on economic growth, in particular when firms face credit constraints warranting policy intervention to curb their effects.[21] Exchange rate appreciations can even nullify the effort in various countries to stimulate innovation, create new productive activities and diversify the economic structure.

Policy makers have adopted a series of measures to try to reduce the volatility of nominal exchange rates and reduce possible exposure to capital flow reversal. Among the measures to reduce capital-flow volatility and the consequent instability of nominal exchange rates are those that discourage short-term capital inflows as well as an increase in foreign exchange assets held by the public sector and certain private financial entities.

Measures to deal with capital inflows can be classified according to whether public authorities try to absorb additional flows or reduce their volume through capital controls.[22] Several countries have accumulated significant quantities of international reserves by intervening in foreign exchange markets, including Argentina, Brazil, Colombia, Costa Rica, Guatemala, Mexico and Peru. In addition, countries such as

Figure 1.6. Indices of real effective exchange rates for 7 Latin American countries, January 2008-March 2011
(December 2007 = 100)

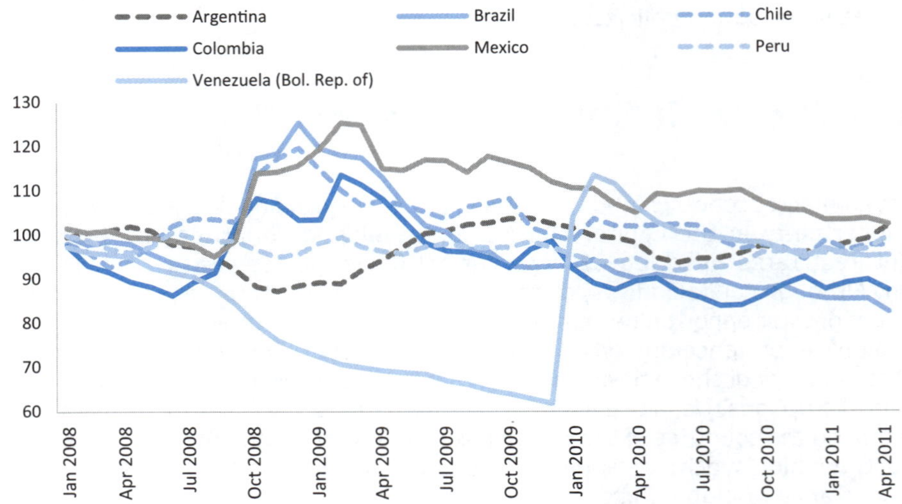

Source: Based on official figures.
http://dx.doi.org/10.1787/888932522436

the Plurinational State of Bolivia, Paraguay and Peru have high levels of reserves as a percentage of GDP (near or above 25%) in comparison to other countries in the region. Some countries have adopted a series of measures directly aimed at reducing capital inflows or increasing capital outflows. For example, Chile has gradually increased foreign investment caps for the country's pension funds, announcing in November 2010 that it would permit up to 80% of these funds to be invested abroad. Peru has adopted similar measures and in September 2010 it announced that it would allow the investment of up to 30% of the funds administered by pension fund managers to be invested abroad. For its part, Brazil increased its financial transactions tax on foreign investment in fixed-rate banking instruments, first to 4% and then, in October 2010, to 6%, while raising the tax on margin deposits in futures markets from 0.38% to 6% and leaving unchanged the 2% tax rate on equity investments. However, other administrative measures were introduced to increase the effectiveness of the tax in terms of curbing speculative capital inflows (see Box 1.1). Argentina, Colombia and Peru have maintained or introduced similar measures, while another instrument has been to increase unremunerated reserve requirements (Argentina, Brazil, Colombia and Peru).[23]

The accumulation of international reserves strengthens the future capacity to cope with sharp drops in terms of trade or a "sudden stop" in capital flows and reduces exchange rate volatility. However, it also increases the challenges for monetary policy in the region. If the region's central banks intervene in the market without sterilising the injections of national currency, they increase the risk of affecting the inflationary expectations of the public. But if they intervene in the market sterilising these interventions (totally or partially), there is the resulting quasi-fiscal cost and risk of damage to their own balance sheet.

Box 1.1. Capital controls as part of the macroeconomic tool kit

"Not only are capital controls ineffective, but in addition they raise domestic interest rates."

This type of internally inconsistent comments is not unusual when discussing capital controls —a subject marked with strong beliefs and weak data. To gain some perspective we must organise our analysis around two basic questions: *i)* Are they effective (i.e. do they affect the market in the desired direction)?, and if so, *ii)* are they efficient instruments (in other words, do the benefits outweigh the costs)? This box begins with the basics, analysing the first question in light of experience with controls on capital inflows through taxation.

These controls, traditionally associated with unremunerated reserve requirements (URRs) on capital inflows imposed in Chile and Colombia during the 1990s, are basically a variation of the Tobin tax on international capital flows. In fact, Chilean authorities at the time offered the option of a tax equivalent to the URRs to those investors who preferred to pay upfront and maintain their liquidity.

The standard argument of the sceptics was that these controls failed to stop capital inflows and currency appreciation. However, this appreciation seems to be biased, since we do not know what the inflows and appreciation would have been if there were no controls. Yet, there are ways to quantify what capital controls aim to introduce in the first place.

The simplest and most natural way to measure the effect of capital controls is through deviations from covered interest parity, in other words, the differential between the difference in interest rates and the *forward* discount (or the "carry" in local currency that international investors receive).[a] A study for the Chilean case shows that this difference oscillated between 2% and 3% during the period of controls, close to the value of the equivalent Tobin tax.[b] A similar exercise for the most recent case of the Brazilian financial transactions tax (*Imposto sobre Operações Financeiras*, IOF) leads to the same conclusions: a 6% tax on capital inflows creates a 6% gap between the differential in interest rates (the difference between the Selic rate [the Brazilian reference rate] and the short-term rate on US *treasuries* that are near zero) and the *carry* of the Brazilian currency, the real (Figure 1.7, left panel). Similar behaviour is also found in the cases of the Turkish lira (Figure 1.7, right panel) and the Israeli shekel.

Figure 1.7. Effects of capital controls in Brazil and Turkey

(Interest rates in annual percentage and exchange rates in national currency per dollar)

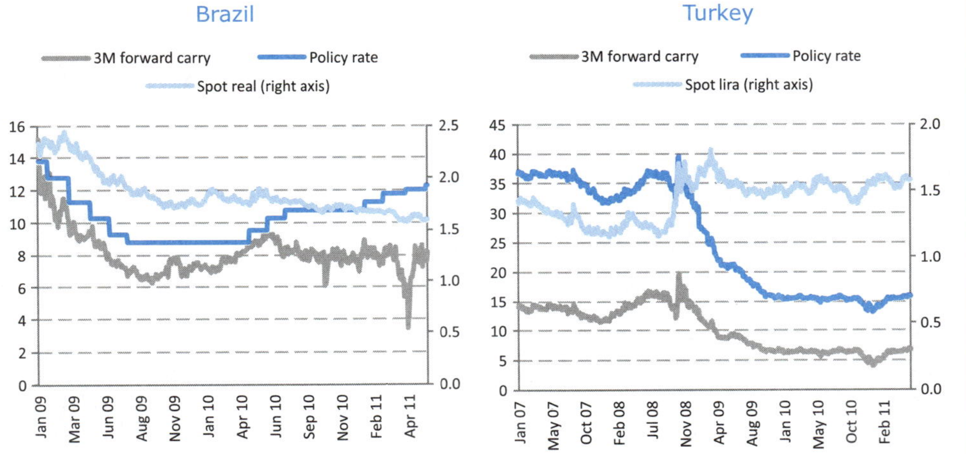

Source: Prepared on the basis of data from Thomson Datastream.

http://dx.doi.org/10.1787/888932522455

Capital controls are also effective, as they impose a toll on traffic in and out of domestic markets. Their effectiveness depends on the cost of the toll (and the volume of traffic). For example, a 2% tax will not obtain much more than a 2% cut in the value of local assets (including the local currency); a 10% tax will obtain a proportionally (but probably not linearly) stronger effect; meanwhile, a 2% tax opened to future adjustments (as recently seen in Brazil) should have an effect somewhere in between, as it affects the expectations of short-term speculative investors.

Summing up, capital controls are not irrelevant, as their opponents argue, nor are they as influential as their defenders say. Rather, they are an additional element in the toolkit of macroeconomic counter-cyclical policies that should complement monetary, fiscal and exchange-rate policy and prudential regulation.

Source: Produced by Eduardo Levy Yeyati.

[a] From a technical perspective, the covered parity implies that the *carry* for currencies (alternatively, the future discount) must be equal to the rate differential plus transaction costs, which include taxes on international capital flows.

[b] De Gregorio *et al.* (2000).

For many countries in the region, a major challenge for current economic policy is to maintain financial stability if the increased availability of funds feeds a boom in bank lending or potential bubbles in certain asset markets. In this regard, stock prices in several local exchanges have shown a strong performance since early 2009.

Given the rapid expansion of credit, rising profits in the financial sector in some countries (such as Brazil), and the upward pressure on currencies in the region, it would be prudent for the authorities to adopt measures to slow credit growth (Figure 1.8). These measures could include, for instance, raising reserve requirements, bank capital requirements, or both, such as those implemented by Peru starting in June 2010. Peru raised the minimum legal reserve to 9%, increased the minimum demand-deposit requirements for banks, raised the marginal reserve requirement in soles and in foreign currency, and increased the reserve requirements for deposits of non-resident financial entities (up to 120%).

Figure 1.8. Real credit growth in seven Latin American countries, 2010
(Percentage rates)

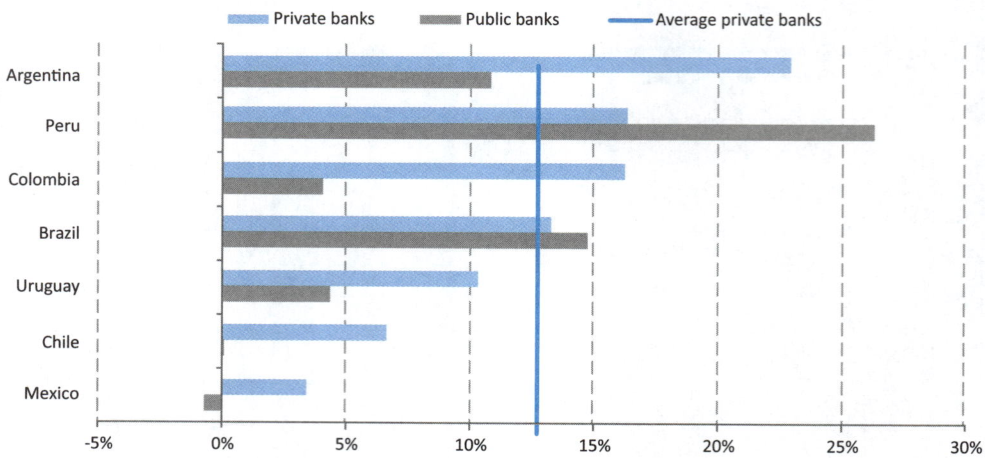

Source: Based on official figures.
http://dx.doi.org/10.1787/888932522474

1.5. Challenges for macroeconomic policy

A greater effort to understand the structural situation, eliminating the transitory effects of the business cycle and other associated factors, can help guide policy decisions. Many indicators, such as fiscal balances, debt-to-GDP ratios and credit ratings, tend to be very pro-cyclical as they are influenced by economic growth, commodity prices and real exchange rates.[24] It is therefore important not to give excessive weight to the "success" of purely domestic factors and to maintain a prudent perspective on the duration of the favourable context, which allows rebuilding policy space.

In designing fiscal stabilisation policies in Latin America it is necessary to differentiate between normal shocks, which induce stationary fluctuations around a trend, and extraordinary shocks, which are long-lasting and may have irreversible effects. One obstacle to designing fiscal measures for exceptional events is that measures for dealing with non-stationary shocks, and due to the weakness of automatic stabilisers in the region, must have a significant degree of discretionality. In the case of a non-stationary event, it is impossible to know beforehand precisely how the trend will evolve —much less how the economic structure and its forms of governance may change as a result of the shock.[25] Thus, it is important to distinguish between strictly counter-cyclical policies and macroeconomic adjustment policies. The former aim to counter temporary shifts away from the current trend; the latter manage the consequences of permanent shocks through changes in rules. The objective may be to structurally reduce excessive volatility, or (in the case of multiple equilibriums) to co-ordinate decisions in order to put the economy in an equilibrium that is considered superior to another.[26] For commodity export economies, similar arguments also apply to the fluctuations in prices of international exports.

The recent international financial crisis has revealed the importance of fiscal policy as a tool for macroeconomic stabilisation. Most countries, including those that recorded positive rates of growth in 2009, have tried to combat the recession with larger fiscal deficits; this has in part been generated by automatic stabilisers, but primarily through the application of discretionary measures due to the weakness of the former in the region. This has allowed for a growing consensus on the legitimacy of applying transitory fiscal deficits as tools for macroeconomic stabilisation in periods of sharp decline in demand. Once the emergency is over, the strategies to exit the crisis must include goals for sustainable public debt that are consistent with the public investment and social policies required to accelerate progress towards sustainable development.[27]

Clear counter-cyclical fiscal rules can help to reduce aggregate volatility and expand the tax base to increase spending and social investment needed to reduce inequality in the region. It is important not to reduce fiscal policy to mere quantitative control over public accounts (public debt, spending and deficit) so that the impact of public finances on crucial development objectives is not forgotten. The links between quantitative and qualitative aspects of fiscal policy must also be incorporated in the quality of public finances with the aim of ensuring the effective and efficient use of public resources.[28]

The credibility of fiscal policy must be reaffirmed, given the region's vulnerability of public finances to the economic and social situation and its institutional and political limitations. A tendency towards excessive discretionality must be avoided, and a limited and responsible discretionality encouraged. Nevertheless, recent experiences show that when rules are rigid and not adjusted to the economic cycle, they often end up being difficult to implement and therefore have little credibility. A recommended guiding principle on fiscal policy is the use of the structural balance indicator to complement effective balances. A temporary co-existence between fiscal deficits and macroeconomic stabilisation is part of a medium-term strategy that takes into account the performance of social indicators and productive development, giving more weight to goals related to structural balance than to current effective balance. In addition, reality has shown that there are exceptional circumstances in which active discretionary policies are justified. The goal of any macro-fiscal rule must be to achieve structural balance (or balance in public debt) in the medium-term (sub-national governments included); it must also contain escape clauses and transition periods for significant macroeconomic fluctuations. Although fiscal rules do not assure per se fiscal credibility and solvency, if they have enough credibility and are part of a country's fiscal architecture, they can become powerful counter-cyclical tools. For this to happen, it is important to develop mechanisms that institutionalise counter-cyclical fiscal policies in the face of excessive fiscal discretion during periods of prosperity.[29]

Funds aimed at stabilising tax revenues generated from the export of natural resources, whose prices are characterised by instability, are part of the fiscal stabilisation framework. When well-run, these funds can help stabilise recurrent expenditures, add financing in critical situations, and regulate the supply of foreign exchange. In turn, the smooth operation of stabilisation funds requires full co-ordination between fiscal and exchange-rate authorities. Its absence could be an obstacle to the match between the macroeconomic environment and achieving sustained development, causing imbalances between different objectives, such as inflation, employment, export quality and growth.

Despite its heterogeneous situation, this is a period of opportunity for more and better growth in Latin America and the Caribbean, but co-ordinated policies on various fronts are necessary in order to achieve this; among these, macroeconomic policy stands out. The history of Latin America shows that there has been a close relationship between the direction of macroeconomic policy and the region's volatile, poor development, its limited productive investment and low productivity growth. A macroeconomy at the service of development focuses on fiscal, monetary and exchange-rate policies and capital markets. There must be co-ordinated management of all these areas of economic policy if the macroeconomic environment is to stimulate capital formation, innovation and the creation of quality jobs.

Notes

1. ECLAC (2011).
2. Kacef (2009) and OECD (2008).
3. ECLAC, (2010a) and OECD (2009).
4. ECLAC (2010b).
5. With the exception of the Bolivarian Republic of Venezuela (where a fall was recorded), El Salvador and Colombia, the value of capital goods imports increased by two digits in the countries of the region, with the highest increases in Argentina, Chile, Ecuador, Guatemala, Honduras and Paraguay.
6. Regarding the composition by institutional sector, the evidence available for the countries that provide quarterly information (Mexico, Peru and Uruguay) indicates that during 2010, private investment was the component that exhibited the greatest expansion in comparison with 2009.
7. ECLAC (2011).
8. OECD (2010).
9. Blásquez *et al.* (2006).
10. Lederman, Olarreaga and Perry (2007).
11. The simple correlation coefficient between real GDP growth in 2007 and 2010 and China's contribution to the total trade of each country is 0.61,.
12. OECD (2010).
13. The ranges of price changes vary considerably depending on the type of product, but four situations can be identified: *i)* sustained increases in the case of tropical products (sugar, bananas and coffee) and non-food raw materials (cotton and rubber); *ii)* beginning in the second half of 2008, a stabilisation of prices in a range of 50%-100% above the average for 2000-05 for edible oils and soybean complex products; *iii)* an increase below 25% in the case of meat products; iv) wide variation for cereals and fertilisers (see ECLAC, FAO and IICA, 2010 and OECD 2011).
14. OECD (2010).
15. ECLAC, FAO and IICA (2010)
16. Jiménez, Jiménez and Kacef (2008).
17. However, uncertainty in the global economy and indications of a slowdown in domestic and external demand at the beginning of the second semester of 2011 has lead most central banks in the region to move towards a more neutral or easing stance.
18. OECD (2011).
19. Other countries in the region that find their currencies appreciated with respect to the average for the first decade of the 2000s are Costa Rica, Guatemala, Paraguay and Uruguay.
20. ECLAC (2011).
21. Caballero and Lorenzoni (2007).
22. Cárdenas and Levy Yeyati (2011).
23. Although instruments for capital controls exist in Chile, they are not currently being used.
24. Reisen and von Maltzen (1999).
25. Daude and Roitman (2011).
26. Fanelli and Jiménez (2009).
27. Carranza, Daude and Melguizo (2011).
28. ILPES (2011).
29. ECLAC (2010c).

References

Blásquez-Lidoy, J., J. Rodríguez and J. Santiso (2006), "Angel or Devil? China's Trade Impact on Latin American Emerging Markets", Working Paper, No. 252, OECD Development Centre, Paris.

Caballero, R. and G. Lorenzoni (2007), "Persistent Appreciations and Overshooting: A Normative Approach", Working Paper, No. 13077, National Bureau of Economic Research.

Cárdenas, M. and E. Levy Yeyati (2011), *Latin American Economic Perspectives: Shifting Gears in an Age of Heightened Expectations*, Brookings Institution, Washington, DC.

Carranza, L., C. Daude, and A. Melguizo (2011), "Public Infrastructure Investment and Fiscal Sustainability in Latin America: Incompatible Goals?", Working Paper, No. 301, OECD Development Centre, Paris.

Daude, C. and A. Roitman (2011), "Imperfect Information and Saving in a Small Open Economy", Working Paper 11/60, IMF (International Monetary Fund), Washington, DC.

ECLAC (Economic Commission for Latin America and the Caribbean) (CEPAL) (2011), *Economic Survey of Latin America and the Caribbean 2010-2011*, ECLAC, Santiago, Chile.

ECLAC (CEPAL) (2010a), *Economic Survey of Latin America and the Caribbean 2009-2010*, CEPAL, Santiago, Chile.

ECLAC (CEPAL) (2010b), *Preliminary Overview of the Economies of Latin America and the Caribbean 2010*, ECLAC, Santiago de Chile.

ECLAC (2010c), "Time for Equality: Closing Gaps, Opening Trails", 33rd session of ECLAC, 30 May - 1 June 2010, Brasilia.

ECLAC (2010d), *Social Panorama of Latin America and the Caribbean 2010*, ECLAC books, Santiago, Chile.

ECLAC, FAO (Food and Agriculture Organization of the United Nations) and IICA (Inter-American Institute for Cooperation on Agriculture) (2010), "Price Volatility in Agricultural Markets (2000-2010): Implications for Latin America and Policy Options", Bulletin no. 1, ECLAC/FAO and IICA.

Fanelli, J. and J.P. Jiménez (2009), "Crisis, volatilidad y política fiscal en América Latina", in O. Kacef and J.P. Jiménez (comp.), *Políticas macroeconómicas en tiempos de crisis: opciones y perspectivas*, ECLAC (CEPAL), Santiago, Chile.

ILPES (Latin American and Caribbean Institute for Economic and Social Planning) (2011), "Panorama de la Gestión Pública en América Latina: En la hora de la igualdad", ILPES, Santiago, Chile.

Jiménez, F., J.P. Jiménez and O. Kacef (2008), "Volatilidad de los precios de productos energéticos y alimentarios: impacto macroeconómico y medidas de política en América Latina y el Caribe", seminar: "Crisis alimentaria y energética: oportunidades y desafíos para América Latina y el Caribe", 4-5 September 2008, Santiago de Chile.

Kacef, O. (2009), "Crisis y políticas públicas en América Latina y el Caribe", en O. Kacef and J.P. Jiménez (comp.), Políticas macroeconómicas en tiempos de crisis: opciones y perspectivas, ECLAC (CEPAL), Santiago, Chile.

Lederman, D., M. Olarreaga and G. Perry (2007), "Latin America's Response to China and India: Overview of Research Findings and Policy Implications", Revista de Economía y Estadística, Facultad de Ciencias Económicas, Instituto de Economía y Finanzas, Universidad Nacional de Córdoba, Vol. 0 (1), pp. 149-193.

OECD (2008), *Latin American Economic Outlook 2009*, OECD Development Centre, Paris.

OECD (2009), *Latin American Economic Outlook 2010*, OECD Development Centre, Paris.

OECD (2010a), *Perspectives on Global Development: Shifting Wealth*, OECD Development Centre, París.

OECD (2010b), *Latin American Economic Outlook 2011*, OECD Development Centre, Paris.

Reisen, H. and J. von Maltzen (1999), "Boom and Bust and Sovereign Ratings", *International Finance*, Vol. 2 (2), pp. 273-293.

CHAPTER TWO

Public administration for development

Abstract

This chapter assesses public administration in Latin America. The region faces many important and common issues such as the quality of civil service, managerial transparency and the high level of centralisation in public administration. In addition, the Latin American state has limited resources to tackle some of the larger goals such as the supply of goods, the fostering of social equity, the delivery of social services, the re-allocation of resources and the stabilisation of the economy. However, Latin American countries are now better positioned than ever to reform their public sector and create states that are able to meet their development needs. This requires proper co-ordination of public policies such as the mobilisation of fiscal resources, the professionalisation of civil service, the appropriate use of new technologies and the mobilisation of diverse public and private actors.

2.1. Introduction

The set of institutions, norms and rules that determine how state agencies and human resources are managed plays a central role in the development of Latin American countries. This chapter assesses public administration in Latin America within the framework of the functions assumed by the state. These functions do not differ much from those of the OECD economies; they include the provision of public goods, the fostering of social equity, the delivery of social services, the redistribution of resources, and the stabilisation of the economy (section 2.2). What differentiates Latin American states from more developed countries is the magnitude of the needs that must be met and the limited resources available to accomplish this task. This creates a substantial and complex challenge. The region also faces other common challenges such as the quality of civil service, excessive bureaucracy, the transparency of governance and greater centralisation than in OECD economies (section 2.3). Policy makers in Latin America should be particularly mindful of the nature of the trade-offs between the short-term costs of addressing these challenges and the long-term benefits of public-sector reform. There are no shortcuts for developing an effective, efficient, transparent public sector (section 2.4).

This chapter confirms that Latin America is now well positioned to reform its public sector and build states that are able to meet their development needs. The economies of the region are growing, the volatility of public finances has been reduced and the burden of debt service is smaller. There have also been significant advances and innovations in public policy in the social sector, in infrastructure and in productive development. The consolidation of democratic institutions and technological development have created new opportunities for improving public administration. This must not, however, lead to complacency or an underestimation of the magnitude of the challenges faced by the countries in the region.

Bearing in mind differences between countries, the creation of states that meet the region's development needs requires special attention to various areas of public policy (section 2.5). The fundamental elements of the reform agenda in Latin America include: *i)* improvements in the mobilisation of fiscal resources, *ii)* a professional civil service, *iii)* the mobilisation of different actors, *iv)* appropriate use of new technologies, and *v)* mechanisms to make government more transparent. Around these elements, mechanisms can be established for inter-regional dialogue that will help disseminate best practices and identify lessons learned. International agencies have an important role to play in the articulation of these networks and in the promotion and dissemination of the reforms.

Fiscal reform is a necessary condition for states to increase the resources they need to fulfil their responsibilities. There are also significant challenges in budgetary management, human resources, access to electronic government systems, information, transparency, and the integrity of public administration. The limited use of evidence in budgetary decisions in Latin America requires the development of new budgetary management systems based on outcomes. This calls for the development of monitoring and evaluation systems capable of generating timely and relevant information on outcomes and adjusting budgetary processes so that this information is used in decision making.

Given that states depend on their staff to perform their functions, Latin America needs to professionalise its civil service. It is important to distinguish between the various functions exercised by state employees and to develop appropriate working arrangements for each function, combining the objectives of merit and flexibility on a case-by-case basis. Appropriate use of new information and communication technologies can help governments shape a more flexible, agile and transparent public sector that has a greater capacity to respond. Information technology must be considered as a means of communication in both directions, able to facilitate transactions but also offering a space for citizen participation; public administrations must be adapted to achieve this.

At the same time, it is necessary to strengthen the citizens' trust in the state. Solutions encompass a combination of instruments, both public and private, that countries can use to reduce the risk of mistrust in the state, such as declarations of interest, information-access systems and codes of ethics. Latin American countries can also benefit from the participation of different stakeholders and actors in public policy. In order to provide public services more effectively and efficiently, governments can combine their inputs, policies and knowledge with those of other actors, including non-state actors, sub-national administrations and commercial providers of public goods.

2.2. Key aspects of public administration

The increase in the provision of services and transfers has made effectiveness a key element in public administration. The capacity of public administrations to meet commitments set out in the political process and to meet the growing demands of citizens has become a central concern.

Public services must also meet high standards of transparency. Governments are financed with taxpayers' money and must act in accordance with specific restrictions and legal mandates. Modern states are accountable to their citizens for the use of public resources and for the results of their actions. The funding mechanisms of many public services often impose transparency requirements that exceed those of the private sector but that are essential to maintaining trust. Transparency is key to limiting the risk of corruption. The predictability of public interventions increases market confidence, reduces risk premiums, and facilitates compliance with regulations. The increased transparency of modern states is also a by-product of information technologies, as citizens of many countries can now access services online and compare situations between countries.

Efficiency is another important element of public administration. Achieving the same level of public services with fewer inputs will free up resources to address other development deficits. Improved efficiency can also help create public support for state reforms, even those that require a heavier tax burden. While citizens, as voters and users of public services, may deem public services (provided directly by the state or under its supervision) to be scarce and of low quality, as taxpayers they may not be willing to pay the cost of resolving this.[1] As a result, states are under increasing pressure to do more with less, making efficiency a third key element in public administration.

As societies become more heterogeneous, the demands on the state become more diverse. In Latin America, states are responsible for the provision of public goods, delivery of social services, the promotion of social equity, redistribution of resources and the stabilisation of the economy to the same extent as in high-income countries. In recent years, Latin American states have begun to address needs in the areas of environmental protection, economic integration, gender equality and social and productive development. The resources available to perform all these functions are scarce, not only compared to high-income countries, but also to countries with similar levels of development.

Box 2.1. Responsibilities and resources of modern states

Countries rely on the state for the provision of essential public goods, such as maintaining law and order, defence, protection of intellectual property rights and the awarding of contracts. States also fulfil the function of economic orientation by sending signals to markets, offering incentives through the granting of business licenses and permits, and by the regulation of energy, transport, food security and innovation. Education and health are essential public services and state benefits provided for the welfare of citizens. States also promote culture and recreation and create systems that protect individuals from unemployment, disease and poverty in old age.

The allocation of responsibilities for these functions reflects social preferences. However, it seems that differences among states are more a product of the heterogeneity with which they carry out these functions —through direct provision, regulation or incentives to the private sector— rather than the actual scope of government responsibilities, which, surprisingly, are similar between countries.

States developed considerably during the 20th century, becoming major service providers. This trend over the past hundred years reflects an increase in the size of the state. During the past century, expenditures and the number of employees grew from less than a tenth of national income to slightly less than half of national income in most developed countries. In many countries the state was transformed with the consolidation of democracy, the development of a market economy, the creation of the welfare state and globalisation. However, these changes have not been linear, and many countries have faced a substantial redefinition of the role of the state as a result of fiscal constraints, the need for competitiveness and social change. The most notable feature of the transformation of the public sector during the last seventy years has been its massive development as a major service provider. Since this transformation, the interaction between the state and its citizens has become a daily activity.

Expectations and standards for public services are now significantly higher. Even though modern states do more and spend more, it is worth asking if they are providing better services and meeting the expectations of citizens and the business community. Given current fiscal constraints, the answer is not necessarily "more State" but "better State", focusing on what the state does best and on building trust and sustainable economic growth. These issues are attracting increasing interest from social scientists. Economists and policy makers are also devoting more attention to the public sector economy because of its growing share of national income and its macroeconomic impact.

States are complex organisations that often pursue many policy objectives simultaneously and that are faced with multiple goals and stakeholders. Public entities and organisations, in lieu of running their own programmes, must respond to the mandates and functions assigned to them by the political process through legislation as well as attend the needs of citizens. This is a process that can generate demands, mandates and objectives that are sometimes vague or even contradictory. Public administration must recognise this reality and reconcile objectives with possibilities. Public administration must integrate the diverse nature of modern states that reflects the relationship between networks of different public bodies. The economy of public choice has helped to improve the understanding of the role and functions of bureaucracy, which is able to pursue precise sectoral objectives on behalf of the general interest.

The complexity of the public sector apparatus requires political responses that are modest yet pragmatic, the implementation of systems of checks and balances, the fostering of openness and transparency, and control mechanisms to reduce the risk of corruption and capture. Similarly, co-ordination is necessary so that, with the contribution of different bodies, the strategic objectives of the state can be accomplished and resources, commitments and implementation are aligned to achieve the expected results.

The gap between the need for public intervention and available resources is considerably higher in Latin America than in developed countries. Making the most of scarce public resources is therefore crucial if governments are to fulfil their contribution to development in the region. Whether it is the management of public programmes or the use of private resources for public purposes, public administration is fundamental for states to meet their objectives.

2.3. Challenges of public administration in Latin America

Availability and efficient resource management: Many countries in the region (probably with the exception of Argentina, Brazil and Uruguay) require more fiscal resources to meet the needs of the public sector and contribute more effectively to development. This also requires greater efficiency in the administration and implementation of spending. And in the context of public administration, greater planning, co-ordination and risk assessment is needed to generate sufficient resources. Given that the structure of public policy evolves with the country's level of development, countries may be increasingly challenged to expand services and transfers. This may be implemented within increased decentralisation, but needs to be accompanied by regular monitoring of the volume and quality of services.

The professionalisation of the civil service: As shown in Figure 2.1., as a percentage of the total workforce, Latin American countries have far fewer public employees than OECD economies. In some countries, the percentage is slightly more than half that found in the OECD economies with the highest levels of public employment. The biggest difference, however, is that the Latin American states are normally pre-bureaucratic, in that they are characterised by the lack of a formal, professional civil service and by a high proportion of political appointments among civil servants. Some countries seem to have developed a highly distorted bureaucracy, with low-skilled workers protected by strict contractual arrangements and managers appointed on the basis of their political affinities. This situation generates levels of job rotation and patronage of little use to the development of public policies that require a high degree of coherence and continuity if they are to be effective. Under this regime, the flexibility that might be necessary to better meet different public needs can easily become discretionary and a source of incoming influences. In many countries the proportion of public employees with high skills and high motivation could be much greater. Some countries such as Brazil, Chile, Mexico and Peru have recently undertaken reforms to establish a highly professional civil service, though they are more the exception than the rule in the region. The reforms in these countries are very recent and still have many hurdles to overcome.

Another indicator often used to identify the size of the state —public spending as a percentage of GDP— shows that the region is behind OECD states. Public spending has increased, but the differences remain substantial, and have even widened in recent years (Figure 2.2).

Centralisation: Latin American countries have a level of fiscal and administrative decentralisation below that of the OECD economies. Municipal spending in Latin America is less than half that of OECD economies as a percentage of GDP (9.5% and 20.6%, respectively), and their revenues constitute slightly less than one third. This reflects significant vertical imbalances. Regional figures are more balanced but with great variations between large federal countries (Argentina, Brazil and Mexico) and smaller unitary states which may not even have a regional administration.[2]

Beyond its impact on the efficiency of public administration and equity in the distribution of public resources, centralisation seriously limits the ability of citizens

Figure 2.1. Latin American and OECD countries: public sector employment in the labour force, 2008
(Percentage of the labour force)

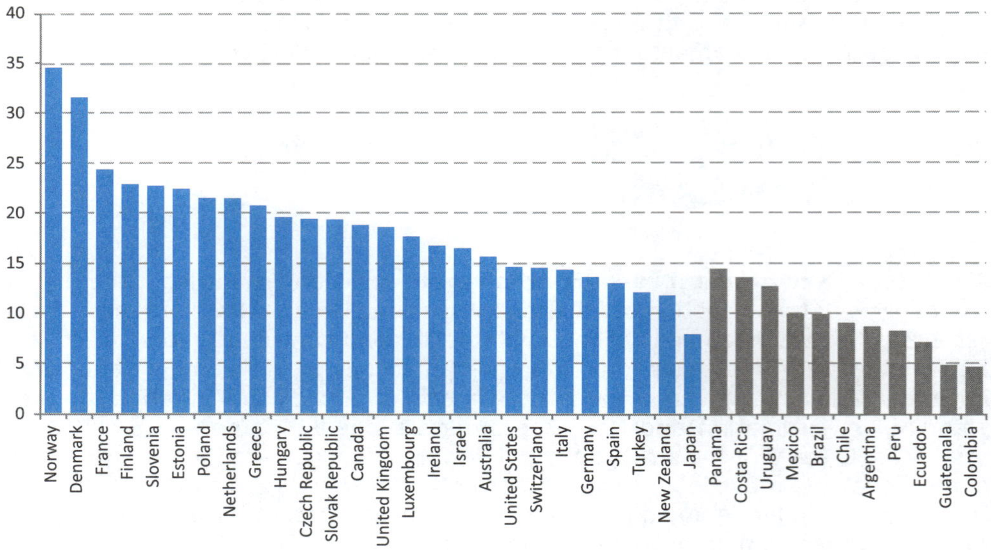

Note: Data for Finland, Israel, Mexico, Panama and Poland correspond to 2007; France, Japan, New Zealand and Uruguay to 2006; and Brazil to 2003.

Source: Laborsta database (ILO).
http://dx.doi.org/10.1787/888932522493

Figure 2.2. Latin America and the OECD: public expenditure, 2000, 2007 and 2009
(Percentage of GDP)

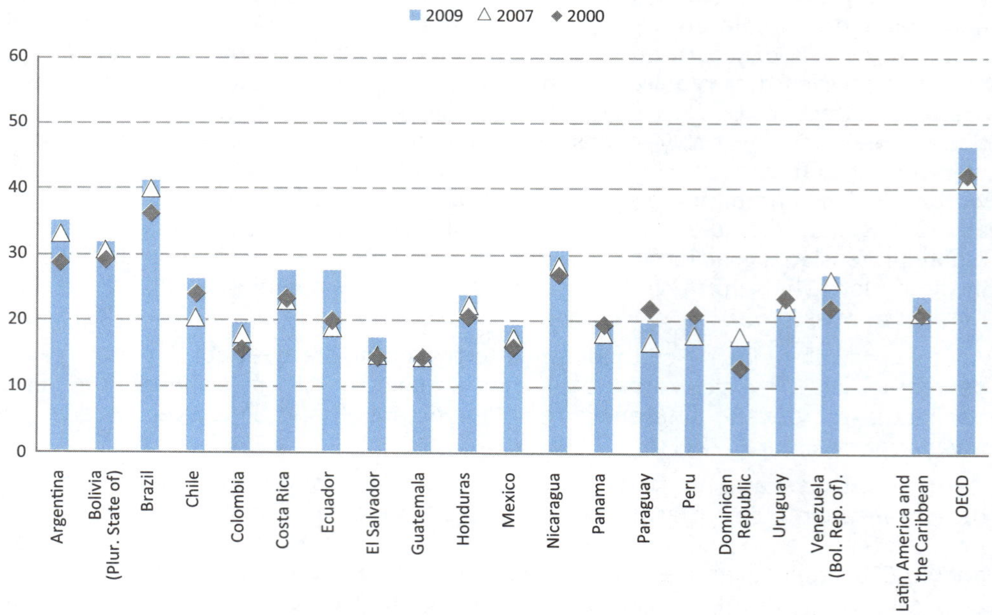

Note: The statistics refer to general government in the case of Argentina, Bolivia (Plur. State of), Brazil, Chile, Costa Rica, Nicaragua and Peru and the central government in Colombia, Ecuador, El Salvador, Guatemala, Honduras, Mexico Panama, Paraguay, Dominican Republic, Uruguay and Venezuela (Bolivarian Rep. of).

Source: CEPALSTA Statistics on public finances for Latin America and the Caribbean and OECD (2011) for other countries.
http://dx.doi.org/10.1787/888932522512

to participate in state affairs. If sub-national governments provide a significant part of services required by citizens and the investments of greatest interest to communities, then their lack of resources and powers, as well as their over-reliance on central government transfers, are structural constraints on citizen participation that the government will struggle to overcome.

Lack of transparency and trust: Latin America has been on the path of democratic consolidation since the early 1980s. Democracy as a political system has the strong ideological support of the Latin American population.[3] According to opinion polls, satisfaction with democracy increases steadily with ascendance in economic status. However, the middle classes, though in relative solidarity with the tax system and a strong supporter of democracy, are not satisfied with the public services they receive. They are "dissatisfied customers" of the state.[4] Despite progress in some areas, high inequality, a lack of transparency and poor-quality public services undermine trust in the government and in the social contract in Latin America.

The institutions in the region often suffer from a lack of trust. Trust in democratic institutions, such as the judicial and legislative system, is very low and the degree of satisfaction with local services almost never exceeds 50%.[5] This can trigger a vicious circle of distrust and weakened legitimacy, which in turn limits the possibility of raising taxes and impedes the provision of more universal services. When people have the means to afford private services, they may come to completely abandon public services, thereby contributing to their stigmatisation. In fact, in Latin American countries, the private provision of basic services in education, health and even security is high compared to in OECD economies.

Comparative international studies suggest that in a large majority of Latin American countries there is a significantly higher perception of corruption than in OECD economies. Whatever the causes, the recent progress made by some countries in the region is commendable. For instance, according to Transparency International, the levels of corruption perception in Chile and Uruguay is similar to the level recorded in European countries such as Belgium, France and Slovenia and only marginally below the levels recorded in the United States and the United Kingdom.[6]

Regulation as a policy instrument: Many countries in Latin America developed their systems of regulation in the 1980s and 90s to adapt to the process of privatisation of public services and state-owned enterprises. During this process, some countries created independent bodies responsible for regulation in the energy, telecommunications and water sectors. However, this wave of reform failed to build a coherent regulatory system. The degree of implementation depended largely on the importance of the institutions responsible for regulation. A common problem for many countries in the region was the imbalance between the power of industry and the fragility of the regulators, who had limited resources and a workforce paid below market wages, as is the case of concessions in transport. In some of the smaller countries in the region, the ability to manage regulations and regulatory processes remains limited, affecting the rationalisation and effectiveness of regulatory frameworks. Thus, regulation as a policy instrument is used less in Latin America —and is often less effective— than in most OECD economies.

2.4. New paradigms and pragmatic responses[7]

The bureaucratic model created hierarchical organisations based on uniform standards for service. The need to improve effectiveness, efficiency and accountability drove many countries to implement innovative practices that would improve public-sector performance. This led to a modernisation of public-management structures and good governance. This caused a change in paradigm, referred to as "new public management" (NPM), which gave greater autonomy to managers and provided incentives for results-based management. This in turn has led to important reforms including the creation of executive agencies, the introduction of semi-contractual models with central government bodies and performance-related pay. This trend had a major impact in redefining the role of the State, which began to focus less on providing services and more on a leadership role that offered global strategic frameworks for markets. Market mechanisms were also used in the provision of services within the public sector. Strategic and preventive management of human resources served to strengthen the capacity of the State and to enable it to exercise its new functions.

Practice has shown that public administration requires its own techniques and instruments. While the NPM model shifted the emphasis in public administration reforms and governance, it did not always provide a clear response to the needs of public administration and often failed to address transparency in governance. Moreover, the NPM model focused on efficiency, sometimes at the expense of effectiveness. The need to create institutions and procedures intrinsic to the state to minimise trade-offs and face new challenges became apparent. As a result, the second wave of reforms emphasised the evaluation of results and sought to strengthen the link between the key processes of public sector management (budget, human resources management, audits) and results, with a particular focus on accountability. The role of regulatory reform increased in importance as it began to be recognised as an instrument of policy implementation. For instance, OECD economies introduced a system of checks and balances to define new rules as well as extensive mechanisms for updating and filtering existing regulation in the interest of consistency.

Fiscal consolidation has increased the pressure on public administration. The crisis has affected the balance between the State, markets and society, and has led governments to assume greater responsibilities. The current priority is to improve the capacity for strategic outlook, collective commitment and flexibility of resources to achieve greater coherence in policy action and recover sustained long-term development. Countries rely more than ever on a culture of performance. This makes it necessary to improve competitiveness and expand the range of options in providing services in order to improve public sector efficiency and promote greater participation of users in the design and delivery of public services.

The spread of new technologies has opened the window to new opportunities. Technological change has provided new tools to manage information and improve communication – two basic elements in the provision of public services. This requires innovative and effective solutions in collaboration with citizens and businesses. The public sector must become more agile and improve its productivity without additional costs while relying more on e-government, telematics in government and the strategic management of human resources. New technologies also provide opportunities to transform the public sector into a "transparent entity" that facilitates citizen participation and improves the provision of services focused on users' needs.[8]

Latin American countries are now better positioned than ever to reform their public sectors. The countries of the region weathered the financial crisis well thanks to prudent decisions taken in recent years. For this reason, they now have the financial strength and credibility needed to undertake long-term reforms. The three Latin American G-20 countries – Argentina, Brazil and Mexico, enjoy the privileged position of participating in the construction of a new economic order and forming part of a group of countries that seek excellence in policy making (Box 2.2).

To create States able to meet development needs, Latin American countries do not necessarily need to follow the same path travelled by today's developed countries. The last twenty years in Latin America have left a legacy of experiences that constitute a good basis for learning and to continue advancing. It is important to avoid the reproduction of management tools without taking into account institutional differences. It is necessary to learn, adapt and innovate.

Box 2.2. The process of reform in Latin America

It is important to study not only *what* practices should be adopted to foster development, but also *how* these reforms are achieved. This is the dilemma of the process of reform, which can be best understood terms of a "reform cycle" in five phases: *planning*, *dialogue*, *adoption*, *implementation*, and *sustainability*.[1] Although these phases do not always unfold in a sequential pattern, it is useful to distinguish between them to assess the relative strength of each player and reform efforts and avoid pitfalls in the future (Diagram 2.1).

Diagram 2.1. The stylised reform cycle: stages, main actors, and bottlenecks

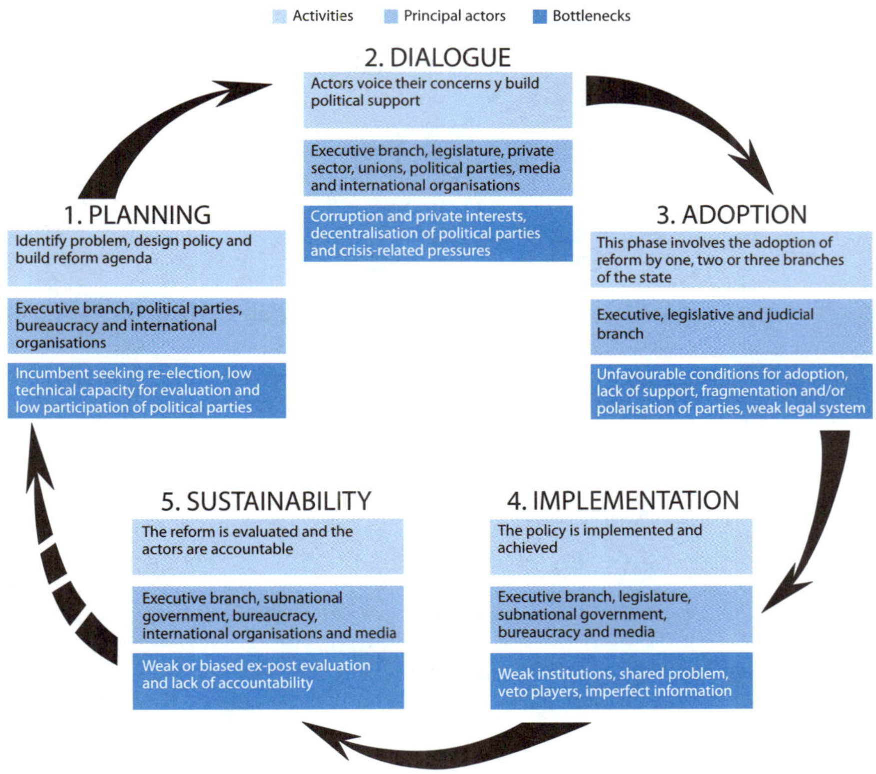

Source: Dayton-Johnson J., J. Londoño and S. Nieto-Parra (2011).
http://dx.doi.org/10.1787/888932522626

In the *planning* phase, the actors identify the problem, design the policy and build the reform agenda. In Latin America, this stage tends to be a creative and disorganised process. Executives have a near monopoly in the formulation of policy proposals, and only occasionally receive input from other actors. Regarding political parties, the low levels of party institutionalisation and high party fragmentation have created clientelistic, weak and short-lived political parties. Non-programmatic parties present challenges for reform planning, as policies will lack *ex-ante* planning and consistency over time. Co-ordination failures can be improved by promoting an increased participation of technical agencies, international organisations, and political parties. The technocracy of bureaucracy improves the quality of the *ex-ante* evaluation and the design of reforms, while international organisations help identifying the bottlenecks in the reforms and disseminating information on different country experiences.

1 See Dayton-Johnson, Londoño and Nieto-Parra (2011) for an analysis of the cycle of reorms in Latin America.

Box 2.2. (continued)

Once designed, there is generally an inclusive and comprehensive dialogue between the stakeholders of a reform. This provides a space for public deliberation and debate, which helps build political support for the reform. In some Latin American countries there have been recent efforts to improve party discipline. Additionally, recent administrations are taking advantage of media influence on public opinion by using "strategic communication" and "news management" techniques to increase public support for the reform. Indeed, presidents have reinforced a direct communication with the public. However, excessive pressure by the media and the public opinion to reform adversely affects the quality of policies, as incumbents might prioritise high-visibility in reforms.

The socio-economic context and the organisation of the reform agenda are key elements in the *adoption* phase. The reforms are adopted by the three powers of the State, although the involvement of different branches depends on the reform in question. The Latin American experience confirms that the economic context affects the chances of adopting policy reforms. In general, crises beget reform — though not necessarily of a structural nature — and launching a "package" of reforms can aid in the correct adoption of policy. The end of millennium crisis triggered fiscal responsibility and transparency frameworks (e.g., Argentina in 1999, Brazil in 2000, Colombia in 2003, Mexico in 2006, and Peru in 1999) and well-designed structural balance fiscal rules (e.g., Chile in 2001, and Colombia is in the process toward approval). In the financial policy-making front, some Latin American countries improved the regulation and supervision of financial systems in the aftermath of the banking crises of the past decade (e.g., Colombia in 1999, Peru in 1999, and Uruguay in 2002). Additionally, leadership and a high degree of legitimacy of the incumbent are crucial at this stage.

Once the policy is adopted, it must be executed and implemented in the *implementation* phase. On the one hand, the executive branch is responsible for implementing the approved policies, while the legislative branch monitors, reviews and investigates in detail the activities of the government. However, the power of interest groups, weak institutional structures, coordination failures between sub-national and national governments, and soft sub-national budgetary constraints have led to policy obstruction in Latin America. This distorts the overall quality of policies and increases the national deficit. Fulfilling its role as watchdog, the media exposes bad policy implementations, rendering actors accountable for their actions. Thus, the wide gulf between *de jure* reforms and *de facto* implementation serves to encourage Latin America to make significant institutional changes in the policy making process.

Ex-post evaluations of reforms must improve the *sustainability* of policies in Latin America. From a political standpoint, sustaining a policy is difficult because it challenges policy makers to maintain the policy until it has proven successful, and to prevent its reversal by the following administrations. Evaluations can help to sustain reforms that bear fruits beyond the political cycle and to facilitate changes to make policies more effective by learning from the implementation process. Increasingly in Latin America, independence in *ex-post* evaluations has been guaranteed by technocracy and international organisations, allowing for greater accountability and enhancing the legitimacy of the State throughout the policy making process. In spite of this, there is still room for improvement.

Source: Dayton-Johnson, J., J. Londoño and S. Nieto-Parra (2011), "The Process of Reform in Latin America: A Review Essay", *OECD Development Centre Working Paper*, No. 304, Paris.

Latin America has been a pioneer in the field of public policy, especially in social sectors. Latin America also pioneered programmes that provide conditional cash transfers to poor households as an incentive to adopt certain patterns of behaviour that would improve their living conditions, opportunities and social capital. After almost a decade since their introduction in many Latin American countries, conditional transfers are now being implemented in Africa and Asia. As shown in Figure 2.3., the degree of coverage varies by country, though a significant percentage of the total population can benefit, as is the case of the current programmes in Ecuador, Brazil and Mexico, among others.

Figure 2.3. Latin America: coverage of selected conditional cash transfer programmes

(Beneficiaries as a percentage of the total population)

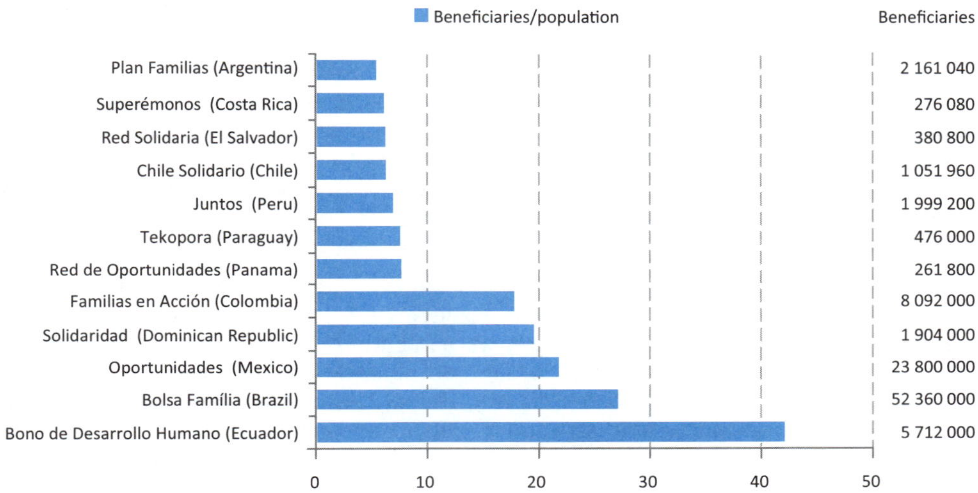

Source: Johannsen, J., L. Tejerina and A. Glassman (2009), Conditional Cash Transfers in Latin America: Problems and Opportunities, Inter-American Development Bank, Washington, D.C.
http://dx.doi.org/10.1787/888932522531

Due to fiscal constraints, many reforms sought to mobilise private resources in order to increase the efficiency and coverage of public policies. The countries of Latin America were early proponents of the creation of social investment funds, public-private partnerships, subsidised schools and private social protection systems. These initiatives were meant to bridge the wide gaps in the financing and management capacity of public policy by incorporating the private sector on the supply side. While not all of the experiences were successful, they have left a legacy of teachings that constitute a good base for further improving public policies. The three main conclusions from these experiences are: *i)* private provision does not absolve the authorities of their responsibility in developing these policy areas, *ii)* public service delivery by private providers raises a number of problems between principals and agents that should be properly solved with incentives and effective monitoring, and *iii)* public-private partnerships and other systems with external involvement should be evaluated according to the same principles as other elements of public policy.

The experience of OECD economies shows that there are no shortcuts nor is there only one path to developing an effective and transparent public sector. The road to public sector reform is long, rocky and requires prolonged cumulative efforts. Too often, political candidates promise sweeping changes in the public sector through very simple measures. And many governments come to power with the promise of starting public sector reform from scratch, dismissing the work of their predecessors.

However, Latin American countries should be willing to continue on the path that has been set, aware that public reform will not be the product of a single government or leader, but the constructive work of many political actors and stakeholders.

In this process, policy makers should be aware of the many obstacles they will face, evaluating the costs and benefits in the short- and long-term. The centralisation of power is a good example of this. Due to the weight of presidential systems and the need for strong leadership to escape the crisis, Latin American countries have tended to concentrate decision-making power in a few actors in the executive branch. This is especially true in the area of fiscal management, where the balance of power between the executive and legislative branches largely favours the former. Even in countries where parliament has the final say on approving the budget, as in Brazil, the executive branch can substantially amend the budget during its execution and alter expenditure items. These provisions may have contributed to fiscal discipline, but have also introduced a high degree of discretionality, which could lead to abuse. Some authorities may also become particularly vulnerable to influences or pressures. Such risks could be mitigated by joint decision-making and by holding authorities more responsible for their decisions.

Policy trade-offs will not be resolved only with legislation —however well designed it may be— but with modifications to the very functioning of public institutions. To achieve this, it is necessary to go beyond local solutions and reform the systems of public administration, or develop others that are more appropriate. Systems need rules to function, but they are also characterised by a series of incentives and institutional structures that determine human behaviour.

Well-structured public administration systems can generate the main asset for governance: trust between the state and society. Distrust is a persistent element in the relationship between citizens and the state in Latin America. Special interests are likely to influence legislation, regulation and administration, but distrust can extend to basic state institutions like the judiciary, the legislature and the police. Distrust is very harmful for public administration not only because it makes the relationship between public agencies and the state difficult, but also because it increases the transaction costs with the government. Policy trade-offs must be carefully monitored with special attention to how institutional systems could overcome them, while at the same time increasing trust in public institutions.

2.5. Policies to improve public administration

Without infringing on the role of the market, the state needs to occupy a central role in the response to development needs and should focus on various areas of public policy. These include: *i)* improving the mobilisation of fiscal resources; *ii)* professionalising the civil service; *iii)* engaging several actors; *iv)* making appropriate use of new technologies; and *v)* promoting mechanisms to make government more open and transparent.

The development agenda of the region presents various challenges to the state. In order to confront them, the State needs the support of its citizens and a long-term vision that can guarantee a certain level of political, social and technical continuity. Five fundamental challenges can be identified:[9]

- The State must guarantee a stable macroeconomic environment capable of dynamising economic growth.
- The State needs to play an active role in promoting changes to the productive structure. This should incorporate technical progress and promote consistent policies for the reduction of productivity lags between sectors and between levels of the productive structure.

- The State needs to play a key role in reducing regional disparities regarding productive capacity, articulation with market and access to services, and move towards decreased inequality of well-being. In order to rationalise the diversity of institutions and actors involved in territorial development, agreements for territorial cohesion must be established to harmonise regional and local development efforts from the top and the bottom. Reversing regional inequalities will inevitably contribute to surmounting inequality nationwide. This highlights the need for public policies that rely upon coordination between different levels of regional disaggregation, contributing to the promotion of greater regional equality.
- The State needs to promote active employment policies that will protect against the contingency of unemployment, close wage gaps in the interest of equality, and increase participation and employment rates. Active policies are needed to improve the quality of jobs and the capacities of the workforce, as are policies regulating the minimum wage, productive support and protection of the informal sector.
- The State should intervene more boldly in the social sector, so as to guarantee better access to welfare and capacity development for the most vulnerable and thus close the gap in this area. Moreover, the state plays a defining role for social protection and promotion, an area where the design and implementation of a universal basic social protection system (basic income security and health) should be explored. Such a system could generate or maximise non-contributory social pension mechanisms, increase the offer of cash transfer programmes, formulate policies to reconcile paid and unpaid work and facilitate women's access to the labour market.

These proposals must be examined in light of the level of resources available to public administrations in the region. The level of public spending is conditioned by capacity for tax collection. Taxes constitute a decisive policy area for increasing the financial capacity of the State to proactively promote development and social equality, as proposed in this report. It is also necessary to study governance of natural resources. At least in the case of many South American countries, the rise of raw materials should motivate a debate on the use of income derived from the exploitation of natural resources.

2.5.1. Expansion of fiscal space and better resource mobilisation

Without additional resources, many Latin American States cannot meet the expectations of society or their global commitments. The functions of the State are already very diverse and will continue to change over the coming years. Some countries will become more urbanised, and others will see substantial demographic changes, such as an increase in life expectancy, requiring governments to make the challenge of providing better living conditions for the elderly a priority objective. The expansion of secondary education will generate more demand for higher education. The empowerment of women will limit the role of families in caring for the elderly, children and people with disabilities. In order to carry out all the functions resulting from the development process, States will need additional resources.

Public administration of finances also plays a crucial role in this area. The recovery of a proper budget process in the region has been significant. The budget process has been transformed into the main instrument of control and allocation of public expenditure, a characteristic lost during the years of heavy indebtedness and high inflation. Progress in terms of planning and multi-year investment allocation is notorious. The resource allocation function has been reinforced with the recent development and consolidation of public-investment and programme-evaluation systems. It is positive that the capacity for medium-term macroeconomic and fiscal planning has been restored in the region. Both planning and multi-year programming in the public sector, based on strategic objectives, represent an opportunity and necessary condition for the promotion of sustainable economic and social development. Efforts to control public finances and short-term budget programming in a volatile environment are therefore in the process of defining development strategies and goals.[10]

Despite the strong improvement in fiscal performance since 2000, countries in the region still have an extensive agenda of budgetary and fiscal-space improvements to increase effectiveness and efficiency in resource allocation and transparency. Budgets suffer from institutional rigidity and high volatility, which undermines public spending management. The fiscal space objectives should not contradict the objectives of redistribution and economic efficiency in fiscal reform.

A comparison of budgetary institutions in Latin American countries and OECD economies reveals that in Latin America there is a greater centralisation of authority and greater restrictions on the executive body when modifying the budget (see figures 2.4a and 2.4b).

Figure 2.4a. Latin America and the OECD: does the executive body have veto power over legislation?

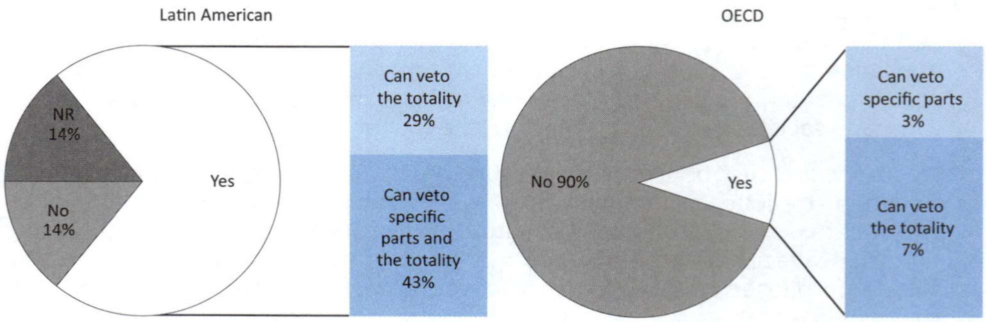

Note: The Latin American countries covered in the survey were Argentina, Brazil, Chile, Costa Rica, Mexico, Peru and Venezuela (Bolivarian Republic of).

Source: OECD International Budget Practices and Procedures Database, 2005 and 2007.
http://dx.doi.org/10.1787/888932522550

Figure 2.4b. Latin America and the OECD: can the executive body increase spending after the budget is approved?

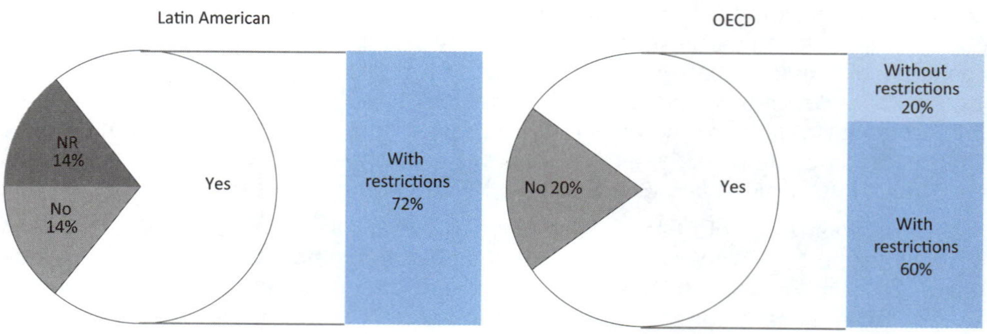

Note: The Latin American countries covered in the survey were Argentina, Brazil, Chile, Costa Rica, Mexico, Peru and Venezuela (Bolivarian Republic of).

Source: OECD International Budget Practices and Procedures Database, 2005 and 2007.
http://dx.doi.org/10.1787/888932522569

The limited use of evidence in budgetary decision-making requires more in-depth budgetary management with result-oriented objectives. Only a minority of countries in Latin America perform a thorough analysis of the economic assumptions of budgetary data and annual evaluations of their long-term fiscal projections. In the area of legislation, parliaments generally have no specific technical support to assess the executive body's budget proposals, which can foster clientelism. Strengthening decision-making and analytical capacity in the ministries of finance and in line ministries in Latin America can help push through reforms that are centred more on the adoption of management decisions based on transparent evidence and less on detailed budgetary control. This must be part of a change in mentality to secure the effectiveness of fundamental budget reforms, such as the creation of medium-term budgetary frameworks, expanded flexibility in ministries that execute spending plans, and implementation of fiscal responsibility laws that lay the groundwork for budget and spending transparency.

Result-oriented objectives for budgetary management should take into account the particular challenges and institutional frameworks of these countries. Because governments in Latin America focus more on programmes and investments compared to OECD economies, budgetary management should strengthen ties with strategic planning, investment programmes and more intensive use of outcomes assessment. Consequently, the challenges are to move forward in developing shared, cross-cutting objectives, promote comprehensive, strategic and institutional planning, and establish performance and management agreements for key public bodies.[11]

2.5.2. From public employment to the professionalisation of the civil service

As service organisations, governments depend heavily on their workforce to meet their mission. This especially applies to public employees who represent the state in the exercise of statutory powers, and whose behaviour, therefore, cannot be based solely on efficiency but also on transparency and fairness. Public employment reform in Latin America is a major challenge that requires a break with the history of patronage and the politicisation of public administration. This challenge is not alien to many OECD economies that over the past century have created a civil service with similar goals.

A good starting point for policy makers in the framework of civil service reform is to have a clear idea of what is expected of public sector employees and what motivates them. To solve the problems in the public employment sector, many countries in Latin America have begun to use modern management tools such as performance-related pay, schemes for senior public administration levels, and executive agencies. However, it is important for policy makers to ensure that the use of these instruments is justified by the nature of the problem and by the reality of the countries where they will be applied.

Before designing reforms and specific instruments, policy makers should distinguish between at least four categories of public employees: professional bureaucrats, service providers, public officials and support staff. In order for these categories to function efficiently, a variety of provisions are required that should be included in the legal and contractual framework of public employees. Because the reality in Latin America shows many discrepancies in this regard, a restructuring of labour agreements should play a leading role in reforming the public sector.

In order to boost the skills and capacities of civil servants and to achieve the goals of the institutions for which they work, it is essential to understand their principal incentives. Studies indicate that public-sector employees are not necessarily motivated by the same factors that motivate private-sector employees. Many people are attracted to the civil service because of the nature of the position or the contribution it can make to their professional development. While this cannot be used as an excuse to reduce pay, it does suggest that an incentive programme should encompass issues such as strategic planning, outcome assessment, training, feedback, recognition and professional mobility, at least to the same extent as compensation systems and performance-based pay.

The central pillar of human resource management in the public sector should be to establish a strong link between corporate objectives, responsibilities and recognition. To achieve this, there must be consistency from entry to exit (hiring, work scheduling, evaluation, compensation, promotion and departure). This needs to be supported by an ongoing study of employee motivation and market conditions. Preference should therefore be given to the process and its institutionalisation, which is unusual in Latin American states.

2.5.3. Inclusion of other actors

In order to provide public services more effectively and efficiently, governments can combine their inputs, policies and knowledge with those of other actors, including non-state actors, sub-national administrations and commercial providers of public goods. Government support helps to introduce incentives to increase efficiency, expand user options, facilitate access, and find new ways to improve the quality of and proposals for public services. Partnerships with private or non-profit entities that offer risk-oriented and innovative thinking can create alternative routes to innovation in public-sector organisations.

The use of market mechanisms in public administration is increasing, although there are marked national differences. This phenomenon is driven by the need for governments to ensure their operations are profitable. Some market mechanisms, such as vouchers, set as their main objective to expand the options for service users.

Information on the use of public services provided by non-government providers is limited. The two Latin American members of the OECD, Mexico and Chile, rely much less on outsourcing than other OECD economies. With outsourced goods and services at 22.9% (Mexico) and 31.1% (Chile), these two countries are well below the OECD average of 42.8% (see Figure 2.5).

This may be an opportunity to open new avenues for innovation in public service delivery through greater use of market mechanisms and partnerships. In addition, low levels of public spending in most countries could provide new opportunities for public-private partnerships aimed at attracting more private capital and expertise and better risk management.

Public-private partnerships are complex instruments that require a range of competencies on the part of government. For example, there should be a solid system to evaluate the profitability of the public sector, and for this purpose there should be transparent, coherent guidelines on non-quantifiable elements. It is also necessary to classify, evaluate and assign risk to those most able to bear it. In addition, strong budgetary and accounting practices are needed. This perhaps requires specific administrative competencies, such as units dedicated to public-private partnerships.

By adopting a market mechanism model, governments in the region face significant challenges in management, especially in its divided role as recipient and provider of services. Latin American governments should ensure that they have the capacity to determine which services and management skills they need to acquire. This requires new technical skills and a complete change in mindset in the public sector. Furthermore, the use of market mechanisms —in addition to traditional government provision— raises questions regarding accountability, transparency, regularity and access to redress mechanisms by society.

In addition to market mechanisms, there are other forms of partnership with citizens and civil society that can contribute to the incorporation of public input and facilitate effective implementation. The evaluation of these types of activities remains a challenge, although there are examples in some Latin American countries that can

Figure 2.5. OECD countries: outsourced production in the public sector, 2009
(Percentage of total public costs)

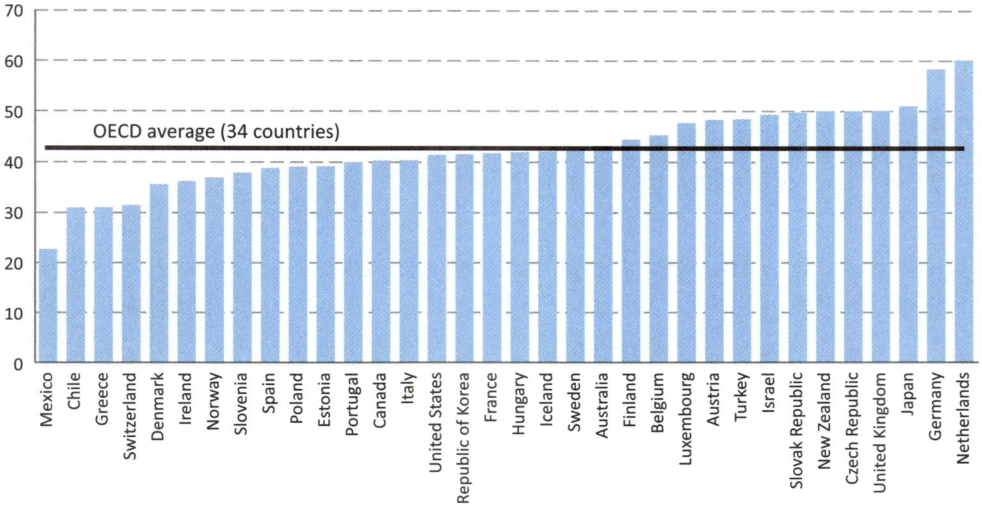

Note: Data for Australia, Korea, Japan, New Zealand and Russia are from 2008.

Source: National Accounts Statistics Database (OECD). The figures for Australia are a combination of the IMF's Government Finance Statistics' database and national accounts provided by the national statistics agency (Australian Bureau of Statistics).

http://dx.doi.org/10.1787/888932522588

help assess new approaches. For example, Brazil has established a partnership between government, public entities, civil society and private-sector organisations to improve water supply in the north-east of the country. Civil society organisations have adopted joint decisions on social issues during the process of integration of the San Francisco River with the river basin of the north-east. This has led to the incorporation of issues related to health, education, sanitation infrastructure and irrigation into the socio-economic impact study and has helped to mitigate local resistance to the project.

2.5.4. Using new technologies to improve dynamism and responsiveness

New information and communication technologies can help a public sector be more flexible, dynamic and transparent. If Latin American countries make full use of the potential of new technologies, they can reduce the gap with developed countries. Because these technologies often require new structures, additional benefits could be obtained with more user-focused administrative machinery. This is part of a paradigm shift that involves the technological revolution already taking place, opening up new opportunities to accelerate the pace of development.

Over the past ten years, most OECD economies have developed strategies and infrastructure for e-government. This is a moving target, given that mobile technologies already have the potential to generate a second wave of innovative approaches that can advance a dynamic and mobile public agenda.[12] The goal is to improve access to information, reduce paperwork and facilitate the delivery of services. E-government is not just limited to the computerisation of existing processes, but also seeks to transform the administration, ensuring that citizens and users have easy access to public services, while the administrative machinery re-organises and streamlines internally to take full advantage of new technologies. The main objective is to avoid overloading the user by requesting the same information multiple times and to use public records that are inter-connected.

In general, the development of electronic administration is linked to the dissemination of information and communication technologies (ICTs), the development of telecommunications infrastructure —such as mobile phones and devices) and access to the Internet. To date, countries in the region have developed infrastructure in line with capacity, but new improvements will only be possible in a context of increased economic development. The strategies to bridge gaps in this area will need to take into account wide income disparities, and consequent issues related to the digital divide and support to disadvantaged groups.

Figure 2.6. Latin America and the Caribbean, OECD economies and other emerging countries: e-government index and per capita GDP, 2008

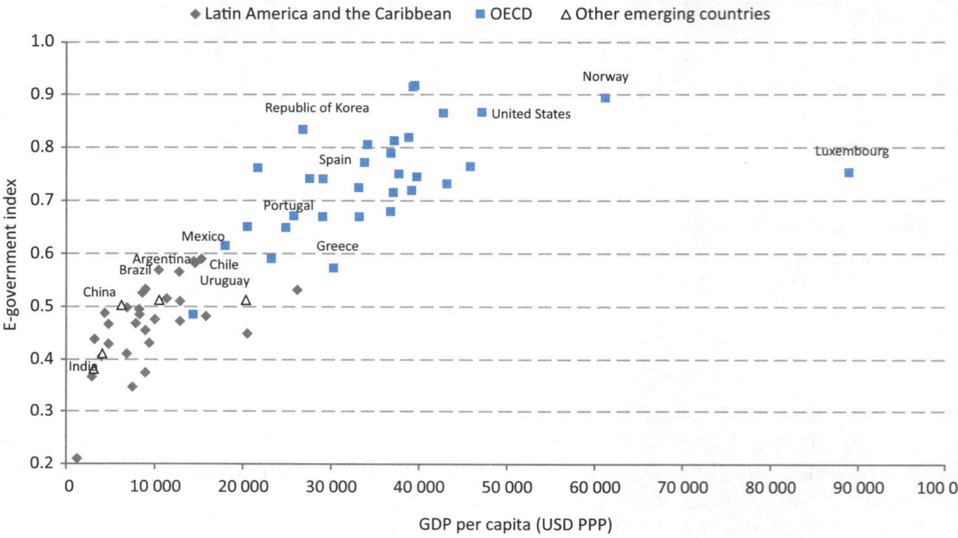

Source: UN e-Government Survey 2008 for e-government index and database, World Development Indicators of the World Bank for GDP figures.
http://dx.doi.org/10.1787/888932522607

The implementation of an ambitious agenda for e-government requires countries to act on several fronts. They must strengthen public-sector capacity to promote the spread and use of new instruments, modernise public services, foster the use of peer platforms, introduce legal and regulatory changes to facilitate electronic processes —such as electronic signatures— and certify procedures for the verification of users. E-government also has the potential to strengthen democracy and the rule of law; for example, through electronic voting and e-justice.

Some Latin American countries have played an active role in this area. E-government opens a window of opportunity to the region. Mobile services make some of the new technologies available even for the lowest income groups. However, access to broadband Internet remains fundamental to more advanced applications in e-government, such as interactive transactions with large sectors of the population.

Some examples from the region encourage optimism in this regard —Argentina, Chile, Mexico and Uruguay have developed significant e-government infrastructures that are comparable to those found in some OECD economies.

Box 2.3. Mobile technologies for good governance and connected societies in Latin America

Brazil: The SMS employment information service (CELEPAR) notifies job seekers registered with the government about job vacancies they are eligible for; in addition, it sends a notification 24 hours before the time of the interview.

Mexico: In Mexico City, the SMS broadcasting system sends information alerts to citizens in the area about weather hazards, rain, low temperatures, possible disasters, emergency locations and contact numbers.

Furthermore, the citizens of Mexico City can express their concerns directly to the mayor through ESCUCHA DHM. Through this service, citizens can send complaints about government services, projects and civil servants, as well as voice their opinions on new policies, ask questions about new programmes and report on possible acts of corruption and illicit enrichment.

Bolivarian Republic of Venezuela: During the 2006 presidential election, about 8 million voters used SMS to find their polling stations. 7.8 million of the 16 million registered voters used the SMS application. The National Electoral Council also used SMS to inform 350 000 electoral witnesses where and when to receive their training.

Source: Adapted from OECD (2011c).

2.5.5. Improving trust in the public sector through open and transparent governments

Transparency consists of making government information accessible to the public and subject to the scrutiny of society. Consequently, making government information accessible to citizens so they can review, analyse and, if they wish, use it as a sanctioning mechanism is a democratic practice. This promotes accountability, providing the public with information on what the government is doing.

Information regarding the allocation of resources and the results of their investment is a necessary condition for transparent government action. The Open Budget Survey implemented by the International Budget Partnership (IBP) is an international reference in this field. It is an independent and comparative survey of budget transparency and accountability, based on a questionnaire that evaluates public access to budgetary information, social participation in the budgetary process, and the capacity of supervising institutes to request explanations from the executive branch. Recent IBP data (2010) reflects important differences between countries. Despite major steps forward in budgetary transparency, the countries of the region continue to face an important challenge in this field.

Access to and the use of public information are changing the way in which citizens interact with their governments. This interaction adds value to public initiatives and contributes to decision-making by communities and political authorities.[13]

The consequences and the impact of this recent evolution are unknown, but will surely go beyond the mere simplification of administrative procedures and more transparent administration. Within this framework, the most pressing challenge will be how to direct the benefits of this gained openness towards the citizen, in a real and concrete manner.

It will also be fundamental for countries in Latin America and the Caribbean to monitor the risk of corruption. Rather than one single remedy, there is a whole range of instruments, both public and private, that countries can use to reduce risks. This requires multidisciplinary approaches that facilitate access to information and transparency, promote the dissemination of information and streamline internal regulations by eliminating concentrations of power and margins for discretion. It is essential to have a satisfactory level of transparency throughout the procurement cycle to minimise the risk of fraud, corruption and mismanagement of public funds. These tools are resorted to internationally and their use is spreading in the region.

Evidence from the region shows that countries are already taking steps to increase transparency and strengthen integrity, such as in the case of Brazil, Chile, and Mexico. For example, Chile's government is proactive in disseminating information. The government encourages the publication of budgetary documents and audit reports and publishes lists of public officials and their salaries. In addition, they make public the names of beneficiaries of social programmes. The country uses different publishing channels, including portals and websites.

Box 2.4. Improving integrity in public administration: the case of Brazil's Federal Government

During the past decade, the federal government of Brazil has adopted a series of measures to improve integrity and prevent corruption in public administration. The actions include: *i)* increased transparency and citizen participation in public policy, *ii)* the introduction of a system of internal control in the provision of services based on risk, and *iii)* the incorporation of high standards of conduct for civil servants.

Transparency and citizen participation in public policies has increased through the free distribution of up-to-date information on public spending in government programmes via the *Transparency Portal*. This has been complemented by the obligation of all federal government agencies to publish information about the services they provide, ways to access them and the standards that can be expected through Citizens' Service Charters. Moreover, citizen participation in monitoring public policies has been facilitated by an expansion in the number of ombudsman units (Ouvidoria), from 40 in 2002, to nearly 160 in 2010.

Public administration is introducing internal control mechanisms in the provision of services based on risk. For example, they have strengthened ex ante and ex post controls for agreements concerning the provision of public services by civil society organisations and the use of federal government credit cards to purchase off-the-shelf goods and for services.

Codes of conduct and other guidance materials, such as orientation courses for public officials, have been published to promote high standards of conduct. In addition, actions have been taken to actively monitor the conduct of civil servants through forensic auditing techniques to identify potential conflicts of interest and situations of unjust enrichment. The federal government has also improved the quality, speed and impact of internal investigations of violations of integrity and administrative misconduct.

Source: Adapted from OECD (2011).

Chile and Mexico, which spend between 5% and 6% of their GDP on public procurement, have also taken steps to publish information on this activity on their main government websites. The countries of the region also rely on structures of checks and balances, which include the offices of the controllers-general. Chile is in a fairly advanced stage given that it publishes justifications for the awarding of tenders, and allows for the online tracking of recruitment spending, activities which are carried out by only 59% and 32% of OECD economies, respectively.[14] Mexico also has a website, updated in June 2010, which offers most of the national information on procurement with the objective of increasing the number of possible transactions. The country also allows online monitoring of procurement spending. In Brazil, the federal procurement portal and the federal portal on transparency in public administration are examples of sites that provide information to the public, although they do not yet function as one-stop shops. Brazil, like Chile, also allows for the public tracking of procurement expenditure. The next step is the obligation to disclose conflicts of interest of senior decision makers.

Notes

1. OECD (2010).
2. De la Cruz, R., C. Pineda and C. Pöschl (2010).
3. In all countries of the region, a large majority of citizens claim to support democracy. The widespread perception in all countries for which ECLAC data is available is that a significant level of democracy has been reached. (CEPALSTAT 2010)
4. See OECD (2010).
5. Data taken from the "Americas Barometer" of the Latin American Public Opinion Project (LAPOP).
6. See Transparency International's Corruption Perceptions Index 2010 (www.transparency.org/policy_research/surveys_indices/cpi/2010/results).
7. This section is largely based on OECD (2006 and 2011b).
8. Many of these key points are reflected in the recent conclusions of the ministerial meeting of the OECD Public Governance Committee, held in Venice in 2010 (www.oecd.org/governance/ministerial2010).
9. CEPAL (2010).
10. ILPES (2011).
11. Martner (2008) and ECLAC (2011).
12. OECD (2011c).
13. Naser and Concha (2011).
14. OECD (2010).

References

ECLAC (Economic Commission for Latin America and the Caribbean) (CEPAL) (2010), *Time for Equality: Closing Gaps, Opening Trails*. Thirty-third period of ECLAC sessions. Brasilia, 30 May - 1 June 2010, (LC/G.2432 (SES.33/3)), ECLAC, Santiago, Chile.

Dayton-Johnson, J., J. Londoño and S. Nieto Parra (2011), "The Process of Reform in Latin America: A Review Essay", *OECD Development Centre Working Paper 304*, Paris.

De la Cruz, R., C. Pineda and C. Pöschl (eds) (2010), *The Local Alternative: Decentralization and Economic Development*, Inter-American Development Bank (IDB).

Johannsen, J., L. Tejerina and A. Glassman (2009), *Conditional Cash Transfers in Latin America: Problems and Opportunities*, Inter-American Development Bank, Washington, DC.

ILPES (Latin American and Caribbean Institute for Economic and Social Planning) (2011), "Panorama de la Gestión Pública en América Latina: En la hora de la igualdad", ILPES, Santiago, Chile.

Martner, R. (ed.) (2008), "Planificar y presupuestar en América Latina", Serie Seminarios y Conferencias, No. 51, (LC/L.2859-P), ILPES/CEPAL, Santiago, Chile.

Naser, A. and G. Concha (2011), *El gobierno electrónico en la gestión pública*, CEPAL/ILPES, LC/L.3313-P and LC/IP/L.308, Serie Gestión Pública, No. 73, Santiago, Chile.

OECD (Organisation for Economic Co-operation and Development) (2005), *Modernising Government: The Way Forward*, OECD, Paris.

OECD (2011a), *OECD Public Governance Reviews: Public Sector Integrity in Brazil, Managing Risks for a Cleaner Public Service*, OECD Publishing, Paris.

OECD (2011b), Conclusions of the Ministerial meeting of the OECD Public Governance Committee, www.oecd.org/dataoecd/1/50/47231930.pdf, accessed 8 October 2011.

OECD (2011c), *M-Government: Mobile Technologies for Responsive Governments and Connected Societies*, OECD Publishing.

OECD (2011d), *Government at a Glance*, OECD, Paris.

OECD (2010), *Latin American Economic Outlook 2011: How Middle Class is Latin America?*, OECD Development Centre, Paris.

United Nations (2008), *UN Global E-Government Survey 2008: From E-Government to Connected Governance*, Department of Economic and Social Affairs, United Nations, New York.

CHAPTER THREE

Fiscal policy reform

Abstract

The countries of Latin America and the Caribbean have made significant progress over the past two decades in the area of public finances. Higher tax revenue has made it possible to reduce debt and increase spending on productive investment and in programmes to fight poverty. The recent crisis has not interrupted this progress, as the fiscal space accumulated in the boom years has made it possible to finance fiscal stimulus programmes similar to those of OECD economies.

Despite the progress made, Latin America continues to face major fiscal challenges. Low levels of personal direct taxes, limited targeting of public spending and the small size of transfers explain the lack of redistribution of public finances. In addition, low tax revenues in most countries are an obstacle to the development of a modern state.

This chapter contends that a combination of advances in fiscal institutions in Latin America could help to address these challenges. It highlights the need for transparent fiscal statistics, multi-year budgetary frameworks and fiscal rules to ensure sustainability, stabilisation and medium and long-term objectives. This could be structured around a fiscal pact to strengthen citizens' trust in their governments.

3.1. Introduction

In the past two decades and even during the recent crisis, progress in Latin America and the Caribbean in the area of public finances has been remarkable, although significant challenges remain. The level of public debt has been reduced and tax revenues have increased, thereby reducing budget rigidities and expanding fiscal space. However, levels of spending on social programmes and productive support are still very uneven, both within countries and between countries in the region. This reflects different institutional designs, but also insufficient coverage in health, education, employment protection, pensions and infrastructure.

This chapter discusses these major trends in public finances (section 3.2) and their recent development. These advances have led to increased public spending, contributing to poverty reduction in the region. However, the level of inequality in the distribution of personal income remains substantially higher than in other regions of the world. Low levels of personal direct taxes, limited targeting of public spending and the small size of direct transfers to poor households explain the low redistributive role of public finances (section 3.3). In addition, low tax revenues in most Latin American and Caribbean countries, with certain exceptions mainly in South America, represent a major obstacle to the development of a modern state that provides the public goods and services needed to accelerate economic growth and reduce inequalities. This limited tax revenue —due to high levels of evasion, informality and tax expenditures— reflects the weak social contract in the region between citizens and the state. As a result, in order to regain citizen confidence and restore the transformative role of the state, it is necessary to strengthen the social contract through a fiscal pact that focuses on resolving socio-economic challenges in the short and long term and on obtaining the material means to do so (section 3.4).

In countries with high levels of inequality the redistributive function of fiscal policy must be reinforced. In most OECD economies, fiscal policy is able to significantly reduce income inequality both because of the importance of transfers to lower income sectors and because of progressive tax systems. In Latin America, fiscal policy must also close regional equity gaps (present in both federal systems —Argentina, Brazil— and in decentralised unitary systems such as Colombia) as well as gender and intergenerational gaps. To do this, the region's states need to extend income-transfer programmes for low-income citizens (following the good practices of conditional transfer programmes for health and education in Brazil and Mexico), and the solidarity pillars of social protection systems. Of particular importance are pensions (which must be designed not to discourage formal employment) and the implementation of stable policies for the development of infrastructure, innovation and education. These programmes should be complemented with better social safety nets, which reduce vulnerabilities in the events of unemployment, illness or retirement.

The state requires stable resources to perform its functions. States must strengthen their capacity for macroeconomic stabilisation —both automatic and discretionary— and their regulatory capacity. They must also expand their tax base, especially from income and assets, reducing tax evasion, avoidance and exemptions, and strengthen tax administration. Other innovative proposals in the area of taxation must also be considered in order to increase revenues, such as environmental taxation. This should be done while considering its impact on long-term growth.

The fiscal financing gap in the region is still significant. However, there are important differences among countries. Argentina, Brazil and Uruguay have levels of tax collection similar to the average for OECD economies, while in Central America and the Caribbean the rates are lower. But on the whole, the tax burden is low, as the structure is biased towards non-progressive taxes and levels of non-payment are significant.

The main difference in tax revenue from OECD economies is a result of the lower contribution of personal income tax, the base of which is severely limited by the combination of high income inequality, high labour informality, a multiplicity of tax expenditures, the high concentration of revenue from income from wages, weak tax administration, as well as tax evasion and low tax morale. However, according to the *Latinobarómetro* survey, Latin Americans who perceive a higher quality of public services (for example in health care and education) are less likely to justify tax evasion or to consider the tax burden excessive. States must therefore strengthen tax administration and expand the income-tax base in conjunction with increasing the quality of public services.

Tax bases are also limited by the extent of tax expenditures in the form of exemptions, deductions and reduced rates. The effectiveness of existing tax expenditures need to be quantified and evaluated. Some of them could be transformed into more transparent spending policies, in accordance with criteria of efficiency and relative management capacity across government revenue and expenditure departments.

The transformative role of the state requires planning tools and greater co-ordination of policies, programmes and projects. Institutionalisation must be strengthened based on fiscal rules and medium-term frameworks, transparent accountability, mechanisms to evaluate policies and programmes, and national systems of public investment. Additional measures include strengthening human resources by developing a body of well-trained and motivated civil service professionals.

One of the greatest challenges for the countries in the region is to regain public trust. A fiscal pact can strengthen the social contract between citizens and the state. These pacts can be comprehensive, or it may address a specific sector such as education, employment, social protection or infrastructure. Or they pact may also be focused on a specific issue such as equality, public safety or the fight against poverty or hunger. Parliaments have a key role in these pacts, in the definition of public policies and their linkages with the budget, and in the negotiation of tax reforms that aim to improve tax systems.

3.2. Main trends in the region's public finances

Despite the recent crisis, progress in public finance in the last decade has been remarkable. Public spending has been more efficient, especially in terms of poverty reduction and income redistribution. This has been possible thanks to increases in tax revenue and a reduction in the level of public debt. Not only has the public debt fallen since the 1990s, from levels of almost 80% of GDP to levels close to 30% in recent years, but its composition has also changed, with a greater proportion of domestic debt (Figure 3.1A). In addition, public investment and social expenditure have increased in almost the entire region.

The generation of primary surpluses during the last boom phase helped reduce public debt levels as a share of GDP. Economic growth, discretionary adjustments and to a lesser extent the appreciation of currencies and a fall in interest rates also contributed to reducing debt levels. The period 2003-08 was characterised by a strong widespread reduction of public debt, with governments applying both discretionary and rules-based policies to that end.[1] This allowed countries to face the crisis under better conditions, and it is also a factor explaining the dynamism of Latin American economies seen in 2010 and into 2011.

Moreover, the increased public deficit that followed the international financial crisis that began in 2008 did not lead to an increase in public debt as a percentage of GDP, in contrast to what happened in most OECD economies. In fact, this deficit was financed primarily with existing financial assets. Although the crisis resulted in a deterioration in the public sector balance sheet, the outlook is for a quick recovery of tax revenue, at least in much of South America.

Figure 3.1. Latin America and the Caribbean (19 countries): increase in fiscal space, 1990-2009

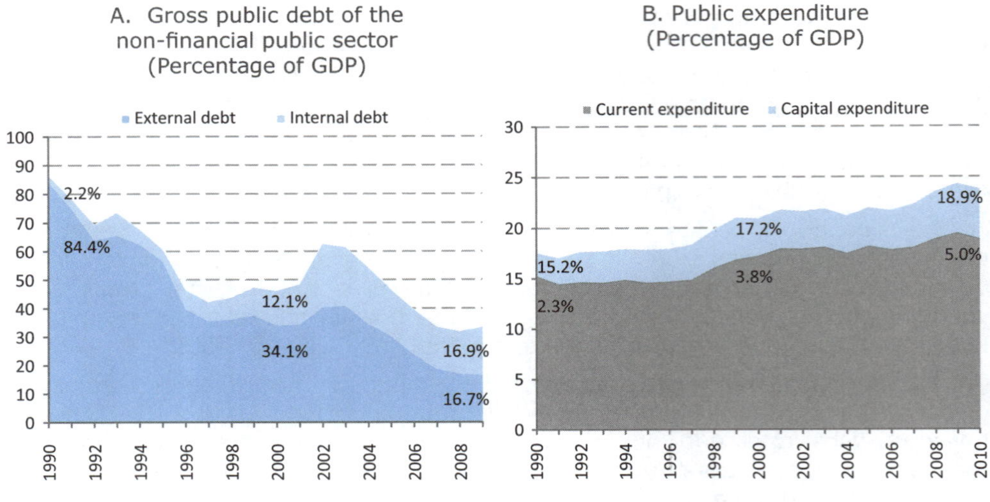

Note: Simple average for Latin America. The average for public expenditure does not include Cuba.

Source: Based on data from CEPAL STAT Statistics and Economic Indicators.

http://dx.doi.org/10.1787/888932522645

As a result of greater tax revenue, since 1990 public spending has increased in most Latin American countries, augmenting by almost six percentage points of GDP on average in the region (Figure 3.1B). Capital expenditure has increased considerably from a low of 2% of regional GDP in 1990 to almost 5% in 2009. In regard to current expenditure, there has been a notable drop in interest payments on public debt as a percentage of the total; the regional average has dropped from 15% to 7%, reflecting the overall reduction in debt and changes in its cost and maturity profile. These changes have resulted in a decrease in budget rigidities and therefore the expansion of fiscal space.

Given regional infrastructure gaps, public investment is an important indicator of the quality of public spending. On this dimension, the Plurinational State of Bolivia, Chile, Ecuador, Panama and Peru have significantly recovered their levels of capital expenditure, compared to 1990. National public investment systems in these countries have acquired a leading role to evaluate the quality and relevance of this investment spending. By contrast, Colombia, Costa Rica, Haiti, the Dominican Republic, Mexico and Uruguay have seen investment spending decrease or slower growth in this type of expenditure, although development plans in these countries include ambitious targets for the expansion of public infrastructure in the coming years that could reverse this trend.

Levels of public social spending in the region continue to vary (Figure 3.2). This in part reflects the diversity of models for the provision of public goods and services, especially in pensions and health care. But it also reflects the low level of coverage in some countries of essential public goods. However, the region has made significant progress in this area in aggregate terms, with an average increase of more than 5 percentage points of GDP according to ECLAC estimates.[2]

Although spending at the sub-national level in terms of GDP is lower than in OECD economies (9.5% vs. 18.6% of GDP, respectively), own revenues are proportionally lower (Figure 3.3), generating significant vertical imbalances. In many countries, the states, provinces, regions and municipalities are heavily dependent on central government transfers. There are significant regional differences in terms of per capita income, which reveal deep horizontal imbalances. As financial compensatory

Figure 3.2. Latin America and the Caribbean and the OECD average: structure of social spending by sector, 2008[a b]
(As a percentage of GDP)

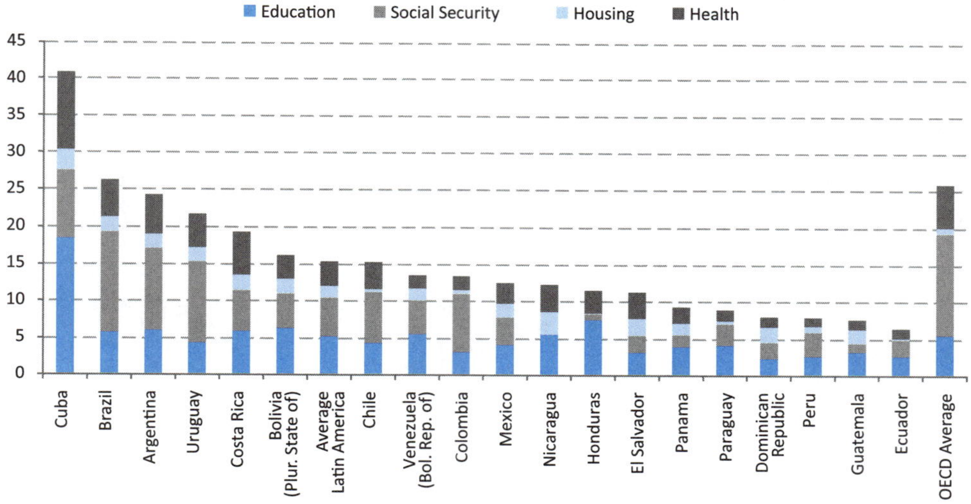

Note:

[a] Institutional coverage of non-financial public sector for Argentina, Bolivia (Plurinational State of), Brazil, Colombia, Costa Rica, Panama, Peru; central government for Chile, Cuba, Ecuador El Salvador, Guatemala, Honduras, Dominican Republic, Uruguay; budgetary central government for Mexico, Nicaragua, Paraguay and Venezuela.

[b] Most recent data available is 2006 for Bolivia (Plur. State of), Ecuador, and Venezuela (Bol. Rep. of).

Source: Based on CEPALSTAT Statistics and Social Indicators and OECD National Accounts.
http://dx.doi.org/10.1787/888932522664

Figure 3.3. Latin America and the Caribbean and the OECD: tax revenue by level of government and tax category, 2008
(Percentage of GDP)

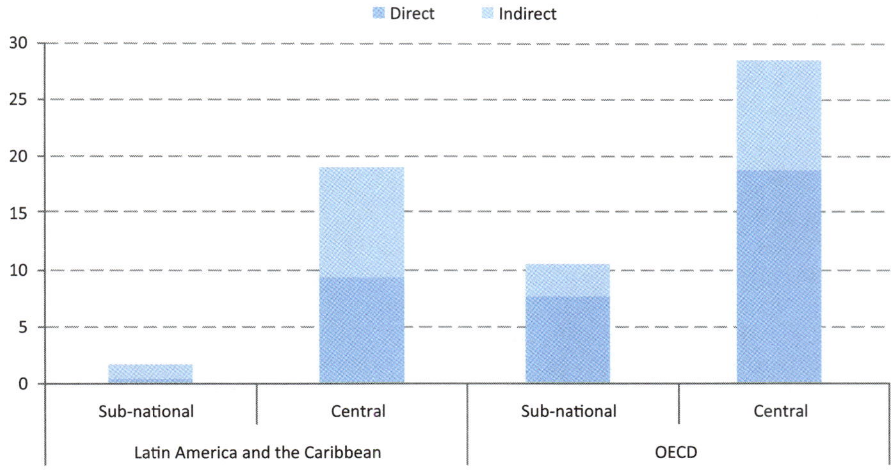

Source: Based on the *Revenue Statistics in Latin America* database, ECLAC-CIAT-OECD.
http://dx.doi.org/10.1787/888932522683

mechanisms are limited in Latin America, in contrast to many OECD economies, these regional disparities are not mitigated.

Latin America and the Caribbean face significant fiscal challenges: the tax burden is generally low, the structure is biased towards non-progressive taxes and the non-payment of taxes is significant.[3] In comparison with OECD economies, in most countries in the region the low tax burden limits the scope for action on the expenditure side (Figure 3.4). In this regard, there is no single formula for all countries;[4] for example, in Guatemala, Peru and the Dominican Republic, the lower tax burden is a constraint on increasing public spending, while economies such as Argentina and Brazil could aim for a higher quality of spending in terms of both allocation and effectiveness.

Figure 3.4. Tax and non-tax public revenue and social spending in Latin America and the OECD, 2008

(Percentage of GDP)

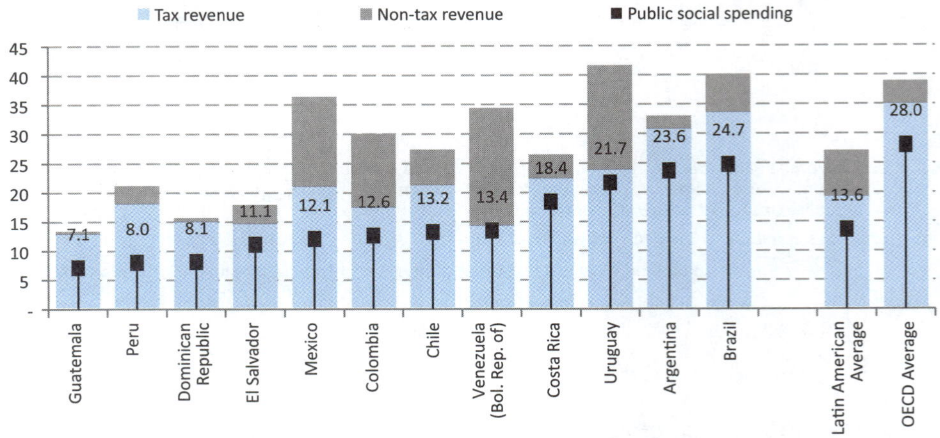

Note: The statistics refer to the non-financial public sector in Argentina, Colombia, Costa Rica, El Salvador, Mexico and Venezuela (Bol. Rep of); government in general in Brazil, Chile and Peru; and central government in Guatemala, Dominican Republic and Uruguay; tax revenues in Mexico include a certain portion of the income from oil production.

Source: Based on data from CEPALSTAT and Revenue Statistics in Latin America, ECLAC-CIAT-OECD.
http://dx.doi.org/10.1787/888932522702

This lower tax burden in Latin America and the Caribbean in comparison to OECD economies is not only explained by the region's lower level of development. It is evident that countries with a higher GDP per capita tend to have a larger public sector and a greater tax burden. However, several studies that take "level of development" into consideration show that the revenue potential of countries in the region is considerably higher than their actual collection.[5] This is explained by a number of factors: the importance of productive activities that involve raw materials, which result in non-tax revenues that can make it less important to increase tax revenues; the level of informality in the labour market, tax evasion; and different designs for health and pension reform (the latter significantly impact on the collection of personal income tax and the social security contributions of workers and employers).

Box 3.1. Tax statistics in Latin America

A comparison of the tax systems of Latin American countries with those of OECD economies shows that there are significant differences in terms of level and structure. While the tax burden was 34.8% of GDP for OECD economies in 2008, the corresponding figure for selected countries in Latin America was only 20.6%. Additionally, in comparison to the OECD, Latin America has a low rate of direct tax collection, offset by higher revenue from indirect taxes. Given the high correlation between a government's policy space and the level and structure of its tax revenue, knowing the reasons behind this difference may help in the design of fiscal policy reforms.

In order to provide better statistics for international comparison, the Centre for Tax Policy and Administration and the Development Centre of the Organisation for Economic Co-operation and Development (OECD), the Economic Commission for Latin America and the Caribbean (ECLAC) and the Inter-American Centre of Tax Administrations (CIAT), in consultation with the Inter-American Development Bank (IDB), are carrying out a joint project to produce tax statistics in Latin America that can be compared among countries in the region and the OECD.

The objective of this project is to provide comparative data on tax revenue by type of tax and sub-levels of government for a sample of Latin American and Caribbean countries (Argentina, Brazil, Chile, Colombia, Costa Rica, Dominican Republic, El Salvador, Guatemala, Mexico, Peru, Uruguay and the Bolivarian Republic of Venezuela) from 1990 to the present. This group of countries represents a high percentage of the region's GDP and population (around 90% in both cases). The data obtained (from data published by Latin American governments and in some cases by participating organisations) have been edited and reclassified based on the methodology defined in the OECD publication *Revenue Statistics*. This has enabled the comparison of tax systems among Latin American countries for the first time, as well as a comparison between these tax systems and those of the OECD.

The main task in designing the new database was to collect tax information, classifying each item of public revenue under the new analytical framework by determining the nature of each tax and its resulting classification. Special emphasis was placed on the analysis of legislation and the regulatory frameworks of the tax systems of the countries involved in order to determine whether a specific category of income is from taxes or not, and if so, its classification based on the corresponding tax base. Detailed discussions between all organisations involved have taken place in order to reach agreement on a common methodology. In addition, special efforts were made to collect data at sub-national levels of government or from social security systems, in light of the limited coverage of certain institutional units.

This effort has resulted in a high-quality, highly detailed and internationally comparable database. The forthcoming publication *Revenue Statistics in Latin America* represents the first result of a broader OECD initiative (the so-called OECD LAC Initiative) to promote policy dialogue and peer review in the region, initially supported by Spain, Mexico and Chile. The continuity of this initiative in the coming years, including the possible expansion of the database to more countries in Latin America, the eventual creation of a parallel database on public spending and networks for dialogue between policy makers, would contribute to improving public debate on fiscal policy in the region.

Less than a third of tax revenue in Latin America comes from direct taxes, while the largest part arises from consumption taxes and other indirect taxes. The average tax burden in Latin American countries is virtually half of that found in OECD economies. This difference is mainly explained by lower revenue in terms of GDP from direct taxes (on income and property). On average, the direct tax burden of the countries of Latin America as a share of GDP is 9 points below that of developed countries. In fact, the direct tax burden in Latin America (relative to GDP) is lower than that of most African countries (Figure 3.5).

Figure 3.5. International comparison of the level and structure of tax burden
(Percentage of GDP)

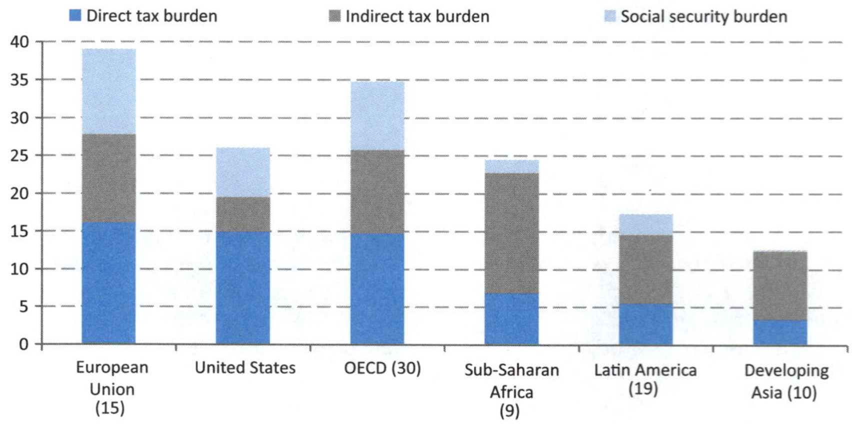

Note: Country coverage by region is indicated in brackets. The data for the OECD, European Union and the United States is from 2008; 2004-09 for developing Asia; 2002-09 for sub-saharan Africa; 2009 for Latin America.

Source: Data for OECD countries from *OECD Revenue Statistics*. For developing countries in Asia and Sub-Saharan Africa, *IMF Government Finance Statistics*. For Latin American countries, based on data from official national sources.
http://dx.doi.org/10.1787/888932522721

In Latin America the largest share of income tax revenue comes from corporate income. By contrast, in OECD economies taxes on personal income provide the largest share. While corporate tax revenue in the region as a share of GDP is close to the OECD average (3.4% compared to 3.9% of GDP, respectively), the region lags far behind in the case of personal income tax. Latin American countries collect on average only 1.5% of GDP from personal income taxes. (Even in Uruguay, the country with the highest personal income tax for which data are available, revenue from personal income tax is equivalent to only 2.2% of GDP.) In comparison, in OECD economies, revenue from personal income tax as a share of GDP is over 9%.

The income-tax base is very limited due to the combination of high income inequality, high labour informality, tax expenditures and tax evasion. Most revenue from personal income tax comes from salaried employees. This is mainly a consequence of the greater possibilities for tax fraud and avoidance among the self-employed and the preferential treatment given to capital income in most countries. This situation, also found in OECD economies, is offset in developed economies by, on the one hand, their greater capacity for control over a larger number of taxpayers (given the lower informality), and on the other, because their higher level of per capita (or family) income results in a higher percentage of the population subject to income taxes.

In Latin America, with the exception of Mexico, the income of most individuals falls below the threshold for taxable personal income.[6] In broad terms, a family with labour earnings starts to be a net payer of personal income tax when its income reaches more than two times the average income for the country. By contrast, in the OECD, this threshold is placed at around half the national average income. For this reason, only a minority of households in Latin America (between 10% and 30% of households with wage earnings) provide all the revenue from personal income taxes.[7] In addition, the vast majority of countries give preferential treatment to capital income, reducing the tax base and increasing the complexity of tax systems, thus affecting horizontal equity.[8]

Income tax non-compliance rates are very high, making it essential to monitor payment of income tax. These rates vary between approximately 40% and 65%, representing an average loss of 4 to 5 percentage points of GDP for these countries.[9] Tax evasion affects both horizontal equity (as taxpayers with equal capacity to pay end up paying different tax amounts) and vertical equity (as taxpayers with greater capacity to pay end up paying proportionately less than those with less capacity to pay). An increase in tax rates without adequate control may however result in an increase in hidden activities if there is a shift of firms and workers from the formal to informal sector, further hindering the ability of governments to generate resources. To combat tax evasion, which is of an increasingly international character, it is necessary to promote transparency and international co-operation based on dialogue on tax legislation.

Social contributions are low in many Latin American countries due to the aforementioned labour informality and to the implementation of private pension systems. Faced with the prospect of increased public spending because of an ageing population and inequality arising from the multiplicity of systems, the region has generally opted for reforming "pay-as-you-go" pension systems, introducing mandatory individual capitalisation accounts managed by the private sector. There are institutional differences among the countries of the region that impact on collection levels: replacement systems (the Plurinational State of Bolivia, Chile, El Salvador, Mexico and the Dominican Republic), where the old public system is closed to new registrations; parallel systems (Colombia and Peru), where workers must choose between one system and the other; and mixed systems (Costa Rica and Uruguay), where the pension comes from both systems. In all cases, new members make their personal contributions to their pension fund, not to the public sector (in some countries, corporate contributions have also been eliminated). However, in contrast with expectations, the introduction of these accounts has not resulted in increased participation in the systems, especially among low and middle-income groups most affected by unemployment and informality.[10]

Tax bases and collection are also limited by the extension of various tax expenditures, of which there is insufficient information and evaluation. According to official estimates, tax expenditures vary widely among countries in Latin America. Some countries show figures of around 2% of GDP (Argentina and Peru), others between 3% and 5% (Brazil, Chile, Colombia and Ecuador), while in Mexico and Guatemala the figure reaches 5.4% and 8.6% of GDP, respectively.[11] These variations and levels are similar to those observed in OECD economies. While originally tax expenditures were aimed at encouraging investment (domestic and external), over time objectives became more diversified, and exemptions were extended to new taxes.[12] While in Brazil, Guatemala and Mexico there is a strong concentration of tax expenditures on income taxes, in Argentina, Ecuador and Colombia VAT exemptions are larger. There is a growing consensus in the region on the need to identify and estimate tax expenditures in a manner that allows for comparison among countries (with sufficient breakdown by type of tax, sector of activity, region of destination, level of government and income group). This will make it possible to evaluate their effectiveness and integrate them into the budget cycle.[13]

Increases in tax revenue during the last decades have come from strengthening tax collection on goods and services (especially value added tax, VAT) and from corporate taxes (Figure 3.6). VAT was adopted very early by most economies in the region to replace the cascading sales-tax; this was the most important tax reform in the 1980s and early 1990s. Since 2000 this has been complemented with increased revenues from income taxes, thanks to booming commodity prices, which significantly benefitted taxation associated with the exploitation of natural resources in certain countries of the region, and to the introduction of simplified regimes for small taxpayers and property taxes based on imputed income. This trend contrasts with the decrease in specific consumption taxes because of trade liberalisation and the reduction of the range of goods and services subject to selected taxes. Additionally, during this period extraordinary tax schemes have emerged, such as bank withdrawals and deposits and financial transactions.[14]

Figure 3.6. Latin America: tax structure, 1990-2009
(Percentage of GDP)

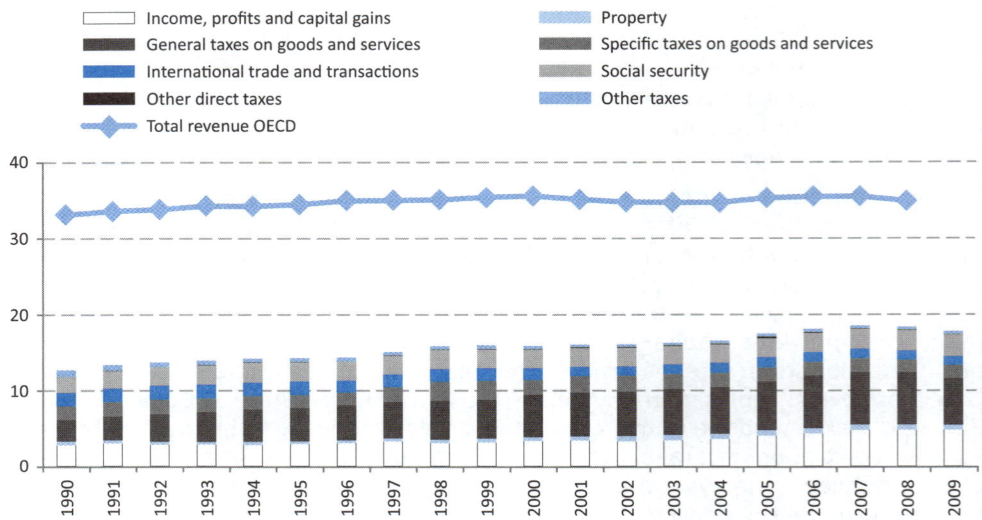

Source: Based on data from CEPALSTAT, Revenue Statistics in Latin America, ECLAC-CIAT-OECD and OECD Revenue Statistics.
http://dx.doi.org/10.1787/888932522740

The recent boom in international commodity prices has driven certain types of tax revenue upwards, especially those associated with oil (Colombia, Ecuador, Mexico and the Bolivarian Republic of Venezuela), minerals (Chile and Peru) and food (Argentina and Peru). This increase in tax revenue is the result not only of these rising prices in raw materials, but also the implementation of new tax instruments. In the case of agricultural products, Argentina has financed a significant portion of its spending with the resources generated from export duties. New instruments were introduced to raise more funds from non-renewable resources, such as a direct tax on hydrocarbons and derivatives and a windfall profits tax (Plurinational State of Bolivia), a specific tax on mining (Chile), a reform of the Hydrocarbon Law (Ecuador) and increased royalties and income taxes on the oil sector (Bolivarian Republic of Venezuela).

There are significant differences among countries in Latin America and the Caribbean in levels of taxation. One group of countries (mainly those in the Southern Cone) has tax collection levels close to the average found in OECD economies, while a second group of countries (mainly in Central America and the Caribbean) has much lower levels. The tax burden as a percentage of GDP ranges from 9.2% in Haiti to about 35.4% in Brazil. Focusing on tax revenue potential in terms of GDP per capita, Mexico stands out with a tax burden that is less than half of what the country's level of development would suggest. Other countries whose tax burden falls below this standard are Ecuador, Guatemala, Panama and the Bolivarian Republic of Venezuela. With the exception of Guatemala, the other three countries have significant non-tax revenues (from oil or the Panama Canal) to partially offset low levels of tax collection.[15]

By contrast, there are fewer differences among countries in Latin America and the Caribbean in terms of the structure of the tax burden. Focusing on direct taxation, if social security contributions are excluded, Mexico is the only country in the region where more than 60% of tax revenue comes from income tax, while its VAT collection is the second lowest (relative to GDP) in the region. Mexico is followed by those countries where the revenue generated from taxes on income and on capital is between 40% and 50% of the total tax revenue collected, such as Chile, Colombia, Panama, Peru and the Bolivarian Republic of Venezuela. These economies specialise in the exploitation of natural resources, and their high level of income tax revenue is related to the taxation of companies engaged in such activities. At the other extreme are Haiti and Paraguay with direct taxes below 20%; they are among the poorest countries in the region, which limits their tax base.

Major differences in the territorial distribution of wealth and economic activity lead to significant differences in tax revenue. In recent years, sub-national levels of government, like central governments, have improved their public finances, reaching surpluses and reducing debt levels. This improvement, however, is strongly tied to a rise in intergovernmental transfers based on the growth of economic activity and higher prices for natural resources. From a structural perspective, a potential area of development for sub-national governments to raise revenue would be through the collection of property taxes. On average, they account for about 0.4% of GDP in the region, a fifth of what is collected by developed countries. In particular, taxes on real estate could be strengthened by reducing exemptions, eliminating tax breaks, and improving tax administration through the use of new technologies to improve cadastral records, update property values and improve tax collection itself.[16]

3.3. Fiscal policy and income inequality

Low levels of revenue from direct personal taxes, limited targeting of public spending and the small size of direct transfers to the poorest households explain the low (almost non-existent) redistributive impact of public finances. The region has a level of inequality in the distribution of personal income that is substantially higher than in other regions of the world, with an average Gini coefficient of 0.53. The country in the region with the least inequality is still more unequal than any member of the OECD. Recent studies[17] show that since 2000 there has been some decline in inequality as a result of increased social spending, and in particular due to the impact of conditional cash transfer programmes (the *Jefas y Jefes del Hogar* programme in Argentina, *Bolsa Escola* and *Bolsa Familia* in Brazil, *Progresa* and Oportunidades in Mexico, and programmes providing benefits in kind in Peru). There has also been a reduction in earnings by educational attainment (relationship of salary to additional years of study). However, the latter is temporary, while the majority of public spending continues to be neutral or even regressive.

The tax structure in Latin America does not favour the redistributive function of public finance. There is a fiscal "empty box" (which is occupied in the more developed countries), as even countries that have higher tax rates (*e.g.* Argentina, Brazil and Uruguay) have tax structures biased towards indirect taxes.[18] Assessments of different taxes in three countries in the region (Ecuador, Guatemala and Paraguay) show VAT to be mostly regressive, while income tax is progressive, but represents a smaller percentage of total revenue.[19] In general, income distribution improves through taxation and spending in industrialised countries, while in developing countries there are not adequate redistributive policies to achieve a comparable degree of equality.[20]

The level of income inequality in Latin America, measured by Gini coefficients before taxes, transfers and public services, is not too much higher than in OECD economies.[21] However, once the effects of the limited effective redistribution from the tax system and economic and social benefits are included, the differences are significant (Figure 3.7).

The redistributive effect of fiscal policy between Chile and Mexico is different from that of the other OECD economies. The low effective redistribution of the tax system in these two countries can be explained mainly by the limited effect of cash transfers. In the OECD, the reduction in the Gini index due to cash transfers is about eight points, while in Chile and Mexico the reduction is less than two points. This is a result of lower social spending in the region on these types of instruments (in OECD economies social spending on cash transfers is about 12% of GDP versus only 6% and 3% of GDP in Chile and Mexico, respectively). In addition, the combined impact of social security contributions and income taxes on reducing the Gini is greater in OECD economies. While in the group of industrial countries this decline is on average about 3.5 points, in Mexico the reduction is about 2.0 points and in Chile, only 1.0 point.

Figure 3.7. Latin America and the OECD: gini indexes before and after taxes and public spending

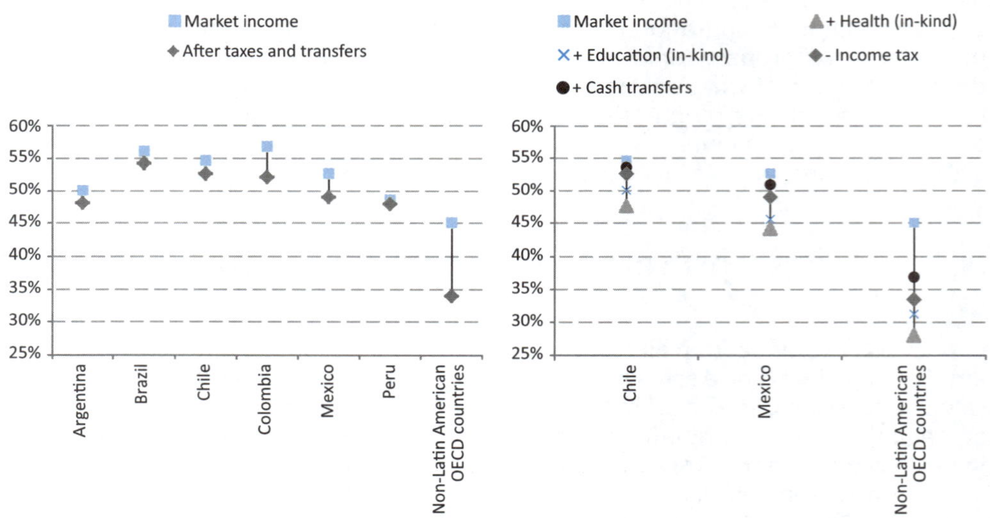

Source: OECD (2008a) for non-Latin American OECD countries, OECD (2008b) for Argentina, Brazil, Colombia and Peru, and estimations based on household surveys for Chile and Mexico.
http://dx.doi.org/10.1787/888932522759

3.4. Towards a strong social contract and an improved fiscal pact

3.4.1. Foundations for strengthening the social contract

High levels of inequality and low redistribution in Latin America contradict economic theory. When inequality is high before taxes and government transfers, the median voter theorem states that democracy should lead governments to increase revenue and carry out significant redistribution.[22] In this situation median voters would benefit from progressive income taxes —which would have more effect on higher-income voters— and from transfers and progressive spending, which would be favourable to them.

Democracy would in this sense be a necessary though not sufficient condition to establish a more generous public sector and more redistributive policies in low- and middle-income countries, even in situations of high inequality. Preferences for redistribution stem from numerous sources, from individual history (experiences and perceptions of social mobility may affect political attitudes towards redistribution), the political system, the organisation of the family, and social and cultural values at both national and regional levels.[23]

Some challenges remain, such as speeding up improvements in the quality of democracy, making progress towards efficient budget systems and strengthening tax administrations. A democracy that fails to adequately channel the popular will may encourage the erosion of tax bases and/or the capture of social spending.[24] The capacity for fiscal management is also a limiting factor.

The weakness of some of these institutions is reflected in low tax morale and a lack of social support for ambitious fiscal reforms. On average, Latin American citizens are almost three times more likely to justify tax evasion (20% versus 7% in OECD economies), and only 34% of those surveyed in Latin America consider tax evasion to always be wrong, compared with 62% in OECD economies (Figure 3.8).[25]

Figure 3.8. Tax morale in Latin America and the OECD: "do you think that cheating on taxes is justifiable?"
(Percentages)

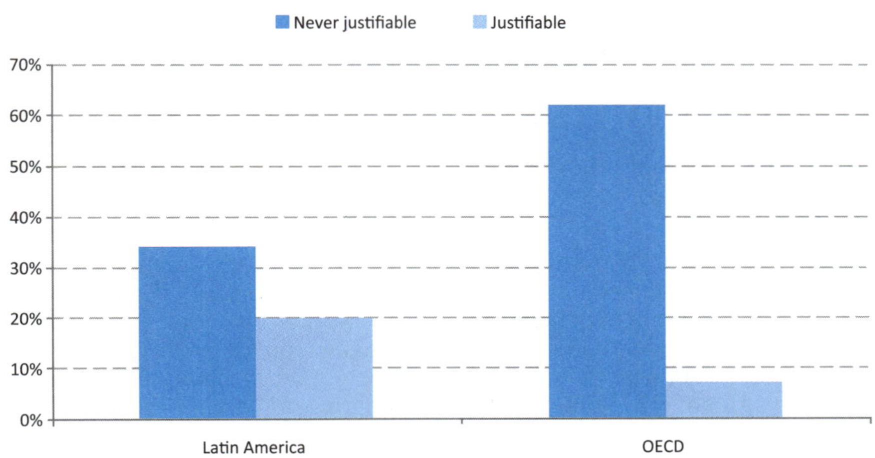

Source: Based on data from Latinobarómetro 2008 and World Values Survey.
http://dx.doi.org/10.1787/888932522778

This low tax morale has traditionally been attributed to corruption and pessimistic perceptions regarding social justice, equal opportunities and mobility.[26 27] The social contract is therefore incomplete. Latin America citizens tend to choose services provided by the private sector such as in health care and education as soon as they can afford it. The principle of sufficiency of tax revenue takes on a different meaning in Latin America, where it is primarily aimed at ensuring adequate revenue to meet minimum standards of quality in the provision of public services.[28] By contrast, in societies with higher incomes, citizens are more aware of the taxes they pay, demanding higher quality in the provision of public services.

Nevertheless, there are reasons to be optimistic about the prospects for strengthening the social contract. Surveys of public perceptions in Latin America reveal a belief in the value of effort, in the benefit of education and in shared responsibility between the state and the individual. These beliefs are also backed by a willingness to pay more taxes to fund social protection schemes.[29]

Latin Americans who perceive a higher quality of public services (particularly in health care and education) are less likely to justify tax evasion and to consider the tax burden excessive. Moreover, individuals who have made progress and/or expect their children to advance socially and economically are more likely to state that good citizens must pay taxes and reject the idea that current taxes are too high. Finally, individuals with higher levels of education are less likely to justify tax evasion and more likely to accept a higher tax burden.[30]

Tax reforms must, therefore, aim to increase the quality and improve the management of public services so that citizens increase their demand and support for these services. This will create an environment conducive to the expansion of public spending and the tax revenue needed to fund it. Assuming a willingness on the part of the middle-income population to support policies adopted by consensus and tax reforms if they are accompanied by better public services, their role in a new social contract is crucial.[31] The state itself must build legitimacy through the use of transparent and participatory planning instruments in the public sector.[32]

Finally, these reforms need to be based on an analysis of the impact that levels of tax and their structure may have on long-term growth. Available evidence for OECD economies show that property taxes, followed by taxes on consumption and environmental taxes, are those that most favour increases in income per capita. Direct income taxes, whether for firms or individuals, seem to be least favourable for economic growth.[34] These results can obviously not be directly extrapolated to the Latin American context, given lower levels of taxation in many of the region's countries, especially with regard to personal income tax. Nonetheless, fiscal reform must incorporate considerations linked to mid- and long-term growth.

3.4.2. Towards a better fiscal pact

A fiscal pact may be seen as a complex "contract" whose clauses express a consensus about what the state can and must do —or not do— in the areas of fiscal, economic and social policy. The metaphor of the fiscal pact as a "contract", which the parties involved may renounce and then redo, fits naturally into Latin America's political landscape.[35]

The policy implications of a fiscal pact go far beyond those from conventional tax or budgetary reforms.[36] It is necessary to reach minimum social and political consensus on the role of the state and the strategies that authorities seek to promote. The fiscal pact is associated with an explicit and agreed-upon design for a medium- and long-term path. It is essentially recovering the notion of development planning. This is, in turn, the expression of a more ambitious and comprehensive design for public policies: *i)* consolidating fiscal solvency; *ii)* raising the productivity of public administration; *iii)* providing greater transparency to fiscal policy; *iv)* promoting equity; and *v)* promoting the development of democratic institutions.

In the current expansionary phase characterised by unprecedented growth in tax revenue, the outlook for reform is quite limited. The incentives for changing tax systems decline when revenue targets are met or even exceeded. In fact, discussion about the inequity of the systems is usually reduced to limited circles of specialists and does not translate into legislative proposals to modify noted defects, despite their being widely known.[37] This is compounded by the fact that in some countries the "elites" have more power than tax administrations. For these and other reasons, the political economy of reform has become the main obstacle to the shaping of tax systems that give support to achieving a fiscal pact.

However, today the idea of a fiscal pact is finding support in the region. There are at least two reasons for this: first, there is evidence that public spending is a powerful instrument for containing the worst effects of external volatility (decline in employment, income and consumption); and second, it has been recognised that a good fiscal policy, backed by strong institutions and adequate public management capacity, contributes to equity, social cohesion and productive development.[38]

These pacts can be comprehensive, or they may refer to a specific sector such as education, employment, social protection or infrastructure. They may also be based on an idea such as equality, public security or the fight against poverty or against hunger. Parliaments have a key role in designing these pacts, defining public policies and articulating them with the budget, and negotiating tax reforms that aim to improve tax systems.

Better fiscal frameworks can foster fiscal pacts and help facilitate the complex political economy of tax reform. These frameworks can range from transparent budgetary practices to second-generation fiscal rules, with clear exit strategies and independent fiscal councils, adapted to the country and the moment. It is especially important to promote transparency and efficiency in the public sector. Parliaments and regulatory bodies must strengthen their watchdog roles where there is greater and better spending.

Fiscal frameworks must be sufficiently comprehensive to address short-term and long-term socio-economic challenges. In the short term they must ensure the capacity for stabilisation, and in the long term they must incorporate social demands (responses to poverty, development of infrastructure and development in general) and the effective management of non-renewable resources. They must also anticipate pressures from social spending associated with ageing. It is not only the composition of expenditure, but also its level and financing that is a key factor in the distribution of income and opportunities throughout society. Accordingly, it is urgent to establish fiscal pacts that define the magnitude of society's contribution to the financing of public policies and how it will be collected, whether through investment or social expenditure.[39] One specific form is the implementation of fiscal rules or the reform of existing ones, coupled with the creation of sovereign funds in certain cases. Fiscal rules must be favourable for medium and long-term development, particularly in key areas of productive investment such as infrastructure.[40]

Better fiscal frameworks should ensure sufficient domestic resource mobilisation, making the tax system an effective tool for development. If the fiscal pact is based on the need to finance public policies by increasing the tax burden, it will be essential to increase public confidence that these resources are being well used.

Institutional reforms must aim to consolidate advances in budgetary frameworks, basing them on international experience. In many Latin American countries, the budget cycle (which lost its leading role in public policy discussions in the years of high inflation) has been rediscovered as a transparent and democratic instrument for the allocation of public expenditure. In this regard, advances have been made in national development strategies and plans, fiscal rules and medium-term frameworks, accountability, multi-year budgets, the evaluation of policies and programmes, national public investment systems and shared indicators of expenditure.[41]

These institutional advances are part of the fiscal pact, in order to ensure the state's role in promoting development. Having a medium- and long-term strategic vision, building alliances among stakeholders and designing a new equation between the State, the market and citizens are the foundations of the fiscal pact.[42]

Notes

1. Martner (2007), ECLAC (2009), Daude *et al.* (2011).
2. ECLAC CEPALSTAT database, based on official national statistics and OECD National Accounts.
3. Gómez Sabaini *et al.* (2010).
4. ECLAC (2010b).
5. Agosín *et al.* (2005), Perry *et al.* (2006) and Gómez Sabaini *et al.* (2010).
6. Cetrángolo and Gómez Sabaini (2007); OECD (2008b, 2010b).
7. OECD (2008b); Daude *et al.* (2011).
8. ECLAC (2010b).
9. Jiménez *et al.* (2010).
10. Rofman *et al.* (2008), Mesa-Lago (2009), OECD (2010b) and Da Costa *et al.* (2011).
11. Villela *et al.* (2009).
12. Jiménez and Podestá (2009).
13. Villela *et al.* (2009).
14. De Cesare and Lazo Marín (2008) and ECLAC (2010a). For an analysis of their effects on economic growth, see OECD (2010c).
15. Gómez Sabaini *et al.* (2010).
16. ECLAC (2010b).
17. González and Martner (2010) and López-Calva and Lustig (2010).
18. ILPES (2011).
19. Jorrat (2011).
20. Chu *et al.* (2000).
21. IDB (2006), Gómez Sabaini (2006) and OECD (2008a, 2008b).
22. See the pioneering work of Downs (1957), for example.
23. Alesina and Giuliano (2009); Alt *et al.* (2010) and Robinson (2010).
24. Elizondo and Santiso (2011).
25. Daude and Melguizo (2010).
26. Torgler (2005).
27. Gaviria (2007).
28. Jiménez *et al.* (2010).
29. Marcel (2008) and OECD (2010b).
30. Daude and Melguizo (2010).
31. Daude and Melguizo (2010); OECD (2010b).
32. ILPES (2011).
33. OECD (2010a).
34. OECD (2010c).
35. Lerda (2009).
36. ECLAC (1998) and ILPES (2011).
37. Gómez Sabaini and Martner (2010).
38. ECLAC (2010b).
39. ECLAC (2010b).
40. Carranza *et al.* (2011).
41. ILPES (2011).
42. ECLAC (2010b).

References

AGOSIN, M., A. BARREIX AND R. MACHADO (2005), *Recaudar para crecer: bases para la reforma tributaria de Centroamérica*, Inter-American Development Bank (IDB), Washington, DC.

ALESINA, A. AND P. GIULIANO (2009), "Preferences for Redistribution", *NBER Working Paper*, No. 14825, National Bureau of Economic Research.

ALT., J., I. PRESTON AND L. SIBIETA (2010), "The Political Economy of Tax Policy", in J. Mirrlees (ed.), *Dimensions of Tax Design: The Mirlees Review*, Oxford University Press, Oxford, pp. 1204-1279.

CARRANZA, L., C. DAUDE AND A. MELGUIZO (2011), "Public Infrastructure Investment and Fiscal Sustainability in Latin America: Incompatible Goals?", Working Paper, No. 301, OECD Development Centre, Paris.

CETRÁNGOLO, O. AND J.C. GÓMEZ-SABAINI (2007), *La tributación directa en América Latina y los desafíos a la imposición sobre la renta*, Macroeconomics of Development, No. 60, ECLAC (CEPAL), Santiago, Chile.

CHU, K.Y., D. HAMID AND S. GUPTA (2000), "Income Distribution and Tax and Government Social Spending Policies in Developing Countries", Working Paper, No. 00/62, International Monetary Fund, Washington, DC.

DA COSTA, R., J.R. DE LAIGLESIA, E. MARTINEZ AND A. MELGUIZO (2010), "The Economy of the Possible: Pensions and Informality in Latin America", Working Paper, No. 295, OECD Development Centre, Paris.

DAUDE C., A. MELGUIZO AND A. NEUT (2011), "Fiscal Policy in Latin America: Countercyclical and Sustainable?", *Economics: The Open-Access, Open-Assessment E-Journal*, Vol. 5, 2011-14. http://dx.doi.org/10.5018/economics-ejournal.ja.2011-14

DAUDE, C. AND A. MELGUIZO (2010), "Taxation and More Representation? On Fiscal Policy, Social Mobility and Democracy in Latin America," Working Paper, No. 294, OECD Development Centre, Paris.

DE CESARE, C. AND J.F. LAZO MARÍN (2008), "Impuestos a los patrimonios en América Latina" *Macroeconomics of Development Series*, No. 66, ECLAC (CEPAL), Santiago, Chile.

DOWNS, A. (1957), *An Economic Theory of Democracy*, Harper, New York.

ECLAC (ECONOMIC COMMISSION FOR LATIN AMERICA AND THE CARIBBEAN) (CEPAL) (1998), *The Fiscal Covenant. Strengths, Weaknesses, Challenges*, ECLAC books, No. 47, ECLAC, Santiago de Chile.

ECLAC (CEPAL) (2009), *La política fiscal en tiempos de crisis. Una reflexión preliminar desde América Latina y el Caribe*, ECLAC, Santiago, Chile.

ECLAC (CEPAL) (2010a), *Economic Survey of Latin America and the Caribbean 2009-2010: The Distributive Impact of Public Policies*, ECLAC, Santiago, Chile.

ECLAC (CEPAL) (2010b), "Time for Equality: Closing Gaps, Opening Trails", 33rd session of ECLAC, 30 May - 1 June 2010, Brasilia.

ELIZONDO, C. AND J. SANTISO (2009), Killing Me Softly: Local Termites and Fiscal Violence in Latin America, available at SSRN: http://ssrn.com/abstract=1400050, accessed 5 October 2011.

GAVIRIA, A. (2007), "Social Mobility and Preferences for Redistribution in Latin America", *Economia*, Vol. 8 (1), pp. 55-88.

GÓMEZ SABAINI, J.C. (2006), "Cohesión social, equidad y tributación. Análisis y perspectivas para América Latina", Políticas Sociales, No. 127, ECLAC (CEPAL), Santiago de Chile.

GÓMEZ SABAINI, J.C. AND R. MARTNER (2010), "América Latina: panorama global de su sistema tributario y principales temas de política", in J. Ruiz-Huerta and M. Villoria (eds.), *Gobernanza democrática y fiscalidad*, Editorial Tecnos, Madrid.

GONZÁLEZ, I. AND R. MARTNER (2010), "Del Síndrome del Casillero vacío al Desarrollo Inclusivo: buscando los determinantes de la distribución del ingreso en América Latina", Working Paper of the Budgetary Policy and Public Management Department,ILPES (Latin American and Caribbean Institute for Economic and Social Planning), ECLAC (CEPAL), Santiago, Chile.

IDB (INTER-AMERICAN DEVELOPMENT BANK) (2006), *La equidad fiscal en los países andinos*, IDB, Washington, DC.

ILPES (Latin American and Caribbean Institute for Economic and Social Planning) (2011), "Panorama de la Gestión Pública en América Latina: En la hora de la igualdad", ILPES, Santiago, Chile.

Jiménez, J.P. and A. Podestá (2009), "Inversión, incentivos fiscales y gastos tributarios en América Latina", Macroeconomics of Development, No. 77, ECLAC (CEPAL), Santiago, Chile.

Jiménez, J.P., J.C. Gómez Sabaini and A. Podestá (2010), "Tributación, evasión y equidad en América Latina", in id. (eds.), *Evasión y equidad en América Latina*, Colección Documentos de proyectos, June 2011, ECLAC (CEPAL), Santiago, Chile.

Lerda, J.C. (2009), "El pacto fiscal visto a sus diez años", in R. Martner (ed.) *"Las finanzas públicas y el pacto fiscal en América Latina"*, Seminars and Conferences, No. 54 ECLAC (CEPAL), Santiago, Chile.

Lopez-Calva, L.P. and N. Lustig (eds.), *Declining Inequality in Latin America: A Decade of Progress?*, Brookings Institution Press and UNDP (United Nations Development Programme), Baltimore, Md.

Marcel, M. (2008), *Movilidad, desigualdad y política social en América Latina*, mimeo.

Martner, R. (2007), "La política fiscal en tiempos de bonanza", Gestión Pública, No. 66, ECLAC (CEPAL), Santiago, Chile.

Mesa-Lago, C. (2009), "Efectos de la crisis global sobre la seguridad social de salud y pensiones en América Latina y el Caribe y recomendaciones de políticas", Políticas Sociales, No. 150, ECLAC (CEPAL), Santiago, Chile.

OECD (Organisation for Economic Co-operation and Development) (2008a), *Growing Unequal? Income Distribution and Poverty in OECD Countries*, OECD, Paris.

OECD (2008b), *Latin American Economic Outlook 2009*. OECD Development Centre, Paris.

OECD (2010a), *Making Reform Happen: Lessons from OECD Countries*. OECD, Paris.

OECD (2010b), *Latin American Economic Outlook 2011: How middle-class is Latin America?*, OECD Development Centre, Paris.

OECD (2010c), *Tax Policy Reform and Economic Growth*, OECD Tax Policy Studies, No. 20, OECD, Paris.

Perry, G., O. Arias, J. López, W. Maloney and L. Serven (2006), *Poverty Reduction and Growth: Virtuous and Vicious Circles*, World Bank, Washington, DC.

Robinson, J.A. (2010), "The Political Economy of Redistributive Policies", in L.F. López-Calva and N. Lustig (eds.) *Declining Inequality in Latin America: a Decade of Progress?*, Brookings Institution Press and UNDP (United Nations Development Programme), Baltimore, Md., pp. 39-71.

Rofman, R., L. Lucchetti and G. Ourens (2008), "Pension Systems in Latin America: Concepts and Measurements of Coverage", Social Protection and Labour Discussion Paper 0616, World Bank, Washington, DC.

Torgler, B. (2005), "Tax Morale in Latin America", *Public Choice*, Vol. 122, pp. 133-157.

Villela, L. (coord.), A. Lemgruber and M. Jorratt (2009), "Tax Expenditure Budgets. Concepts and Challenges for Implementation", Working Paper, No. 131, December 2009, Inter-American Development Bank (IDB), Washington, DC.

CHAPTER FOUR

Reforming education systems

Abstract

The progress that Latin America and the Caribbean has achieved in recent years in terms of coverage, expenditure and performance in education creates the space for new challenges to be considered. The fundamental task for the region involves using the potential of education policies as an instrument for equal opportunities, social inclusion and the shaping of qualified human capital. For this reason, a number of reforms have looked to extend the access, quality and management, with a central role for the State as regulator and provider of quality education. This chapter presents a panorama of the state of education in Latin America, and the role of these reforms to attain this objective: decentralisation policies, national evaluation systems, reforms in higher education and management of teaching staff. The chapter presents a series of recommendations for the design and implementation of policies: allocating more funds for management at sub-national levels; fostering a population trained in the use of new technologies; strengthening technical-university education, adapting it to the demands of the production sector; consolidating national evaluation systems and extending them beyond schools; and promoting efficient management of teaching staff through a true professionalisation of the teaching career through improved selection, evaluation and incentives. These aspects should be at the core of education reforms over the next few years.

4.1. Introduction

Education is a fundamental right and plays a decisive role in development by bringing about greater equality of opportunity and social inclusion by promoting the skills needed for technological progress and development. Education has direct positive effects on economic and social welfare, productivity, income, employment and competitiveness. It is therefore essential that the State carry out the reforms necessary for education systems to play this transformative role.

The aim of this chapter is to present a panorama of the current state of education in Latin America and highlight the principal challenges for the design and implementation of education reform. We will present the trends in coverage, performance, equity and spending on education in Latin America (section 4.2). This will be followed by a description of recent reforms in different spheres of the education systems in the region, analysing four fundamental aspects: decentralisation, national evaluation systems, higher education, and management of teaching staff (section 4.3). The chapter concludes with various recommendations for education policy (section 4.4). Some priority areas are: increasing secondary education coverage for young people from low-income families; reducing the gaps in knowledge and facilitating access to tertiary education; implementing decentralisation policies that avoid increasing inequality and transfer financial, human and management resources to the local level; strengthen mechanisms and institutions to assure the quality of education, particularly at the tertiary level; and finally, implement adequate evaluation systems and ensure accountability regarding educational achievement as well as management and teaching practices.

Educational coverage and spending has increased in recent decades in the region, now benefitting the most vulnerable sectors of the population who did not have access to these services in the past. However, there are still major challenges ahead. There have been significant advances in primary school coverage (where the region is close to achieving the Millennium Development Goals), but major gaps remain in secondary and higher education. The challenges for Latin American education systems not only include expanding coverage, but also improving quality, efficiency and performance. In terms of educational results, the performance of Latin American students on tests such as the PISA (Programme for International Student Assessment, see Box 4.1) continues to be low compared to students in the rest of the world despite improvements in recent years.

The region remains one of the most unequal in the world, not only in terms of income but also in terms of access to education and quality of education services. Differences in access to education and in educational performance due to socio-economic factors are still significant and in some cases (for example, at secondary and tertiary levels) have increased. Income is a significant factor in the segmentation of access to good-quality education services. The current education system often reinforces inequalities in income and opportunities, perpetuating social inequality. The State has an essential instrument to compensate inequalities of origin, providing new generations with better opportunities for occupational mobility, thereby reversing the reproduction of inter-generational social gaps: to build a high-quality education system that is accessible to all at all levels.[1]

Education reforms in Latin America seek to strengthen the social and inclusive role of education. Such reforms have spurred improvements in the management and administration of education systems, integrating new teaching methodologies in school curriculums and generating closer ties with the labour market. Tertiary education has also been the object of important reforms in recent years, which have tried to respond to some of the traditional problems the region faces (such as coverage and funding). Today, universities face new challenges based on changes in the productive paradigm and the demand for scientific and technical knowledge. Strengthening the capacity for applied research and co-ordination with the real sector is now required.

4.2. Trends in education: coverage, performance and spending

4.2.1. Trends in coverage and performance

Primary and secondary education coverage in Latin America has been rising in recent years. Enrolment rates for primary and secondary education have now reached levels close to those of OECD economies. In contrast, higher-education coverage remains low (Figure 4.1).

Figure 4.1. Latin America and the Caribbean (15 countries) and OECD: gross enrolment rates by education level - 2009 or the most recent year for which data is available
(Percentages)

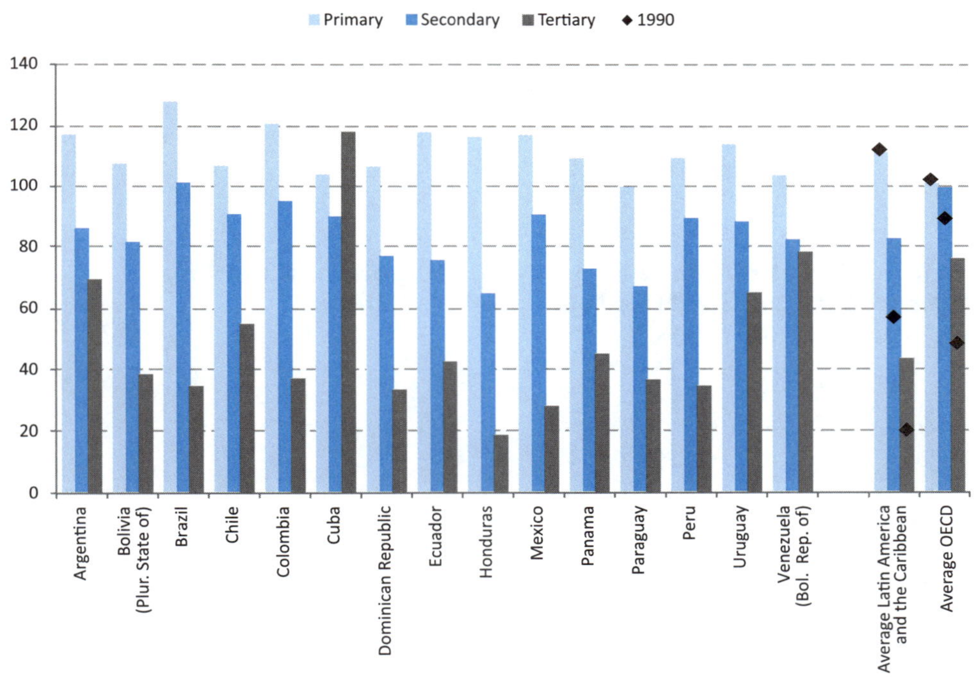

Note: Gross enrolment rate is calculated as the total number of students (of any age) enroled over the total number of children in the official age group corresponding to the level of education. The current rate corresponds to the most recent year available for the countries in the sample. In Argentina, Brazil, Chile, Ecuador, Honduras, Peru and Uruguay this year is 2008, in Bolivia and Panama, 2007, in Peru, 2006, in the Dominican Republic, 2004. The average for Latin America and the Caribbean is 18 countries (the 15 aforementioned countries plus Costa Rica, El Salvador and Jamaica). The higher rates of enrolment for Latin America, relative to those of the OECD may reflect a greater incidence of late entry into school and/or may include students over the standard age group.

Source: Institute for Statistics, UNESCO (2011).
http://dx.doi.org/10.1787/888932522797

The panorama of coverage and performance in tertiary education in Latin America presents multiple challenges. Despite the significant increase in participation at this education level in the last two decades (in particular in Brazil and Paraguay), most countries in Latin America and the Caribbean continue to have tertiary education enrolment rates below 40%. There is also a high level of heterogeneity in the region: in some countries enrolment is over 60% (Argentina, Cuba and Uruguay), while in others it is below 30% (Honduras, El Salvador, Nicaragua, Jamaica and Mexico).[2] These percentages are well below those found in OECD economies, where Finland, the United States and the Republic of Korea all reach coverage of over 80%.

In the last few decades, the demand for higher education has been increasing in the region, reflecting changes in the economic and social structure. An essential component in this increase in demand has been the rise in per capita income, but also significant is the growing awareness of the importance of scientific and technical knowledge and skills to boost competitiveness and long-term development.[3] In higher education, which is aspired to by a much wider section of society than in the past, there is a more important social value, which has contributed to increase its demand. One positive aspect of this increase in enrolment is that in several countries more than half of the university students are the first members of their families to attend university, giving them greater socio-occupational mobility than what their parents had.

Although PISA scores remain low, the performance of Latin American countries has shown a slight improvement in the past 10 years. Recent results confirm two important facts: first, Latin American countries are among those with the lowest scores in the PISA group; and second, the region's performance is improving in comparison to earlier assessments (Figure 4.2).[4] Average reading scores for the five Latin American countries that participated in 2000 and 2009 (Argentina, Brazil, Chile, Mexico and Peru) reveal that over the course of the decade there was a slight reduction in the gap with OECD economies from 23% to 19%.[5] The OECD average increased by 2 points during that period (from 485 to 487), while the average of the Latin American countries increased by 16 points (from 395 to 411). In various countries this progress is the result of improvements among lower-scoring students:

Figure 4.2. Latin America and OECD: evolution of reading performance on the PISA test, 2000 and 2009
(Variation in score)

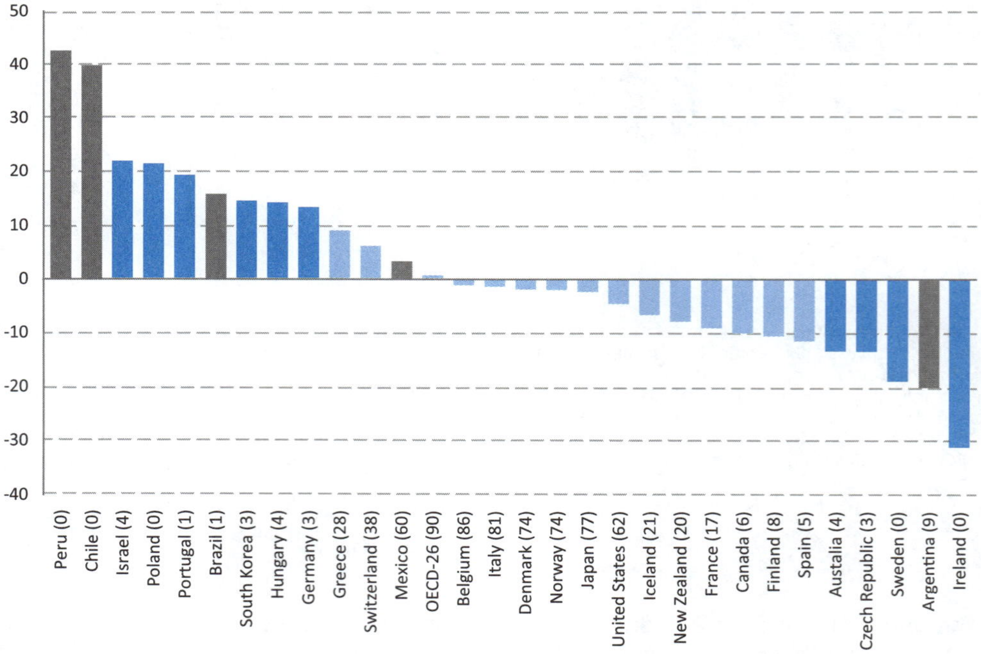

Note: Statistically significant changes are marked in dark tones and P-value is between parenthesis. Countries are organised in descending order based on the change in score. Of the countries that participate in the PISA exam, only those with scores for both years are considered here.

Source: OECD PISA 2009 database, Table V.2.1 (OECD, 2010e).
http://dx.doi.org/10.1787/888932522816

In Chile and Mexico the proportion of low-performing students fell by almost 15%; in Brazil, the best students improved their performance (with skill levels of 5 and 6), and results among low-performing students remained stable. Chile and Peru showed significant improvements in all skill levels.[6] Despite this progress, Latin America continues to be among the countries with the lowest scores on the test. Mexico remains the OECD country with the lowest results, with an average difference equivalent to two years of schooling (114 points) compared to Korea, which had the highest score in 2009. This gap is greater than with other emerging regions, such as South-East Asia.[7]

As in a number of OECD economies, students in state and private schools in Latin America perform similarly. A first glance at the data on student performance shows that students from private schools perform better than those from state schools. However, this result does not take into account socio-demographic and economic factors. Once these factors are considered, students from private schools do not perform significantly better than those from public schools. This confirms, on the one hand, the persistent effect of socio-economic status as a factor explaining performance (more important than public or private management of schools), and on the other, the strong segmentation of public and private schools by socio-economic status.[8]

Performance by gender and region continues to show important differences. As with global trends, in Latin America women are making greater strides than men in terms of enrolment, retention and graduation.[9] On the PISA reading test, girls performed significantly better than boys in all member countries, including Latin America.[10] This gap has at times increased due to improvements in female performance not being matched by improvements among males. On the other hand, geographic differences in performance are also noticeable. Analysis of urban and rural schools reveals higher PISA scores in cities in most OECD economies (after controlling for socio-economic differences) and in countries such as Argentina, Brazil and

Box 4.1. The PISA test: a comprehensive assessment of skills

The PISA programme (Programme for International Student Assessment) began in 2000. It aims to assess the capacity of students to use their knowledge and experience in "real world" situations. The emphasis of the test is on understanding concepts and mastering skills in three areas: mathematics, reading and sciences.

Around 470 000 students from 65 countries completed the fourth edition of the test in 2009. Each student spent approximately two hours completing the different tests, and in addition, they completed a background questionnaire focused on themselves and their home, their learning habits, their attitudes towards reading and their commitment and motivation. The assessment includes tasks that require students to construct their own answers as well as multiple-choice questions. School principals also complete a questionnaire about the demographic characteristics of their students and the quality of the learning environment.

The PISA test provides three essential elements for the analysis of education systems: first, a profile of the knowledge and skills among 15-year-old students in 2009, with a focus on reading, and contextual indicators that associate performance results with personal and school characteristics; second, an assessment of the dedication of students to reading activities, and their knowledge and use of different learning strategies; third, data on changing trends in students' knowledge and skills in mathematics, reading and sciences and on the impact of different factors (*e.g.* socio-demographic factors) on performance.

In 2012, PISA will focus on mathematics and will put greater emphasis on evaluating the ability of students to read and understand digital texts and resolve problems in a digital format, in this way reflecting the importance of information technologies.

Chile. At the regional level, the results in various Latin American countries show a significant difference in performance across regions, which is explained to a great extent by socio-economic differences. These inter-regional differences involve both performance and performance distribution (performance equity).[11]

Box 4.2. ICTs in Latin American education systems: better quality, greater equality

The widespread dissemination of information and communication technologies (ICTs) is producing rapid change in economic, social and cultural life. Today, developing the potential of young people depends to a great extent on their ability to use ICTs.[a] The level of ICT penetration has led to the growing importance of new technology skills in the labour market —the digitally illiterate are increasingly unlikely to be employed in high-wage jobs. This has also made digital competency a necessary condition to achieve social inclusion.[b]

In this regard, the gradual incorporation of ICTs in education systems represents a fundamental challenge for Latin America and the Caribbean. ICTs are important for the curriculum but also for the possibilities they offer to take advantage of opportunities for integration and social mobility and the full exercise of citizenship.

The school is the largest, most effective and most economical institution for reducing the digital gap among young people, in particular for students with fewer resources who do not have these technologies at home. The potential of schooling cannot be reduced solely to its role in digital literacy: ICTs can also be introduced across disciplines in the learning process, facilitating the pedagogical process through didactic tools and lifelong learning.

Thus, an initial challenge is to press forward in expanding access to ICTs. This requires strategies to increase coverage and available technological resources, providing more computers and improving the quality of broadband Internet access. In regard to access to ICTs and their use in education, significant differences remain among countries. But there are also numerous success stories: Brazil's experience with the Broadband in Schools programme; Chile's *Enlaces* programme; and Uruguay's CEIBAL project (Educational Connectivity/Basic Computing for Online Learning), which attempts to universalise student access by supplying computers to students.

Differences are also found in the rate of computers per student in primary school systems: While Uruguay had a rate of 1 student per computer at the primary school level in 2008 and Chile had a rate of 13 students per computer at primary and secondary levels, Brazil and Honduras had rates of 83 and 137 students per computer, respectively. Broadband access in primary schools is also quite unequal, as illustrated by the cases of Costa Rica (40%) and Uruguay (100%).

Training to give teachers the necessary skills to use ICTs in their professional practice and in the classroom is also an important challenge. Policies to develop digital infrastructure should therefore be accompanied by policies to promote teacher training in the use of new technologies in education.[c]

[a] See Kaztman (2010) and ECLAC/IYO (2008).

[b] ECLAC (2010d).

[c] ECLAC (2010d).

4.2.2. Trends in equity

PISA results show a slight improvement in educational equity in the past decade.[12] The PISA test enables us to explore equity in several dimensions: in student performance, in the distribution of resources among schools, and in the distribution of learning opportunities. The variation in performance (estimated as the score total variance in the reading test) by student shows a slight decline (of 3%) between 2000 and 2009 among OECD economies. Most countries that improved their performance in the PISA test between 2000 and 2009, including several Latin American countries, also reduced the variation in results. In breaking down the variation in results, we see that PISA results reflect trends related to equity. In contrast to total variation, variation between schools remained constant between 2000 and 2009, implying stable school inclusion throughout the decade.

Economic and socio-cultural status is an important factor affecting access and educational achievement at all levels of education in Latin America. There is a clear correlation in the region between educational achievement and household education level (expressed in parents' years of education and educational attainment). Only 3.1% of the children of parents that did not complete primary education finish tertiary studies, whereas over 70% of those with parents that completed tertiary education do so.[13]

Despite the advances in coverage, education systems in Latin America have not become a mechanism to promote social equity, as the low rate of educational achievement of secondary and tertiary education shows. Secondary education coverage in Latin America increased significantly between 1990 and 2006, rising from 27% to 51% of young people between 20 and 24 years of age having completed secondary education. However, the picture is less optimistic if we look at the data by income quintile: in the first quintile (lowest income) the percentage is a little over a quarter of the percentage found in the last quintile (highest income) (see Figure 4.3).[14] These differences in educational attainment

Figure 4.3. Young people completing secondary and tertiary education by income quintiles, 2008 or nearest

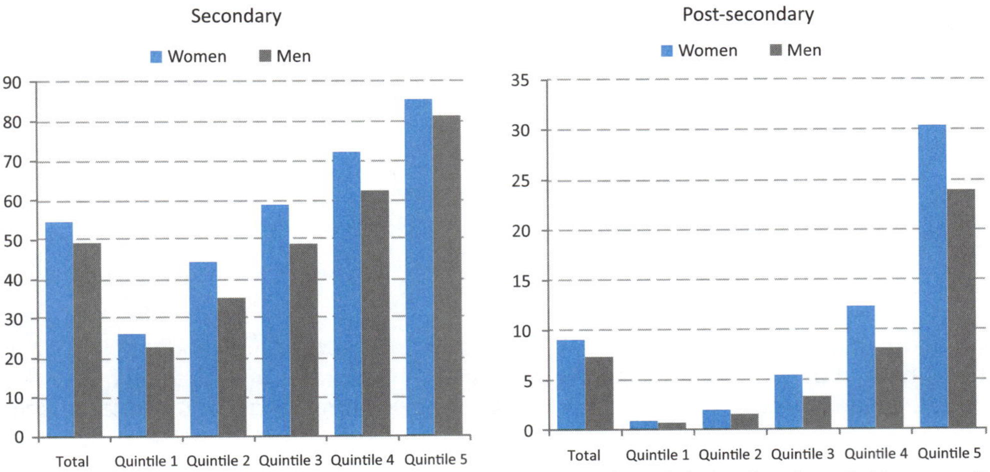

Note: Average from 18 Latin American and Caribbean countries, based on tabulations from household surveys. At the secondary level, the completion rate corresponds to youth aged 20-24 who have completed their secondary education. The post-secondary level considers young people aged 25-29 who have completed at least five years of tertiary education.

Source: ECLAC (2010c.).
http://dx.doi.org/10.1787/888932522835

are even greater at the tertiary level. Among young people aged 25 to 29, only 8.7% have managed to complete at least 5 years of tertiary education, and there are significant differences by income quintile (0.6% in the lowest quintile vs. 22% in the highest). This illustrates the extent to which the high opportunity cost of remaining in the education system impedes young people in lower income quintiles from completing tertiary education.

Differences in income distribution in Latin America and the Caribbean are also reflected in school performance. PISA test results of secondary students distributed by income quartiles show that most students in the first and second quartiles (that is, from the poorest households) perform below level 2. This indicates that they have failed to develop the basic competencies assessed by the test. This seems again to confirm the importance of the socio-economic and cultural status of students' household of origin in generating differences in education outcomes.[15]

Figure 4.4. Latin America and the Caribbean (9 countries) and OECD average: distribution of test score in PISA reading tests, according to socioeconomic and cultural household background quartiles, 2009
(Percentages)

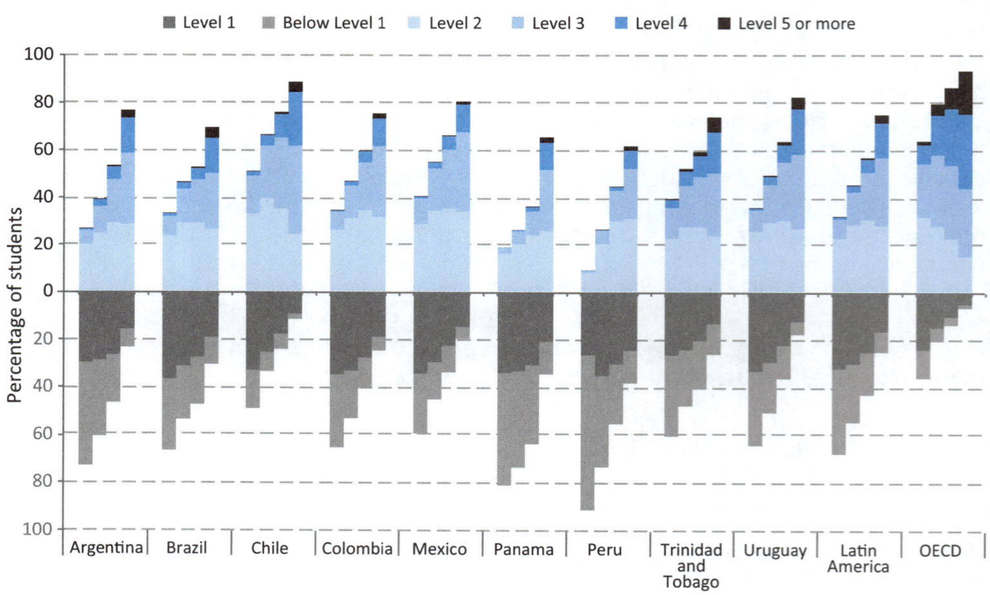

Note: The distribution by performance levels in Latin America and OECD refers to the simple mean of attainment level weighted at the national level for participating countries in PISA 2009.

Source: Based on data from PISA 2009.
http://dx.doi.org/10.1787/888932522854

In some countries of the region (especially in Brazil, Chile and Mexico) the transmission of socio-economic inequalities into inequalities in education outcomes has declined in the last decade. Figure 4.5 shows the change in the relationship between socio-economic and cultural status and reading performance between 2000 and 2009. This result contrasts with that found in OECD economies where the relationship has remained constant.

Figure 4.5. Impact of the index of economic, social and cultural status, 2000-09
(Percentages)

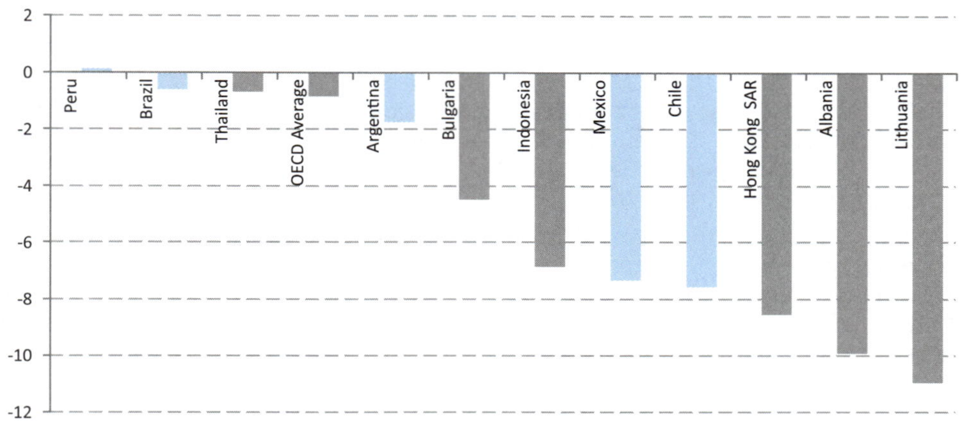

Note: Countries organised based on the difference in the impact of the index of economic, social and cultural status between 2000 and 2009.

Source: PISA 2009 database, Table V.4.3 (OECD, 2010c).
http://dx.doi.org/10.1787/888932522873

Box 4.3. The challenge of expanding education programmes: pre-school education and lengthening the school day

A strategy for equality in education must include the expansion of pre-school education coverage and the introduction of the extended school day in public education. This will help to equalise learning in the early stages of education, a key to performance in subsequent education levels,[a] and counter differences based on family origin, thus promoting equal educational opportunity. The low performance of Latin America in the PISA test reveals the need to improve students' cognitive capacities at early ages. In addition, better pre-school coverage and extending the school day mean that adults, above all women, will not have to dedicate as many hours to taking care of their children. This promotes women's access to the labour market and income for households (above all for those with lower incomes).

Recently, there have been important advances in policies to expand pre-school education programmes in Latin America (0-5 year olds) and —to a lesser extent— extend the school day. However, in most countries these are still outstanding issues. In the countries with greatest coverage, participation in pre-school education accounts for two thirds of the primary-school enrolment rate (except in Uruguay, where it reaches 74%), while it ranges from 20% to less than 50% in other countries in the region.[b] In regard to extending the school day, in countries such as Chile, Colombia and Uruguay significant efforts have been made, at least in primary education (though also in secondary education in the case of Chile). However, the extended school day exists primarily in private schools and, as a result, depends on the capacity of families to pay. This is an additional factor in the reproduction of inequality, as it is precisely children from socially disadvantaged backgrounds who most need early education programmes.[c]

[a] ECLAC (2010b).

[b] ECLAC (2010d).

[c] ECLAC/IYO (2008).

4.2.3. Spending on education

Latin America has begun to invest more in education. Traditionally, total public spending on education in Latin America has been low in comparison with OECD economies. These differences, however, have begun to decline. An average of 4% of GDP in the region is spent on education, representing a slight increase since 2000, while the average for the OECD is 5%. Distribution by levels shows that education spending is concentrated on primary and secondary education; while the level of spending on pre-school education, despite low coverage, is close to that of OECD economies. Spending on tertiary education is below the OECD average, with some exceptions (Colombia, Uruguay and the Bolivarian Republic of Venezuela).

Three factors explain the increase in education spending per student in the region: economic growth, demographic changes and private-sector participation. First, the significant economic growth of the last decade, which has increased GDP per capita in many of the countries of the region, must be taken into consideration. Second, the ageing of the population has led to a decrease in the proportion of school-age population, a factor that is particularly relevant in Argentina, Brazil, Chile and Mexico. Lastly, there has been an increase in private-sector participation in the provision of education services (especially in Argentina and Chile), leading to a higher percentage of students in private schools and freeing up more public resources per student.[16]

The recent increase in public spending per student (on primary and secondary education) is linked to improvements in the education conditions.[17] Since 1990, most Latin American and Caribbean countries have been increasing public spending per student, a trend that has been strengthened in the past decade. Between 1990 and 2000, school coverage was increased (especially in secondary education, as primary education had already been essentially universal since the beginning of the 1990s); thus, a large share of the increase in education spending was concentrated on facilitating the incorporation of new students. This, however, limited the increase in average spending per student. Between 2000 and 2008, the increase in spending was used to improve conditions that affect the quality of education, such as infrastructure, equipment and didactic materials, among others.[18] However, there are still important differences between countries: in primary education, for example, public investment per student as a percentage of GDP oscillates between 8% (Peru) and 16% (Brazil). Similar differences occur with secondary education.

Regarding public investment per student, spending on tertiary education is higher compared to other levels of education. This can be seen clearly in Brazil, Costa Rica, Cuba, Mexico, Panama and Uruguay.[19] On the other hand, for a notable group of countries this indicator has decreased, in particular Argentina, Chile and Colombia. This decrease is much more significant in Latin American countries than in OECD economies. This is partly due to strong differences in investment in education by income quintiles making public spending per student at the tertiary level regressive and higher than spending per student at primary and secondary levels.

Spending on public education remains more important, although some countries do have high levels of spending on private education. On average, public investment in education in Latin America reaches levels similar to those in OECD economies (4% of GDP), with the private sector covering about a quarter of total spending in this area (Figure 4.7). In OECD economies, private spending on education does not reach 1% of GDP, while in Latin America it accounts for 1.3% on average, with Chile, Colombia, the Dominican Republic and Peru standing out.

Figure 4.6. Latin America and the Caribbean: evolution of public spending on education by level between 2000 and the most recent year with available data

A. Spending per student (percentage of GDP per capita)

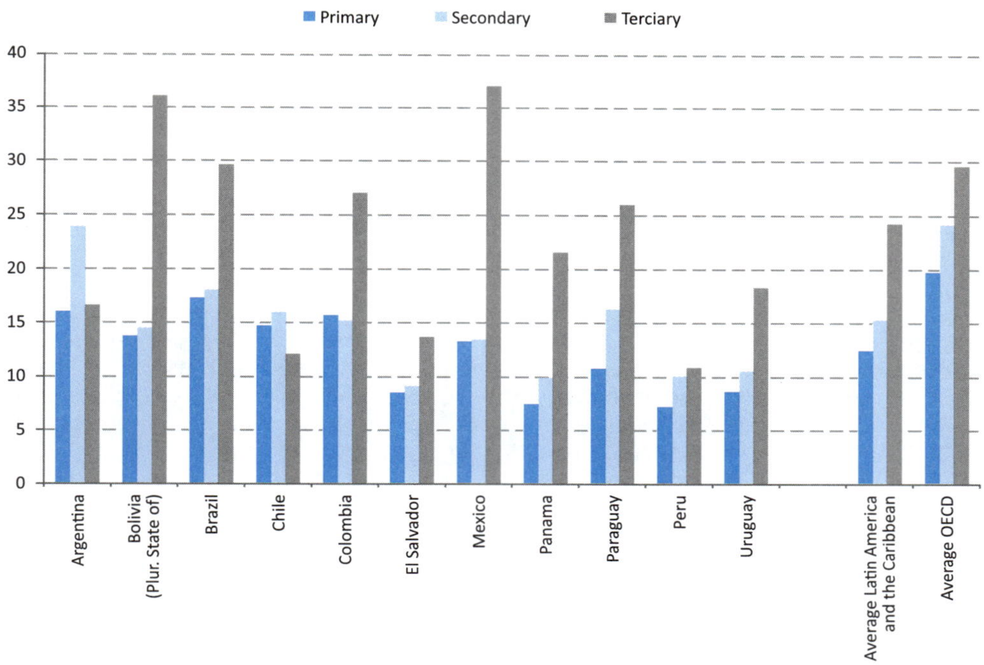

B. Variation between the year 2000 and the most recent year

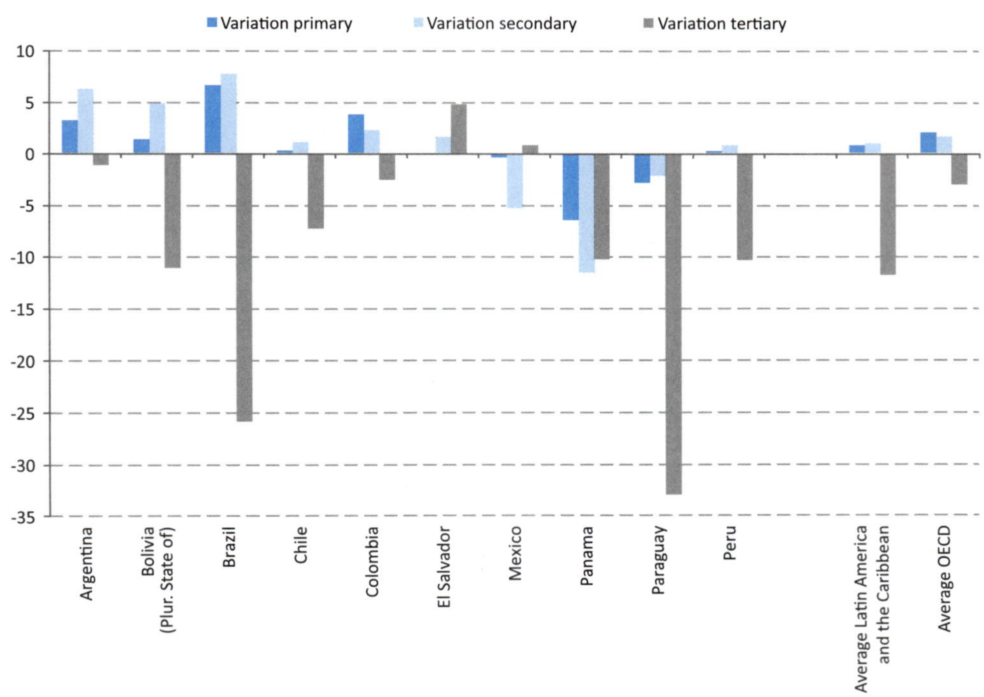

Note: Data correspond to 2009 for Colombia; 2008 for Argentina, Chile, Cuba and El Salvador; 2007 for Brazil, Jamaica, Panama, and Paraguay; 2006 for Bolivia (Plur. State of), Peru and Uruguay.

Source: *Institute for Statistics, UNESCO (2011).*
http://dx.doi.org/10.1787/888932522892

Box 4.4. Demographic bonus and the evolution of public expenditure on education

The growth of GDP and income per capita in the past decade is not the only factor that has made the expansion of public spending on education in Latin America possible; in fact, public spending per student in primary and secondary cycles —considering students that attend public schools— has also been positively affected by the decline in the number of school-age children and adolescents (from 5 to 19 years of age).

The existence of this "demographic bonus" in the region has been apparent since the beginning of the 1990s, as the percentage of the school-age population has decreased from 27% (1990) to 23.4% (2008) of the total population.[a] This demographic transition fostered an increase in public spending on primary and secondary education in the past two decades; for every dollar allocated per potential student in 1990, 2.7 dollars were allocated in 2008.

The existence of this "demographic bonus" in the region represents a great opportunity to strengthen the education of young generations. However, this opportunity must be seized now, as these particular demographic conditions will not last in the long-term. Strengthening the skills of youth becomes even more urgent if we consider that that these generations will have to maintain high levels of productivity in order to sustain the dependent population resulting from the gradual ageing of society. This is the situation OECD economies now find themselves in, as they have completed this demographic transition. A more skilled labour force is one that can incorporate knowledge and innovation to drive sustained economic growth; therefore, it is fundamental to invest some of the resources freed up by this "demographic bonus" into strengthening the competencies of those generations who have recently entered the labour market.[b]

[a] See ECLAC (2010c) and ECLAC/IYO (2008).

[b] ECLAC/IYO (2008).

4.3. Education reforms in Latin America

In order to improve coverage and quality, a number of reforms have been carried out in education systems across Latin America —administrative, budgetary and curricular, among others.[20] These reforms have brought about changes in management on different levels, from the ministerial or central government levels to that of the schools themselves. They have included reforms in programmes (from programmes of universal coverage to programmes giving total freedom to schools to follow the curriculum that best fits their population and their objectives), reforms in the management of teaching staff (*e.g.* selection and incentives), as well as changes in the rules for allocating resources with regard to transparency of information and public accountability, among other areas.

One of the main results of these reforms has been the gradual increase in private-sector participation. In the last two decades the percentage of students enrolled in private educational institutions from pre-school through to secondary school has increased by two percentage points, reaching approximately 20%. For higher education, the percentage of total student enrolment in private institutions is even higher, reaching over 50%.[21] This trend reveals a growing role for the state, which has gradually changed from being a supplier to being a regulator in education. In particular, in countries such as Chile and Colombia where the monitoring of tertiary education has been relatively poor since the introduction of reforms in the 1990s, public administrations must ensure that gains in coverage are not accompanied by a loss in quality.

Figure 4.7. Latin America and the Caribbean (9 countries) and OECD: public and private spending on education as a percentage of GDP, 2008

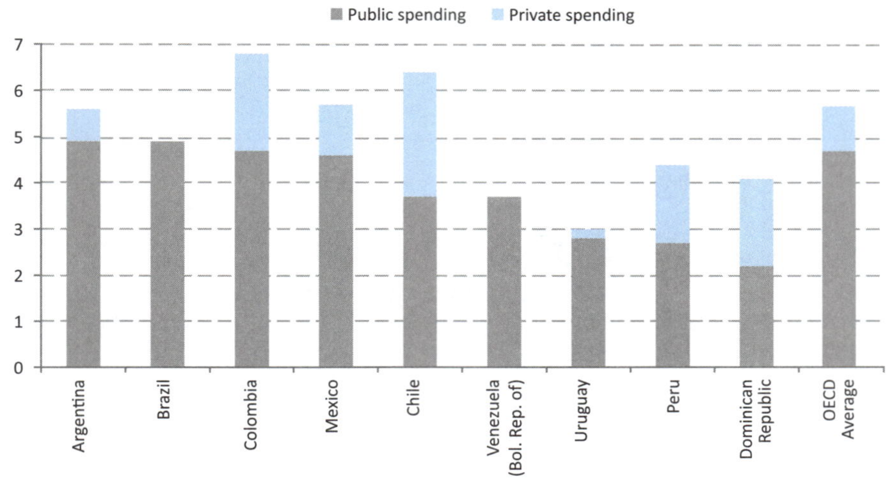

Note: Total spending on educational institutions and administration as a percentage of GDP, based on public and private sources, including all levels (pre-school, primary, secondary and tertiary). Data for private spending in Brazil and Venezuela (Bol. Rep. of) not available.

Source: Institute for Statistics, UNESCO (2011).
http://dx.doi.org/10.1787/888932522911

Given their structure and objectives, education systems require strong state involvement to ensure they function properly. The dynamics of current education systems involve diverse actors (students, parents, teachers, administrators) with different objectives, which private suppliers may not be able to meet. These characteristics make active state involvement even more important for two reasons. On the one hand, the returns from education only become visible in the long-term, making it difficult to quantify the cost and benefit of educational services.[22] On the other hand, important external factors, such as the role of the household, intervene in the educational process. Education reforms must take these particularities into account.

This section focuses on five aspects of the reforms that have been carried out to varying degrees in many of the countries of the region: decentralisation; tertiary education reforms; a strengthening of evaluation systems; teacher selection, career and assessment policy; and private participation in the education system.

Important initiatives have been taken to improve education, but in order to be effective, they must be accompanied by concrete measures with a long-term vision. As with all investment in knowledge, investing in education does not offer immediate returns. It is therefore important to create the fiscal and policy space for reforms to have a real impact, with mechanisms for periodic adjustments so that the course set can be maintained.[23] At the fiscal level, governments must create tools to provide continuity to the programmes and reforms they introduce. Fiscal space must be accompanied by a policy space in which the different actors can reach agreement on the types of measures to be implemented.

"Prioritising" the reforms in education, in order is another key to achieving the desired effects. The sequence in which investments are made, programmes designed and reforms scheduled is important. In the past, Latin American governments often carried out certain reforms without taking into account the implementation sequence. In the case of education, addressing the gap in physical infrastructure is one of the first actions for public institutions. Providing teachers and principals with the necessary pedagogical content knowledge and skills is also key for education policy in the region. A subsequent essential step is curriculum reform, which requires continuity. If it is necessary to lengthen the school day to improve learning, which seems to be the growing consensus in the region, the first step must be to invest in the education infrastructure provided for students.

Box 4.5. The OECD supports reforms to improve education[a]

Carrying out reform is not easy. The evidence shows that the implementation process is as important as policy design. Even the most logical and best designed policies cannot be implemented if the path to reform is not well prepared. The OECD has developed an innovative approach to strengthen capacity for reforms focused on improving educational achievement among member and partner economies. The approach combines: *i)* an OECD evaluation to develop an analysis and contextualised recommendations and *ii)* involvement of stakeholders in the reform process in order to foster consultation and exchange.

Mexico participated in this process. One of the final publications of the project, *Improving Schools: Strategies for Action in Mexico*,[b] presents an action framework for improving the quality of education. Its 15 recommendations offer a framework for education reform that can be used as a reference for other Latin American countries:

- **Better teachers:** *i)* Define effective teaching through standards; *ii)* Attract the best candidates to teaching; *iii)* Strengthen initial teacher preparation; *iv)* Improve initial teacher assessment; *v)* Open all posts to competition; *vi)* Create induction/probation periods; *vii)* Improve professional development; *viii)* Evaluate to help improve.

- **Better schools:** *ix)* Define effective school leadership; *x)* Professionalise training and appointment of directors; *xi)* Build instructional leadership in the schools; *xii)* Enhance school autonomy; *xiii)* Ensure funding for all schools; *xiv)* Strengthen social participation.

- **Implementation:** *xv)* Create an implementation working committee with representation from the different stakeholders involved in the process.

To support reforms and promote genuine capacity-building in Mexico, the OECD also organised the OECD Seminar for Leaders in Educational Reform, held in Chile and in Canada (in the province of Ontario). Both seminars were attended by 30 high-level policy makers from Mexico, including the Secretary of Public Education, national education authorities, parliamentarians, and representatives from the national trade union for education (the SNTE) and civil society organisations. Attendees worked together in teams to extrapolate lessons and design a strategy for education reform.

These seminars are aimed at planting the seeds for reform by facilitating learning among policy makers, analysing international practices, and promoting a process of consultation and contextualisation of recommendations with members economies of the OECD.

[a] Contributed by Beatriz Pont and Diana Toledo, from the Educational Policy Implementation team of the OECD Directorate for Education, based on OECD (2010h).

[b] OECD (2010h).

4.3.1. Decentralisation

Decentralisation reform can strengthen performance, but it can also create greater inequalities. One of the arguments in favour of decentralisation is that local governments know more about local preferences[24] and are, therefore, better able to respond to local needs.[25] In addition, it has been argued that local governments are subject to greater public scrutiny locally, making their decisions more transparent.[26] However, some point out problems resulting from decentralisation, emphasising that local governments are more likely to be controlled by local interest groups.[27] They are also not able to take advantage of economies of scale. In addition, there is greater heterogeneity in decentralised management capacities compared to centralised management, and in some cases it is inferior.[28] If it occurs, decentralisation can have a tendency to replicate the segmentation of local governments in terms of their management capacity of education systems. All these arguments could be used in characterising the range of experiences with decentralisation in the region. However, various voices argue that decentralisation has not led to greater changes in the most important space for public education policies: the classroom.[29]

Experiences with decentralised management of education systems in Latin America have varied in terms of gradualness, magnitude and attributes.[30] Argentina, Chile, Colombia and Mexico began the process of decentralisation before the rest of the region in the 1980s, and other countries later followed suit. The majority of Latin American countries now have some elements of decentralised management in their education systems. Decentralisation is generally a gradual, sequential or incremental process in the sense that it does not come through the passage of a single law, but has a long-term perspective. Decentralisation also varies in terms of the competencies delegated to sub-national bodies and educational institutions. Decentralised functions can be classified as follows: *i)* the function of leading, regulating and supervising the sector; *ii)* the financing function; *iii)* the function of the direct management of the service (personnel policy and investment management, etc.); and *iv)* the "planning" function (educational goals, goals with respect to coverage and quality, curriculum, fixing school timetables and schedules, etc.).[31]

Decentralisation can have an incremental effect on the provision of private educational services. The decentralisation process might not always affect coverage or performance. For example, the decentralisation reform in Colombia in 2001 did not lead to improved enrolment rates, according to an evaluation of the measure. However, municipalities with greater autonomy were more likely to sign subsidy contracts with private schools.[32] In this way decentralisation has served to increase private provision of educational services.

Decentralisation policy implies the need for greater resources for school management. The effective shift of centralised sectoral policies and strategies to the implementation of programmes at the local level requires two key elements: *i)* monitoring and communication links between central, regional and local levels, and *ii)* an updated management information system that is accurate and timely in order to implement a monitoring system.[33] In addition, economies of scale seem to indicate that the following interventions are better when they are the responsibility of central government: *i)* sectoral planning and programming; *ii)* the assignment of additional resources based on certain equity criteria; *iii)* basic curriculum design; and *iv)* the management of teachers and statutes regulating teaching.[34] All of this requires a solid local management capacity. This seems to be the major outstanding challenge of decentralisation: providing local entities with better management capacity, especially in the less economically developed regions (those with higher rates of unmet basic needs, with a higher presence of ethnic minorities, with greater exposure to internal armed conflict and with greater vulnerability to natural disasters).

Disadvantaged schools in Latin American, like those in the OECD, tend to lack resources. Figure 4.7 shows the relationship between the average socio-economic level of students and the school's level of resources. Even when schools have a similar number of teachers, disadvantaged schools tend to receive more resources in some areas (*e.g.* percentage of full-time certified teachers), whereas in other areas (*e.g.* quality of educational resources), the more advantaged schools receive a larger share of the resources. Decentralisation reforms can play a decisive role in balancing the distribution of these resources.[35]

Figure 4.8. Correlation between average socio-economic level and school resources

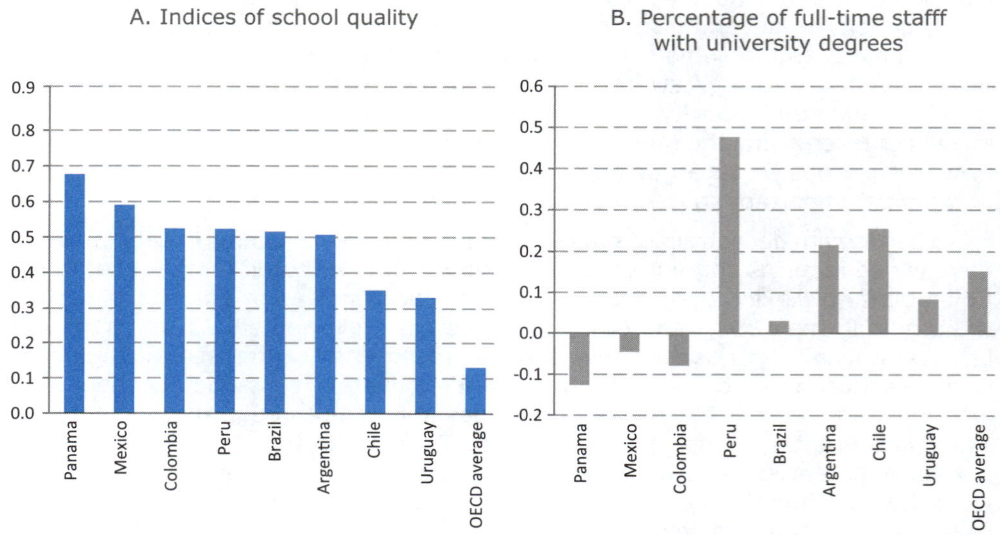

Source: OECD, PISA 2009 database, Table II.2.2.
http://dx.doi.org/10.1787/888932522930

4.3.2. Tertiary education

Deregulation and decentralisation have been the main thrust of reforms in higher education in Latin America. As a result, important changes have been made in university structure, management and funding. These changes include: a decrease in state involvement in providing and financing tertiary education; the creation of systems of higher education accreditation and bodies for quality assurance; the adoption of new criteria for quality and funds allocation; and greater control over the use of resources. In addition, under the strong influence of globalisation, countries in Latin America have been gradually opening up to transnational providers of education services at the tertiary level. In different countries in the region, these changes have been incorporated in a new regulatory framework for education through specific laws, decrees or, in some cases, constitutional reforms, such as in Argentina and the Plurinational State of Bolivia.[36]

These reforms have resulted in a significant increase in heterogeneity in tertiary education, at the expense of average quality. As a result, the need to strengthen the regulatory role of the state through the creation of bodies for quality assurance has become an urgent priority. New outcome-oriented assessment models, which prioritise institutional efficiency and productivity, require public information systems and logistics that can provide comparative data at the national and international level. Under new quality criteria, and with the expansion of privately provided tertiary education, the production of knowledge has lost importance in these institutions.

The growth of the higher education system in Latin America in recent years has increased the pressure to diversify funding mechanisms. New forms of financing have developed, among which four main mechanisms or schemes stand out:

- Direct public funding: in some countries, the allocation of public funding is increasingly characterised by performance-based funding through competitive procedures.
- Public funding based on policy objectives: funds to address specific objectives or advances in research, such as the University for All Programme (PROUNI) in Brazil.
- Private funding: fees paid by families, firms that finance research and post-graduate programmes, or private donations. The cost of education is increasing even in state universities (the most noteworthy case is Chile).
- Mixed model: Chile.

An urgent challenge to resolve in terms of funding higher education in the region is to balance access and equality. If young people from the lowest income quintiles are going to achieve real and lasting social mobility through better employment opportunities, they must have access to and be able to complete university. The challenge for a more egalitarian education system is not to reduce public spending on tertiary education. On the contrary, it involves increasing access for young people from low-income households, identifying alternative forms of funding for those who cannot afford to pay (through cross-subsidisation or scholarships based on ability to pay), having flexible timetables with evening hours and having an adequate supply of publicly and privately provided tertiary education.

Tertiary education in Latin America and the Caribbean is faced with various "traditional" challenges that can only be overcome with the active support of the State. These challenges include: improving the quality of teaching; improving the efficiency of educational institutions; aligning technical education with labour market demand; and complementing the teaching mission with research and extension. The increased private presence in state education has not resolved the problem of obtaining resources for research and for the production of other public goods, which remain in general the responsibility of state universities and others that receive public funding for this purpose.

Along with these challenges, others will be emerging for Latin American universities in the coming years, such as new technological paradigms and the need to strengthen the university's role in development. The transition towards the knowledge-based economy has brought about major changes in productive structures and redefined the function of higher education institutions. Knowledge and technology transfer is beginning through the dissemination and application of academic research results and, in short, the generation of profits derived from them. The public sector in Latin America must therefore take these demands into account in defining coherent and effective policies in education, science, technology and innovation. The role of universities in creating skills in the region is crucial, so they need to become key players in the region's development.

Modernising the university in Latin America involves establishing a solid relationship with the production sector through research and development. Traditionally, higher education institutions have had another mission in parallel with teaching: to carry out research. In Latin America, higher education institutions have a great potential in this respect, given that they account for most of the human resources dedicated to scientific and technological research. However, Latin America has not reached a "critical mass" of researchers. This is illustrated by the number of full-time researchers with respect to the size of the economically active population, which continues to be below the levels of OECD economies. This limitation in resources is also reflected in the poor performance of the region in terms of scientific production and innovation performance (see Chapter 6).[37]

In addition to having fewer researchers, Latin American universities are characterised by the greater weight of the social sciences and humanities. In fact, the distribution of university students in the region is concentrated mainly in these disciplines, while there is a smaller proportion in science and technology. This pattern differs considerably from that of the OECD economies, where we see cases such as Korea and Finland with a greater concentration of graduates in the fields of engineering, science and technology. This is consistent with the strategy in these countries to increase human resources in disciplines with applications in sciences and technology, as they look to develop a productive system based on the development of manufacturing value added.

Given the limited public resources available, closer interaction between universities and the productive sector could help reconcile the traditional missions of higher-education institutions with their new functions related to knowledge and technology transfer. For universities, collaboration with business could strengthen the training and retraining of teachers, in particular in regard to scientific and technological skills and the dissemination and practical application of research results, and promote alternative sources of funding. From a business perspective there are multiple reasons for having more direct contact with universities: to help resolve problems specific to the structure of production, to provide an alternative source for research and development, and to carry out a long-term strategy to maintain and improve competitiveness.[38]

4.3.3. Creating and strengthening evaluation systems

Although they are not perfect, standardised measures of school performance have served as tools for raising the importance of student learning. But there are also measures for teachers. The Teaching and Learning International Survey (TALIS), for example, is the first comparative approach to teaching and learning practices among teachers in secondary education in both public and private schools.[39] Based on information on the attitudes and practices of teachers in 23 countries (Brazil and Mexico in Latin America), TALIS has identified factors needed for effective teaching: professional development for teachers, teacher recognition and other factors that shape the learning environment in schools.[40] Studies of this type have made it possible to quantify various factors, including, for example, the impact of teacher absenteeism and the lack of pedagogical preparation on the quality of the education imparted in the school. These studies also emphasise the importance of job satisfaction, collaboration and professional development for the creation of an effective teaching environment. There are different practices in Latin America to evaluate teachers, such as the *Carrera Magisterial* or the new universal evaluation system in Mexico, or the Sistema Nacional de Evaluación Docente (SNED – National System for Teacher Evaluation) in Chile.

Although these evaluation systems have helped us understand the dynamics of education systems, they must also be evaluated and perfected. Until the 1990s, the systematic measurement of student performance and teaching effectiveness was not a common practice in OECD economies or in Latin America. Today, the evaluation of schools and teaching and management practices has become an essential variable to guarantee the quality of school systems, especially given the proliferation of private institutions, and it has become an important tool in defining policies. Nevertheless, as with other monitoring mechanisms, evaluation systems can have perverse effects, such as the practice of "teaching to the test", the modification of curriculums without a general overview of educational objectives, fraud or other types of irregularities. This dimension, the *evaluation of evaluation*, must continue be considered when implementing these systems to guarantee their reliability.

There must be greater awareness and transparency related to education outcomes. Just as in OECD economies, parents are highly satisfied with the education their children receive, despite poor educational results in the region. This is a generational issue (the youth of today far exceed their parents in years of schooling). It reveals, however, a lack of knowledge regarding education indicators. We must promote a culture of evidence in Latin America to help identify areas for improvement and the support mechanisms required for this, while at the same time recognising the educational achievements that do happen in school.

Accountability and transparency are key elements for the successful performance of education systems. In countries where schools must make their results public, the schools with more autonomy tend to perform better; however, in countries where these transparency mechanisms do not exist, the effect is the opposite.[41] Some countries have implemented their own programmes to evaluate schools: Brazil's National System for the Evaluation of Basic Education (SAEB); Chile's System to Measure the Quality of Education (SIMCE), and Mexico's National Evaluation of Academic Achievement in Schools (ENLACE). There are also regional initiatives such as the Latin American Laboratory for Assessment of the Quality of Education (LLECE). These assessments use different approaches (*e.g.* censuses or sampling) but they have allowed for more accurate and transparent monitoring of student achievement and performance.[42] The use of national evaluation systems also has an impact on the level of equity in school systems. In fact, socio-economic background has less impact on student performance in schools where the use of evaluation systems is more widespread.[43] The proper functioning of education systems is, in short, tied to their transparency.

National evaluation systems are not limited to schools. This is reflected in the recent implementation of the Programme for the International Assessment of Adult Competencies (PIAAC), which studies the learning skills of the adult population in OECD economies and partner countries. The PIAAC assesses the cognitive skills and workplace competencies of adults that actively participate in society and contribute to economic development. The PIAAC will provide a clear picture of the stock of human capital in OECD economies and the distribution of skills among the population according to type of activity and education. The initial results of this study will be available in 2013.

4.3.4. Teachers: selection, career, assessment and incentives

A well-trained and well-paid teaching staff and management, with well-defined career paths and adequate incentives for good performance, are common elements of successful school systems.[44] The training, management and professional development of teachers and principals are fundamental factors in an education system. International evidence points to the teacher as the most important factor in learning.[45] In recent years, reforms in teaching policy in Latin America have concentrated on five fundamental areas: selection, initial training, support, continuing training and incentives. In each of these areas, lack of clarity in the distribution of responsibilities is one of the main problems. Furthermore, co-ordination between the educational and cultural demand of society and teacher training, which is often outdated and not sensitive to educational demands. Consolidating a real professionalisation of teachers and management is also increasingly urgent, as this benefits the quality of the system. Along these lines, it is important to define a set of coherent standards on expectations in terms of knowledge, skills and values associated with effective teaching and management. Improving working conditions, optimising systems for hiring new teachers and principals and offering attractive and flexible career plans can have a major impact on student performance.

In the last two decades, the teaching staff in Latin America underwent a series of transformations. The predominance of women in the profession increased. Towards the beginning of the 1990s one in every four teachers was male, while by the end of the first decade of the 2000s male teachers represented only one in six. During this period, the greater presence of female teachers in pre-school and primary school in comparison to secondary school was maintained. In addition, the average age of teachers has increased. The percentage of teachers over 45 years of age rose from 7% to 28%. At the other extreme, if in the 1990s one in four teachers was 24 years of age or under, by the end of the first decade of the 2000s only one in ten teachers fell within this age range. This confirms that less and less young people are opting for teaching. The percentage of teachers that have completed higher education fell from 17% to 12%. It is interesting to note that this decrease has been among secondary school teachers. The education level of pre-school and primary school teachers has improved slightly.

Selection mechanisms are key to the quality of teaching staff. To attract the best possible teachers, it is important to have a mechanism for the recruitment and assessment of candidates, which in various countries of the region is not well developed. Strengthening the preparation of new teachers is fundamental. The introduction of an accreditation system for teachers' colleges (*Escuelas Normales*) and other teaching institutions is essential. Some studies show that there are great differences among schools in the evaluation mechanisms for new teachers. The use of clearer performance measures to assure a minimum level of teaching skills for all teachers could be an important medium-term objective. Regarding the quality of teaching, there are major differences in the region: in countries currently expanding their coverage, the main problem is the lack of teachers to cover the demand, rather than the quality and selection mechanisms.

Another important element related to teaching careers is competition for teaching positions. Currently, many positions are allocated by special commissions (as is the case in Colombia and Mexico). This results in an inadequate distribution of resources. Other types of mechanisms must be found for assigning teachers to posts; for example, mechanisms to place teachers in those schools where their individual skills are most needed. The schools themselves must be directly involved in these decisions.[46]

Beyond salary, possibilities for professional development for teaching staff are often limited and irregular. The most successful incentives for teachers are those associated with professional prospects and not only factors such as salary or training opportunities. The courses and training available may not always be relevant. It is necessary to provide training that meets teachers' needs. In addition, the involvement of school principals is essential to improve the effectiveness of schools. In addition, the professionalisation of the teaching career must also include school principals. In general there are not adequate training programmes for principals or incentives for them to improve school performance. The appointment and professionalisation of principals must be clear, with transparent selection schemes. Institutional leadership is built from within and across schools. An exchange of experiences among principals has been shown to be effective in other contexts (see Box 4.5) and can reduce significant disparities among different high- and low-performing schools. The autonomy of principals is therefore important in guiding and better supporting teachers in their educational practice. Principals must have the power to hire or suspend a teacher, but also to introduce incentives, make decisions on the curriculum and manage the professional training necessary for the school. Giving greater financial autonomy to schools also means that principals must have better management skills.

A remaining challenge in the region is to assign qualified teachers to schools with the greatest need. Equity in performance is affected by the tendency to concentrate the best teachers in the most privileged schools.[47] In Colombia, for example, less than one third of the teachers in the most vulnerable areas (i.e. poor areas, areas exposed to armed conflicts and those with a higher presence of indigenous people or people of African descent) have higher-education qualifications; in contrast, in departments that are better off, more than three quarters of the teachers do. A better distribution of teaching staff is possible through appropriate incentives tied to pay and career prospects. Another possibility is to focus on policies that help to strengthen the quality of education in the most vulnerable schools. Examples of this approach are CONAFE, the National Council for the Promotion of Education (Consejo Nacional de Fomento Educativo) in Mexico and "Escuela Nueva" in Colombia. These programmes offer syllabuses adapted for students in rural schools, but also provide continuing education for teachers so that they can carry out their jobs in these specific contexts.[48]

4.4. Towards a new agenda of education reforms

Latin America faces multiple complex challenges in education. Recent reforms in the education systems in Latin America raise multiple challenges in regard to the role of the State. The "traditional" challenges remain: extending coverage and access, creating more equal stages of education, and improving teaching and education outcomes. However, there are now new demands based on social and economic needs specific to the knowledge-based society. Policy response must also serve these multiple objectives.

Expanding secondary and tertiary education coverage is a priority. In the last two decades, most countries in the region have implemented reforms in their education systems to expand coverage and improve the impact of their investment in education. One of the achievements that stands out is the universalisation of primary education. However, Latin America continues to lag behind in terms of coverage, progression and educational achievement, in particular in secondary education. The ongoing improvement of the education system also requires expanding pre-school coverage and extending the school day in state schools.

Latin American education systems must be instruments for equality and social mobility. One of the main problems the region faces is the persistence of socio-economic segmentation in terms of school access and academic performance. Latin America has not managed to transform the education system into a mechanism to promote inter-generational mobility, continuing to lag behind other regions. Education reforms must be aimed at improving equity. A number of educational initiatives have sought to reduce the persistent inequalities in the region related to the quality of the education system (public/private, rural/urban, male/female and those faced by ethnic minorities) and to opportunities for access to the labour market or income. To consolidate a more inclusive system, both demand-side measures (*e.g.* conditional transfer programmes) and supply-side measures (such as the distribution of qualified teachers) have been used.

The quality of education in Latin America must be at the centre of a new reform agenda. Today the region is in a particularly favourable situation to increase investment in education, with a favourable economic situation and the existence of a *demographic bonus*. Despite the growth in public spending on education in most countries, great strides have not been made in learning. The reform of education systems is not only about investing greater financial resources or creating fiscal space. Policies must be framed and defined by a long-term vision in order to achieve greater impact and efficiency in the use of these resources. Thus, prioritising reforms is critical, and the sequence of implementation must balance coverage objectives (*e.g.* infrastructure) with quality objectives (*e.g.* management of teachers, schools, and central and decentralised bodies).

To maximise the potential of decentralisation reforms and avoid possible negative effects, states must allocate more resources to sub-national and school level management. Decentralisation policies can improve performance, but they can also increase inequalities. These externalities result from a lack of communication between central and local administrations and limited local management capacity.

Certain interventions, such as basic curriculum design, are better managed at the central level. In contrast, it is necessary to provide local authorities with sound management capacity, particularly in more vulnerable and disadvantaged areas, in order to improve the efficiency of policy implementation. However, federated systems remain essential for the proper functioning of the education system. They generate incentives for performance and the development of skills through the exchange of successful experiences among schools.

An active population trained in the use of new technologies is key to sustaining long-term development. Therefore, the region needs to channel more efforts into increasing the supply of tertiary education (university and technical), especially for young people with fewer resources. In addition, there must be stronger links between the education offered and the productive sectors. In this challenge, it is important to stimulate learning, management and diffusion of new technologies. In this context, tertiary education policies must be geared towards increasing the progressivity of spending at this level; they must also compensate for lack of flexibility and funding resources through instruments such as cross-subsidisation or flexible timetables.

Assessment should not be limited to schools. The implementation of both national and international evaluation systems in Latin America has made it possible to assess the challenges of education, explore mechanisms to address these challenges, find deficiencies in education systems and quantify the impact of pedagogical and management practices. However, assessment schemes must go beyond the school and involve parents more actively. Measuring the skills and competencies of the adult population will provide a clearer picture of the skills needed for integration into the labour market.

Efficient management of faculty is key to improving the performance of education systems. The professionalisation of the teaching career must be a priority. Improving working conditions and hiring systems and offering attractive and flexible career plans can have a significant effect on performance. It is important to increase competition for teaching positions and to improve teacher assessment both when they begin teaching and throughout their teaching careers.

Notes

1. ECLAC (2010a)
2. ECLAC/SEGIB (2010).
3. Gazzola and Didriksson (2008).
4. Since the beginning of this assessment, the countries participating in PISA include all OECD economies and a growing number of associate countries. As a result, from 2000 to 2009 the number of participants rose from 43 to 65 countries.
5. OECD (2010e).
6. In the reading test, Chile and Peru recorded the most improvement in the region during the first decade of the 20th century. In the mathematics test, Brazil and Mexico have improved since 2003, while the performance of other Latin American countries has remained the same. In the science test, results improved in three countries: Brazil, Chile and Colombia. Their improvement was the equivalent of one year of schooling, in part thanks to a decline in the proportion of students with low skill levels.
7. OECD (2010a).
8. OECD (2010i).
9. Duryea *et al.* (2007).
10. For the total PISA sample, 24% of male students have a low performance compared to 12% of female students. There is an average difference of 39 points between males and females among OECD economies. In the group of Latin American countries, both the country with the best (Chile) and worst (Peru) outcomes show a difference between male and female students of 22 points. Colombia has the lowest difference between males and females of all the countries (9 points).
11. OECD (2010j).
12. The PISA test uses two basic measures of performance, one associated with test scores and one associated with equity in the distribution of scores within schools, between schools and across countries.
13. ECLAC (2010c).
14. ECLAC/IYO (2008) and ECLAC (2010c).
15. ECLAC (2010c).
16. ECLAC (2010c).
17. Marcel and Raczynski (2009).
18. ECLAC (2010c).
19. ECLAC (2010c).
20. Jakubowski (2010) and Petrow and Vegas (2009).
21. Pereyra (2008).
22. Psacharopoulos and Patrinos (2004).
23. World Bank (2008).
24. Persson and Tabellini (2000).
25. Faguet (2004).
26. Myerson (2006), Gradstein *et al.* (2004).
27. Bardhan (2002).
28. Galiani and Schargrodsky (2002).
29. Carnoy (1999) and Candia (2004)
30. See Vegas and Umansky (2007) on decentralisation experiences in Central America.
31. Di Gropello (1999).
32. Cortes (2010).
33. Rapalo (2003).

34. Rapalo (2003).

35. Galiani and Schargrodsky (2002); Avendaño and Nopo (forthcoming). One example of resource redistribution policies is the Preferential School Subsidy Law (SEP) in Chile, which provides subsidies for each student classified as a priority student. Thus, a school with more priority students can receive more resources. Another important element is that schools receiving this funding follow a school improvement plan. Another example took place in Mexico with the Quality Schools Programme (PEC) and the Full-Time Schools Programme (PETC), initiatives to improve the quality of teaching in disadvantaged schools and to increase their resources (OECD, 2010h).

36. Gazzola and Didriksson (2008).

37. For example, only a few countries stand out for number of publications and scientific citations on a world level (Argentina, Brazil, Chile and Mexico). (ECLAC/SEGIB, 2010)

38. ECLAC (2010b).

39. OECD (2009).

40. OECD (2010c, 2010g).

41. OECD (2010d).

42. Since 2006, the ENLACE test has measured the level of knowledge and skills of students defined in official programmes of study. This evaluation covers the areas of Spanish, mathematics and a rotating subject. Over 100 000 schools participate. See Campos-Vásquez and Romero (2010).

43. OECD (2010d).

44. OECD (2010d).

45. OECD (2010c, 2010h).

46. Mizala and Nopo (2011).

47. OECD (2010b).

48. OECD (2011).

References

Avendano, R. and H. Nopo (forthcoming), "How Successful were Decentralization Reforms in Latin America? Evidence from the PISA Survey", Working Paper, OECD Development Centre.

Bardhan, P. (2002), "Decentralization of Governance and Development", *Journal of Economic Perspectives*. Vol. 16, No. 4, pp. 185-205.

Campos-Vásquez, R.M. and F.D. Romero Urbina (2010), "Desempeño educativo en México: la prueba ENLACE". Documento de Trabajo, No. 19, Centro de Estudios Económicos, Colegio de México.

Candia, A. (2004), "Razones y estrategias de la descentralización educativa: un análisis comparado de Argentina y Chile", *Revista Iberoamericana de Educación*, No. 34, January-April 2004, pp. 179-200.

Carnoy, M. (1999), *Globalization and Educational Reform: What Planners Need to Know*, Fundamentals of Educational Planning, UNESCO (United Nations Educational, Scientific and Cultural Organization), Paris.

Cortes, D. (2010), "Do More Decentralized Local Governments do Better? An Evaluation of the 2001 Decentralization Reform in Colombia", Working Paper No. 84, Facultad de Economía, Universidad del Rosario.

Di Gropello, E. (1999), "Educational Decentralization Models in Latin America", *ECLAC Review*, No. 68, August 1999, pp. 155-173.

Duryea, S., S. Galiani, H. Nopo and C. Piras (2007), "The Educational Gender Gap in Latin America and the Caribbean", RES Working Papers, No. 600, Inter-American Development Bank, Washington, DC.

ECLAC (Economic Commission for Latin America and the Caribbean) (CEPAL) (2010a), *Time for Equality: Closing Gaps, Opening Trails*, LC/G.2432 (SES.33/3), ECLAC, Santiago, Chile.

ECLAC (CEPAL) (2010b), Science and Technology in the Latin American Pacific Basin: *Opportunity for Innovation and Competition*, ECLAC, Santiago, Chile.

ECLAC (CEPAL) (2010c), *Social Panorama of Latin America 2010*, ECLAC, Santiago, Chile.

ECLAC (CEPAL) (2010d), *Monitoring of the Plan of Action eLAC2010: Advances and Challenges of the Information Society in Latin America and the Caribbean*, ECLAC, Santiago, Chile.

ECLAC/IYO (Ibero-American Youth Organisation) (2008), *Youth and Social Cohesion in Ibero-America: A Model in the Making*, ECLAC, Santiago, Chile.

ECLAC (CEPAL)/SEGIB (Secretaría General Iberoamericana) (2010), *Espacios iberoamericanos. Universidad y empresa: vínculos entre universidad y empresas para el desarrollo tecnológico*, ECLAC, Santiago, Chile.

Faguet, J.P. (2004), "Does Decentralization Increase Government Responsiveness to Local Needs? Evidence from Bolivia", *Journal of Public Economics*. Vol. 88, Issues 3-4, pp. 867-893.

Galiani, S. and E. Schargrodsky (2002), "Evaluating the Impact of School Decentralization on Educational Quality", *Economia*, Vol. 2, No. 2, Spring 2002, pp. 275-314.

Gazzola, A.L. and A. Didriksson (eds.) (2008), *Trends in Higher Education in the Latin America and the Caribbean*, IESALC (International Institute for Higher Education in Latin America and the Caribbean)-UNESCO, Caracas.

Gradstein, M., M. Justman and V. Meier (2004), *The Political Economy of Education: Implications for Growth and Inequality*, MIT Press, Cambridge, Mass.

Katzman, R. (2010), "Impacto social de la incorporación de las nuevas tecnologías de información y comunicación en el sistema educativo", Políticas Sociales, No. 166, October 2010, ECLAC, Santiago, Chile.

Mizala, A. and H. Nopo (2011), "Teachers' Salaries in Latin America. How Much Are They (Under or Over) Paid?", mimeo.

Myerson, R. (2006), "Federalism and Incentives for Success of Democracy", *Quarterly Journal of Political Science*, Vol. 1, pp. 3-23.

OECD (Organisation for Economic Co-operation and Development) (2009), *Creating Effective Teaching and Learning Environments: First Results from TALIS*, OECD, Paris.

OECD (2010a), *PISA 2009 Results: What Students Know and Can Do: Student Performance in Reading, Mathematics and Science*, Vol. 1, PISA, OECD, Paris.

OECD (2010b), *Pisa 2009 Results: Overcoming Social Background: Equity in Learning Opportunities and Outcomes*, Vol. 2, OECD, Paris.

OECD (2010c), *Pisa 2009 Results: Learning to Learn: Student Engagement, Strategies and Practices*, Vol. 3, OECD, Paris.

OECD (2010d), *Pisa 2009 Results: Resources, Policies and Practices*, Vol. 4, OECD, Paris.

OECD (2010e), *Pisa 2009 Results: Changes in Student Performance*, Vol. 5, OECD, Paris.

OECD (2010f), *Improving Schools: Strategies for Action in Mexico*, OECD, Paris.

OECD (2010g), *Economic Assessment of Colombia*, OECD Development Centre, Paris.

OECD (2010h), *Iberoamerica in PISA 2006. Regional Report*, Santillana Educación, Paris.

OECD (2010i), *Education at a Glance 2010: OECD Indicators*, OECD, Paris.

OECD (2011a), *Strong Performers and Successful Reformers in Education: Lessons from PISA for the United States*, OECD, Paris.

OECD (2011b), "The Impact of the 1999 Education Reform in Poland", OECD Education Working Papers, No. 49, OECD Publishing, Paris.

Pereyra, Ana (2008), "La fragmentación de la oferta educativa en América Latina: la educación pública vs. la educación privada", *Perfiles Educativos*, Vol. 30, No. 120, Mexico.

Persson, T. and G. Tabellini (2000), *Political Economics: Explaining Economic Policy*, MIT Press, Cambridge, Mass.

Psacharopoulos, G. and H.A. Patrinos (2004), "Returns to Investment in Education: A Further Update", *Education Economics*, Vol. 12 (2), pp. 111-134.

Petrow, J. and E. Vegas (2008), *Raising Student Learning in Latin America: The Challenge for the 21st Century*, World Bank Publications, Washington, DC.

Rápalo, R. (2003), "Los procesos de descentralización educativa en América Latina y lineamientos de propuesta para la descentralización educativa en Honduras", Colección Cuadernos de Desarrollo Humano Sostenible, No. 13, United Nations Development Programme (UNDP), Tegucigalpa.

Vegas, E. and I. Umansky (2007), "Inside Decentralization: How Three Central American School-Based Management Reforms Affect Student Learning through Teacher Incentives", *World Bank Research Observer*, Vol. 22, No. 2, pp. 197-215

World Bank (2008), "Strategies for Sustained Growth and Inclusive Development", report, Commission on Growth and Development, World Bank, Washington, DC.

CHAPTER FIVE

The State and reform of public infrastructure policy

Abstract

This chapter examines the changes needed in the role of the State in managing infrastructure to increase the effectiveness and efficiency of public investment and support economic and social development. The gap between Latin America and other emerging economies in economic infrastructure such as transport, telecommunications, water and energy hampers economic development potential and social cohesion in the region.

Greater investment alone will not suffice to solve this problem if the way in which public management policy is conceived and implemented is not changed. This chapter analyses infrastructure policies in transport and telecommunications (in particular, broadband Internet) and suggests that to increase the effectiveness of public infrastructure policies, Latin American states must improve policy design through a comprehensive and sustainable framework, fostering a clear and flexible institutional and regulatory framework for an effective participation of the private sector and civil society.

5.1. Introduction

Infrastructure is a key ingredient for economic growth and development. Along with its related services, it impacts significantly economic activity and quality of life. Most infrastructure from different sectors plays a major role in the achievement of the Millennium Development Goals (MDGs) given that improvements in connectivity and mobility enable access to economic and basic services, such as education and health care.

This chapter focuses on analysing the required transformations states must make to increase the efficiency and effectiveness of public investment in transport and telecommunications infrastructure. It begins by identifying the role of the state in the provision and operation of transport infrastructure and the need to establish an integrated and sustainable policy of logistics and mobility at the national and sub-national level (section 5.2). The chapter then examines broadband Internet access and its potential social and economic effects, particularly public policies for its development, and it presents information on the use of broadband and on broadband requirements (section 5.3). Finally, the chapter recommends several public policy measures aimed at providing mass access to information and communication technologies (ICTs) and increasing coherence and co-ordination among the different actors involved in transport and telecommunications infrastructure (section 5.4).

Latin America's economic development is seriously hampered by the lag in necessary infrastructure. Despite increased private-sector participation in the last two decades the region is still behind Asia and other emerging economies. This does not only affect its economic growth but also compromises the possibility to reduce inequality, which is so deep-rooted in the region. To face firms' and households' new demand for infrastructure between 2006 and 2020, Latin America will have to invest around 5.0% of regional GDP, assuming an average annual real growth of 3.9%. To close the gaps with South-East Asia, the requirement climbs to 9.0% of the region's GDP. The effort needed is considerable, given that infrastructure investment in 2007-08 was only 2% of GDP.[1]

The challenge for the region is to supply infrastructure that strengthens the economy and fosters equality in a sustainable manner. Increasing the availability and quality of infrastructure reduces logistics costs and increases productivity and competitiveness of the economies. For instance, by closing the infrastructure gap with other middle income countries, Latin American economies can boost GDP growth by two percentage points per year.[2] Furthermore, improved access to transport infrastructure contributes to reducing inequality and social exclusion. Access to roads, railways and waterways facilitates the connection between agricultural centres and the main internal urban markets. Similarly, provision of electronic services in education, health care and government management increases the efficiency of these services, overcoming geographical and financial barriers that restrict coverage of poor and marginalised segments of the population.

The substantial drop in public investment during the 1990s affected the provision of these infrastructure services. After the debt and fiscal crises suffered by most states in the region in the 1980s, the 1990s saw a reduction in capital investment as part of fiscal consolidation programmes. Simultaneously, fiscal consolidation limited the levels of debt that States were able to assume, which together with low levels of taxation seriously limited financing capabilities. ECLAC figures show that while in 1980-85 public investment hovered around 4% of GDP, in 2007-08 it was only 2%.

This decrease in public investment was not compensated by a proportional increase in private investment. Although there was an increase in private-sector involvement through diverse schemes, this was not enough to compensate for the decline in public investment compared to economic growth in the 2000s. Notwithstanding the associated benefits, private investment was less than the contraction of public investment in most sectors, except in telecommunications and, to a lesser extent, energy. In addition, in some cases public policies were not adequately designed to involve the private sector, resulting in insufficient supply and sometimes causing delays and cost overruns. This complicated the achievement of pre-established goals.

Infrastructure shortfalls differ considerably across sectors and states. Gaps in the region tend to be concentrated in transport and energy, but even in telecommunications, where the aggregate gap is smaller, there are important challenges in specific segments such as broadband Internet access. In transport infrastructure, the whole region presents significant deficits, which could affect economic growth by hindering development and preventing access to the benefits of economies of scale and specialisation at the national and sub-national level.[3] In telecommunications, some countries (such as Brazil, Costa Rica, Jamaica, Panama and Uruguay) have reasonable levels of infrastructure considering their income levels, but have serious problems in terms of equality of access.[4]

To increase the efficiency of the public sector a series of mechanisms to change sectoral public policies and improve co-ordination with the private sector must be defined. The design and implementation of transport infrastructure policies should turn towards an integral, multimodal approach, with the infrastructure provided defined according to the needs of mobility and logistics, regardless of the mode of transport. In transport concessions, it is essential to correct the flaws resulting from dynamic inconsistencies (a situation in which agents' preferences change over time), which are magnified by the fiscal accounting system for concessions and the inadequate management of the risks resulting from the concessions themselves, among other factors. Broadband development requires a complementary goods and services technology system and co-ordination mechanisms to direct the long-term investments by the many private-sector actors who are involved in providing and using the service.

The analyses of transport and broadband Internet infrastructure policies indicate the need for greater policy co-ordination and coherence. Thus, it is important to define a clear framework to articulate policies. This would allow more efficient and effective use of resources and an increase in the quality of public spending. It would also allow for better co-ordination with the private sector under public-private participation schemes. In telecommunications it is necessary to speed up the adaptation of the regulatory framework for it to be consistent with an environment of technological convergence.

5.2. The role of the State in transport infrastructure

5.2.1. Co-ordination of infrastructure policies

One of the main challenges faced by public infrastructure policy is to improve coherence and co-ordination —vertical and horizontal— among stakeholders. Despite the close links between infrastructure and its users, a disassociation is often observed between policies on design and infrastructure provision and policies on the operation and promotion of transport. This seems to be the result of a duplicity of functions and in some cases direct competition between public agencies, affecting the efficiency of the proposed public or private intervention. Latin American governments should therefore strengthen their institutions, increasing co-ordination and policy coherence. There is also a need to reinforce the relationship with the private sector through modern regulatory frameworks that provide balance between planning, evaluation, capacity and the maturing of investments.

According to a survey conducted on the region's policy makers,[5] these challenges are more important than the stability, adaptability and effectiveness of policies and also more important than public-interest considerations. These qualitative results corroborate the opinions of different institutions, stakeholders and public-policy experts, who emphasise that problems of coherence, co-ordination and multimodal strategy in public policies are factors that reduce the efficiency and productivity of economies (Figure 5.1).[6]

Figure 5.1. Policy-makers perceptions compared with those of experts regarding infrastructure policy in Latin America: "what are the characteristics of the principal aspects of public policy in infrastructure sectors?"

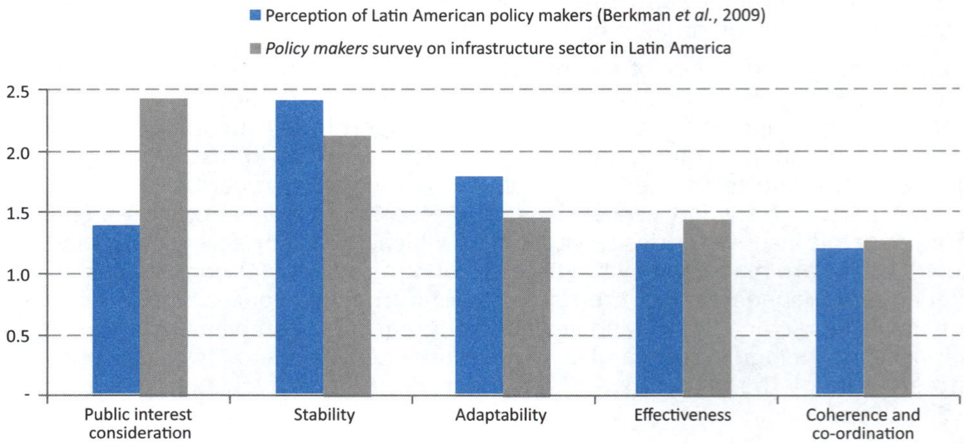

Note: a lower level indicates that these characteristics are still relatively weak points in infrastructure policies.

Source: Based on Berkman et al (2009), "Policies, State Capabilities, and Political Institutions: An International Dataset", Inter-American Development Bank, Washington, D.C. (available at: http://www.iadb.org/res/pub_desc.cfm?pub_id=DBA-012), and Gutiérrez and Nieto-Parra (2011), "The Policy-Making Process of Transport Infrastructure in Latin America: A Review from Policy Makers", OECD Development Center Working Paper, forthcoming publication.

http://dx.doi.org/10.1787/888932522949

Proper policy coherence and co-ordination requires an institutional and incentive framework that is appropriate for each individual country's structure. A greater connection between ministries and public administrations is essential. It is also necessary to strengthen infrastructure planning in accordance with a national development plan created by technicians of the different agencies in charge of infrastructure development. This must be done with a focus on the long term, independently of political cycles and coordinated with sub-national policies.

The main obstacles to proper co-ordination between public infrastructure institutions and the transport sector are a lack of incentives for co-operation and an inadequate institutional architecture. According to the policy makers' survey these aspects are more important than lack of clarity in assigning responsibilities, competition between ministries and a lack of political commitments in the area of infrastructure. The lack of incentives for co-operation is a key factor behind the problems in the relations between the transport, telecommunications, electricty and social infrastructure (such as education and health care) sectors. The countries where this obstacle is greatest are Colombia, El Salvador, Paraguay and Peru. These countries therefore must prioritise integrated policy for the different infrastructure sectors.

5.2.2. Public policy for the development of transport infrastructure

5.2.2.1. Prioritising and planning in the transport infrastructure policy-making process

Evaluating the policy-making process with the intent of identifying bottlenecks is vital to making transport policies more effective. Four distinct phases can be identified in this process: prioritisation and planning, execution, operation and maintenance. In each stage it is necessary to consider assessments, accountability mechanisms and project oversight. Appropriate allocation of responsibilities at each stage and an adequate integration of policies throughout the whole project cycle —with their corresponding technical analysis— help increase the effectiveness of public transport policies.

The transport sector faces different obstacles throughout the project cycle, but especially in the prioritising and planning stage. At this stage low technical capabilities for adequate project design and the lack of a framework for policy implementation stand out (see Box 5.1).[7]

However, states are seeking to improve the selection and evaluation of projects through the implementation of national systems of public investment. Along with improving the quality of public finances, these systems seek to improve resource allocation to develop and strengthen assessment systems for public programmes and investment. Promoting co-ordination between institutional strategic plans where the synergies between different public or private projects are considered can reduce inefficiencies in public infrastructure spending (see Box 5.2).

The selection of projects must be improved. It is also necessary to establish an appropriate balance between new projects and the maintenance of existing ones. An analysis of transport policy-making in various countries in the region points to the challenge of improving the selection process and the quality of roads in Latin America.[8] The overall cost of transport and of investment and maintenance is between three and seven times less for a road in optimal state versus one that is not maintained.[9]

Problems of dynamic inconsistency —the incentive to change the initial rules of the game— have an impact on the efficiency of the transport infrastructure sector. The political cycle may encourage the tendering of projects that are poorly prepared. This can create cost overruns and delays that drastically affect a project's ex post profitability.[10] In addition, the scarcity of professional resources leads authorities to prefer new projects over rehabilitation and maintenance because they can obtain greater political dividends from them. In order to avoid these problems, some countries have established greater budgetary rigidities as a way of guaranteeing the resources needed for road maintenance.

Failures from dynamic inconsistency could be addressed through the development of institutions that broaden the scope of public decision-making.[11] Bias towards new infrastructure projects instead of rehabilitation and maintenance can be reduced through independent assessment of levels of service. Some Central American countries created infrastructure maintenance funds with resources from fuel taxes. However, in practically all instances, these schemes have been difficult to maintain due to a lack of appropriate incentives.

During the first phase —project identification and design— it is necessary to evaluate various alternatives and variants in terms of project profile and pre-feasibility. It is necessary to identify the different possibilities for satisfying demand in the first phase, which has lower costs, before proceeding to the technical and economic feasibility phase, which is more expensive. Once the best option has been selected, the project moves on to the social feasibility phase, where public action should be guided by the principle of multimodal transport —that is, the use of more than

Box 5.1. Road infrastructure policy-making in Latin America

The policy-making process in transport is complex and inefficient. In general, Latin America significantly lags behind other regions with similar economic characteristics in terms of road infrastructure. One of the reasons for this lag seems to be the perception of institutional weakness in this sector in comparison with other areas of infrastructure. This situation is particularly visible in Colombia.[a]

The effectiveness of transport policy is hindered by a lack of prioritisation and planning, information problems that complicate monitoring and evaluation, and the weakness of vertical and horizontal co-ordination. Quantitative data (*e.g.* official data, prior research) and qualitative data (*e.g.* interviews with public employees and analysts) are needed to determine the bottlenecks in each of the road transport policy-making phases. The following failures should be noted:

i) A lack of planning and prioritisation. This is manifested in the construction of projects without preliminary analysis, the adjudication of contracts without definitive designs and prior land studies, often without even having property rights to said land. This causes delays and cost overruns. Furthermore, several countries lack a national system of public investment corroborating the social evaluation of prospective projects as a necessary requirement to initiate them.

ii) Information problems. These make monitoring and evaluation difficult: In general, projects are designed without concrete physical goals (*e.g.* targeted kilometres), which makes it impossible to monitor the physical execution of the project. There is no inventory of existing roads, nor of their current state, especially secondary and tertiary roads. This makes it difficult to carry out estimates of costs per kilometre and is an obstacle in determining the cost-benefit ratio for building new roads vs. performing maintenance on existing ones.

iii) Co-ordination problems. Institutional weaknesses affect the rules of the game for road policy making. Firstly, there are no regulations that favour the development of multimodal transport, and secondly, responsibilities and resources available for road infrastructure are not clearly defined and distributed among the different levels of government (*i.e.* national, regional and municipal).

a. Nieto-Parra, Olivera and Tibocha (2011).

one mode of transport for a journey or group of journeys for people or goods, making journeys as efficient as possible. Multimodal transport is a central part of a modal-shift strategy, which is part of an integrated, sustainable logistics and mobility policy.[12] This assessment should consider as benefits the actual savings of economic resources, including time savings of users, valued according to reasons for travel, and incorporate negative externalities. If the project is economically and socially profitable, different alternatives for its implementation must be evaluated, whether as a public works project, as an integrated public-service concession or as a combination of the two for some infrastructure and services components, bearing in mind the sustainability of the solution.

Box 5.2. The rise in public investment in Peru: the benefits of better regulation and a national system of public investment

Levels of public investment have grown continuously in recent years in Peru. During the 1990s public investment reached similar levels, but it was largely financed by fiscal deficits accompanied by high levels of public debt. At the beginning of the 2000s this scenario changed radically, as public investment fell to below 3% of GDP. The 1999 Fiscal Prudence and Transparency Act (LPTF) established limits on the fiscal deficit of the consolidated public sector, on public spending and on the total debt for the consolidated public sector. In addition, the National System of Public Investment (SNIP) was created, an administrative system of the state charged with improving the efficiency of investment in Peru by following a series of principles, procedures and technical regulations and certifying the quality of public investment projects.

Under this scenario, public investment fell between 1.5 and 2.0 points of GDP between 2000 and 2006 in comparison to the previous decade's figures. This was due to the fiscal restraints imposed by the LPTF and the creation of the SNIP, which significantly decreased the number of investment projects being implemented (projects which previously were carried out without prior socio-economic evaluation).

Extraordinary income from the boom in prices of mining exports and reduction of public debt improved public accounts and enhanced the investment process. Also, in 2006 the limits on public spending were modified to exclude infrastructure maintenance costs, and in 2007 they started to be applied only to government consumption. Thus, public investment no longer faced budgetary constraints beyond those imposed by the fiscal deficit[a]. An Economic Stimulus Plan was implemented in 2009 and 2010 under this new fiscal framework. It focused on infrastructure, and as a consequence public investment rose again to nearly 6% of GDP in 2010. These levels should be maintained until 2013 according to the Macroeconomic Multi-Year Framework approved by the Ministry of Economy and Finance.

[a] Carranza, Daude and Melguizo (2011).

5.2.2.2. Selection and evaluation of public-private partnership projects in transport infrastructure.

Latin America's past experiences with public-private partnerships (PPPs) have led to questions about their usefulness. In Latin America, the model of public works concessions or PPPs[13] in the transport sector has been applied to the development of airports, roads, railways, ports and multimodal terminals. The use of this model began in the late 1980s and early 1990s in Argentina, Chile and Mexico, spreading later to Brazil, Colombia, Peru and countries in Central America and the Caribbean. However, difficulties and challenges encountered in various sectors and countries have led some to question the model.[14]

However, proper use of concessions can improve the provision of services and competitiveness. In its broadest form a concession contract for the provision of infrastructure services includes financing, construction and operation of the infrastructure by a private operator. In general, concessions can help to solve agency problems in traditional public provision and fix important failures of the state resulting from the interaction between the political cycle and the decision-making timeline. The main benefits of the concessions system, which would compensate for its higher transaction and financing costs, are the following:

1) The full project cycle can be planned with a guaranteed balance between initial investment and future maintenance costs. In the planning of public works, maintenance costs are usually excluded; this could be corrected if public oversight of service contracts is established.

2) It limits the development of "white elephants", deriving from the weakness of national systems of investment, if the demand risk is transferred to the concessionaire.
3) Commercial risks are transferred to the private sector, which is better prepared to cope with and mitigate them, so a stronger regulatory framework is required.
4) There is a greater tendency towards "fee for service", which leads to a greater orientation towards service and encourages spending on infrastructure maintenance.
5) There is greater flexibility and efficiency in the management of human resources.

The benefits of concessions are usually associated with failures of the state. The weakness of the state's institutions and the recurrence of dynamic inconsistencies resulting from the political cycle are supposedly intrinsic to the system of public provision. To the extent that this is the baseline for evaluation, the benefits of concessions tend to increase.

The long-term nature of concession contracts carries potentially significant transaction costs. This means that certain infrastructure projects are not appropriate for this modality. Furthermore, concession contracts are by definition incomplete; it is impossible to predict all the contingencies that may arise during the concession. There can be issues with adverse selection in the designation of the concessionaire and post-contractual risks of opportunism that can be magnified by institutional weakness. Another issue is the balance between the transfer of risk costs to the private sector under a scenario of asymmetrical information and imperfect capital markets, which requires designing an adequate incentive scheme.[15]

The State's failures as a direct provider could reappear in the regulatory role that it plays in concessions. These weaknesses could jeopardise the possibility of creating "value for money" through concessions. If concessions are used to create new projects that are used for political ends, contracts will most probably not be supervised appropriately. Given that concessions are usually for fixed terms, the concessionaire with weak oversight has no incentive to spend on maintenance to affect the value of the asset beyond the contract's end.

Exploiting the benefits of concessions requires strong regulatory capacity in terms of evaluating, tendering and managing the concession contracts. Faced with weak contract management, concessionaires offer tendering prices below what they would offer in the absence of renegotiations and match or improve the initially expected revenues during the renegotiation. This continuous renegotiation carries high financial costs and risks that affect the efficiency of this mode of contracting (Box 5.3 and Figure 5.2).

An evaluation based on "value for money" helps to determine which mode of financing is most appropriate for infrastructure works. Following a social feasibility analysis, a value-for-money evaluation can be used to assess whether a concession model is preferable to direct public-sector provision. While most OECD economies do a cost-benefit analysis or use a public-sector comparator, Latin American countries usually limit their analysis to a comparison of tendering results. This creates uncertainty regarding whether the private sector can generate "value for money".[16]

A change in fiscal accounting can improve concession selection, avoiding reckless investments and the transfer of fiscal commitments to the future.[17] Given that the state controls the economic results of the concession through regulations and is also the recipient of the work at the end of the contract, considering concessions as public projects can lend transparency to public accounts. Thus, if investment in concessions is accounted for within a comprehensive framework for public infrastructure expenditure, concession would be chosen based on a value-for-money analysis.[18]

Figure 5.2. Latin America (8 selected countries): renegotiations in concession contracts

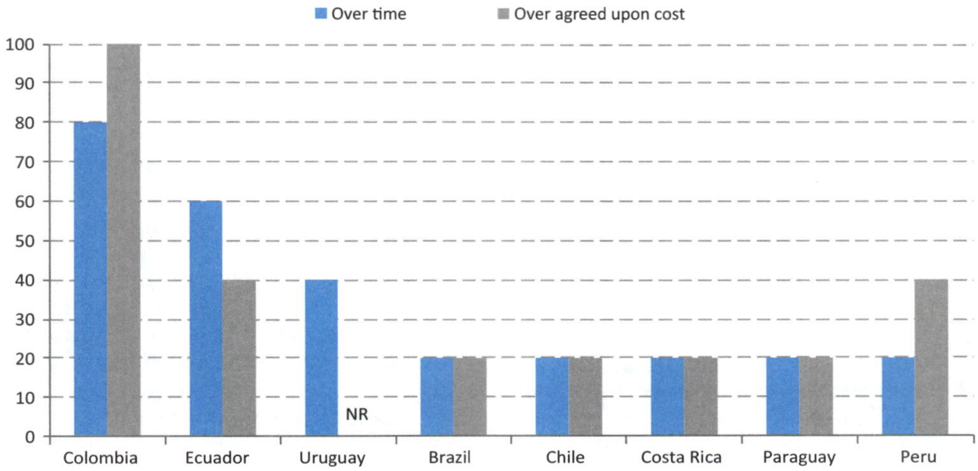

Note: the percentage refers to the proportion of the total number of concession contracts. NR: no response.

Source: Gutiérrez y Nieto-Parra (2011), "The Policy-Making Process of Transport Infrastructure in Latin America: A Review from Policy Makers", OECD Development Center Working Paper, forthcoming publication.
http://dx.doi.org/10.1787/888932522968

Therefore, a priority in Latin America is to establish criteria that are followed before initiating a concession contract. Once the project has been defined by means of a social pre-feasibility study, three critical evaluations must be carried out:[19]

1) Qualitative evaluations of value for money, which justify considering a full or partial concession.

2) Pre-feasibility analysis of the viability of the project for the private sector, which is to determine the subsidies and/or guarantees that would make participation attractive to the private sector.

3) Social feasibility of the concession project, which enables a comparison of the social benefits of a public works project vs. a private one, based on their respective future cash flows and discount rates.

This analysis should lead to an evaluation of a full concession or a mixed scheme, and a determination of which type of contract maximises net social benefits. Ultimately, concessions are the best option when the present net value of cash flows adjusted for the expected increase in efficiency and the increased capital costs to the concessionaire are greater than the net benefits predicted by the traditional social evaluation of the project. This analysis allows the focus to be placed on the issues relevant for decision-making, such as the greater cost of private financing, the mitigations and subsidies necessary to offset it, the benefits of increased efficiency needed to justify the concession and the transaction costs inherent to this modality and in ex post renegotiations.

5.2.2.3. Multimodal interurban transport planning

Each country's geography determines which modes are most efficient for the transportation of goods. In general, the region has a high preference for road transport over other means that could better take advantage of the geographical characteristics of the region, affecting both competitiveness and complementarities among modes of transport. The development of railways has stalled while the existing network has not evolved from its historic coverage as a mode of transport for mines and quarrying. Maritime transport, while actively present for international trade,

Box 5.3. Concession renegotiation in Latin America

The regulatory and institutional weakness of concessions in Latin America has caused continuous renegotiations. In the 1990s close to 50% of transport concessions were renegotiated in Argentina, Brazil, Chile, Colombia and Mexico. In Chile each concession was renegotiated an average of four times between 1993 and 2007, and nearly a quarter of investments in concessions derive from renegotiations.[a]

Today, according to interviews with regional policy makers, an average of 40% of concession contracts are renegotiated (vs. 20% in the UK).[b] Of the 60 road concessions agreed up to 2010 in Colombia, Chile and Peru, 50 have been renegotiated, generating additional fiscal costs of 50% of the initial value of the contracts. A noteworthy case is Colombia, where 21 concessions have been renegotiated 273 times, resulting in additional fiscal costs or the extension of the concession period. These renegotiations are worth 170% of the contracts' initial worth and represent an average increase of 40% of the concession period; 98% of modifications were carried out bilaterally by the administration and the concessionaire, and in over 70% of the cases funds from future fiscal periods were used to pay for these renegotiations. In addition, in all theses cases, the first renegotiation was carried out within the first two years after the initiation of the contract.[c]

Regulatory aspects (such as price cap and tendering processes) as well as institutional and political aspects (such as quality of the bureaucracy, election cycles, lack of independence of regulators and corruption) have been identified as determining factors of renegotiations in the region.[d] The possibility of extending the duration of concessions reduces competition, allowing de-facto monopolies to be formed in road networks and weakening service provision. The asymmetry of unlimited profits and limited losses due to their social distribution through renegotiations leads to problems of adverse selection and moral hazard, which foster high fiscal costs for future administrations.

a. See Guasch, Laffont and Straub (2008) for Latin America, and Engel, Fischer and Galetovic (2009) for Chile.

b. See Gutiérrez and Nieto-Parra (2011) for Latin America, and OECD (2008) for OECD economies.

c. See Bitrán, Nieto-Parra and Robledo (2011) for a recent analysis of renegotiations of road concessions in Colombia, Chile and Peru.

d. Guasch, Laffont and Straub (2007; 2008).

is practically absent in the domestic transport of passengers and cargo. Waterway transport is also practically non-existent, even though the geographical conditions exist for this mode of transport to be used and to provide multimodal solutions and better territorial connectivity.

The traditional view states that short-distance railway and maritime transport are only competitive for distances over 500 km (about 300 miles). However, factors other than distance affect the successful use of both rail freight services and short sea shipping, as international evidence has shown. The success of these services is determined not so much by distance as by the concentration of available cargo volumes and the suitability of services offered in terms of frequency, costs and time.

An inadequate modal partition in Latin America not only increases logistics costs and reduces competitiveness; it also increases negative externalities from transport. In countries with a size relatively comparable to the United States and Canada, there is a preference for the use of road transport for cargo which, in addition to deteriorating roads, weighs considerably on the cost structure of domestic transport (Figure 5.3). The potential of railways and waterways is largely untapped, with road transport having a concentration that is 15 times greater than in the United States.[20]

Figure 5.3. MERCOSUR and countries of north and South America: distribution of freight by type of transport (in volume), 2007
(Percentages)

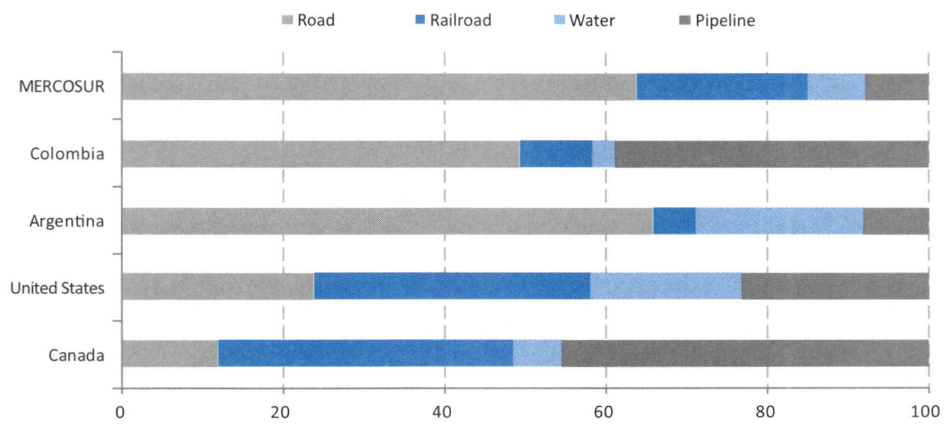

Source: Silva (2007), based on information from the Corporación Andina de Fomento (CAF), Asociación Latinoamericana de Integración (ALADI) and the Bureau of Transportation Statistics of the United States.
http://dx.doi.org/10.1787/888932522987

Private-sector participation has not necessarily improved the effectiveness of investment in the railway sector. Railway reform started in the 1990s in Argentina, Brazil, Chile, Mexico and Peru. Integrated concessions to operate both the track and the transport of freight were made in most cases. The design of the concession areas in Mexico, with restrictions to horizontal integration and open access requirements, created greater competition than in the other four countries, where there is a tendency towards monopoly access in certain disconnected segments of the network. Private participation significantly improved labour productivity in the sector and reduced the fiscal costs of railway operation, but it has not managed to reverse massive underinvestment and the backlog of deferred maintenance. Due to this, the participation of railways in freight transport has not grown in these countries, maintaining a much lower modal share than found in OECD economies with similar geographical characteristics. Another problem has been the concentration in traditional goods, which has not fulfilled its role of expanding the production frontier by introducing new goods, unlike in the United States and Europe, for instance, and has not contributed to sustainibility to the extent that it could based on its potential.

Institutional failures explain the low share of fluvial transport. Maritime and fluvial transport have great potential in countries where underutilization is largely due to institutional failures. For example, in Colombia, fluvial transport on the river Magdalena (which carries 80% of the country's fluvial freight transport, but only 4% of total freight transport and 5% of passenger transport) is planned, regulated and managed by a single entity (*Corporación Autónoma Regional del Río Grande de la Magdalena*), which, by constitutional mandate, is independent from the Ministry of Transport. Under this scheme there is no integrated policy between the management of transport on the Magdalena and other waterways, nor are there incentives for one.[21]

The port system reforms adopted in the region over the last two decades have generally been positive. However, reforms were delayed in several countries, like Costa Rica[22] and Peru, affecting external competitiveness and the development of maritime transport in the corresponding corridors. The current challenge is how to expand and renovate concession contracts, respond to demands for vertical and horizontal concentration of industry and provide port terminals with the required infrastructure to cope with commercial activity. Significant works in connectivity to the hinterland and secondary port infrastructures in the hinterland are also required to efficiently solve the interface between port and city without reducing port competitiveness or the quality of life of citizens. In particular, the development of waterways and river ports lags behind and does not receive proper attention from the public sector.

The lack of a multimodal planning strategy generating incentives for a better distribution of modes of transport and the use of sustainable, carbon-efficient modes distorts transport-related decisions in the region. This has fostered decisions to investment in roads while ignoring other factors. Institutional fragmentation, with its associated weakness in the allocation of responsibilities and institutional co-operation creates distortions in public investment and subsidies among different modes of transport (Figure 5.4). Latin America's institutional structure makes the centralised services of transport and public works ministries responsible for investment in roads, affecting the allocation of resources to other modes of transport.

Figure 5.4. Perception of policy makers in the regions: obstacles to co-ordination of multimodal transport

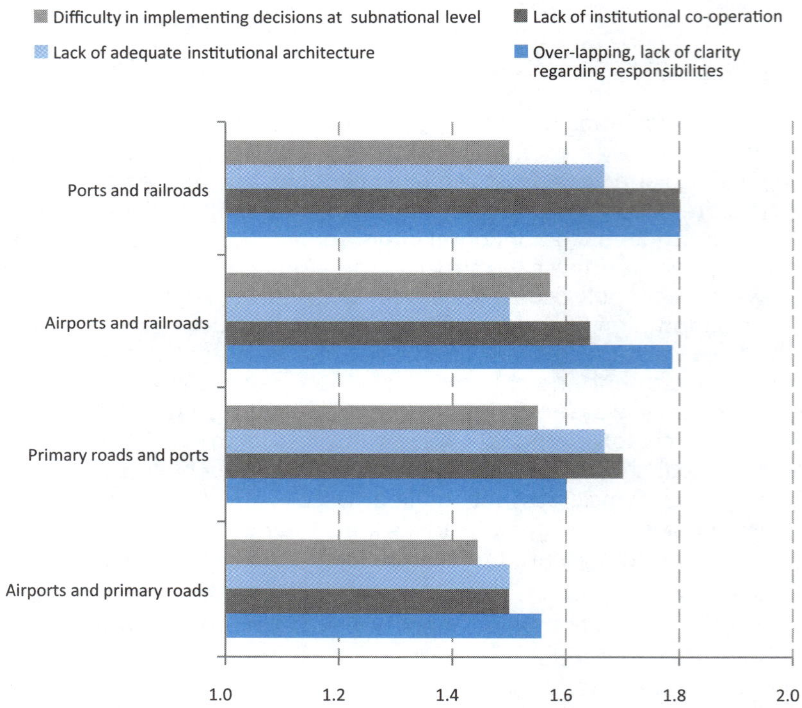

Note: Scale from 1 to 3, where a higher value indicates greater importance.

Source: Based on policy-maker survey, Gutiérrez and Nieto-Parra (2011), "The Policy-Making Process of Transport Infrastructure in Latin America: A Review from Policy Makers", OECD Development Center Working Paper, forthcoming publication.
http://dx.doi.org/10.1787/888932523006

An inadequate institutional framework that does not clearly assign responsibilities and generate incentives for collaboration between stakeholders limits the effective co-ordination of multimodal transport policy. These failures are especially present in multimodal forms of transport that include ports and railways, as evidenced by the lack of integrated pricing schemes for multimodal transport. In countries such as Colombia, Costa Rica and Mexico, the lack of institutional incentives for co-operation is an important obstacle for the link between primary roads and ports, and between ports and railways.

The integration of freight transport policies and multimodal planning that allows comparisons between subsidies and investments in different modes of transport are major challenges in the region. The elevated fiscal costs of road transport (due to high public investment and concessions) have generated unfair competition to other forms of transport. The rail and waterway concession model could maintain open access and finance investment through public contributions in cases where environmental externalities are significant. In the long term it would be desirable to adopt effective price signalling (for example, through adjusting fuel taxes and road tolls), thus avoiding the need for investment subsidies in other modes of transport. In addition, this would lead to more efficient and environmentally sustainable modal shares for the different transport modes.

5.2.2.4. Vertical co-ordination in transport infrastructure

In infrastructure provision, including transport, the actual construction of the infrastructure and the government policies and regulatory framework under which it is developed are equally important. In addition to infrastructure policy co-ordination among different government agencies at the same level of government, co-ordination *between* different levels of government is also needed.

Central government dominates transport infrastructure policy planning. The results of the survey of policy makers cast light on certain phenomena identified in case studies in other regions.[23] Although this may be explained by the type of infrastructure (*e.g.* primary networks and railways), the results show that there is little involvement of sub-national governments throughout the project cycle. It is therefore necessary to strengthen co-ordination between different levels of government.

Heterogeneity in responsibilities at different stages of the infrastructure process points to bottlenecks that limit the effectiveness of public transport policies. In all the countries participating in the survey, sub-national governments were found to carry out a wide variety of responsibilities. These range from policy design to performance monitoring and infrastructure maintenance. Such is the case of Peru, where sub-national governments are legally obliged to report on compliance with transport policy. However, their partial involvement limits the effectiveness of these joint measures.

Clearly defining the responsibilities of each level of government allows a greater level of co-ordination. For example Brazil's *Growth Acceleration Programme*, a vast infrastructure plan now in its second stage (PAC2), provides for the selection of projects by the federal government in consultation with its regional and local counterparts.

Defining technical plans at a sub-national level facilitates territorial co-ordination of investment. Shared objectives among the different levels of government can generate strong incentives for the transfer of resources. In nearly half of the surveyed countries there are such plans, which are usually aligned with national development plans or investment plans. Otherwise, a decoupling of public spending programmes in infrastructure among different levels of government can lead to wasted resources, duplication of efforts, and, in the worst case scenario, conflicting priorities.

A greater link between different government levels exists in countries that have sub-national transport policies. In the surveyed countries that have such plans there is greater co-ordination with the national government. This is evidenced by shared responsibilities for implementation. However, due to the small size of some countries in the region, especially in the Caribbean and Central America, it is not necessarily desirable to have explicit sub-national transport infrastructure plans because it eliminates the economies of scale inherent to large investment projects. Even so, the inclusion of sub-national strategic plans in national investment plans makes more effective co-ordination possible.

The unitary character of public finance in many countries in the region hampers sub-national infrastructure spending, as it often depends on the transfer of resources from the central government. This, coupled with limitations in the technical competencies of sub-national governments, makes the transfer of responsibilities impossible due to financial, operational and administrative factors. This situation allows the central government to concentrate subsidy funding in land transport networks.

In this regard, the formulation of medium-term fiscal and investment frameworks that clearly and expressly define the policies to be implemented in each region/ territory can be a useful tool. These frameworks can provide a benchmark for both national and sub-national governments on how to manage public spending. Improvements in the use of multi-year budgeting, a product of institutional reforms aimed at increasing the effectiveness of public spending, have brought about greater transparency and communication in the formulation of these plans.

5.3. The role of the State in the development of telecommunications infrastructure

5.3.1. Proper use and broadband requirements for a more effective public policy

The social and economic impact of broadband depends on its use by productive and social sectors. The applications with greatest potential for social benefit are those aimed at improving the efficiency and effectiveness of services such as education, health care and governance. However, their development is much more limited than those dedicated to entertainment. The true economic and social potential of electronic applications resides in their advanced use, which is only possible with high-speed broadband Internet, which in turn depends on the type of infrastructure and technology used by the network.

The continuous, secure provision of social services requires high standards of connectivity associated with adequate infrastructure. The connectivity requirements for health care and education applications are particularly high in terms of speed and latency (that is, the delay in Internet communication due to data transmission lag). These sectors require high-level broadband. In comparison, video downloading and social networking applications have varied broadband requirements and are less affected by latency (Figure 5.5).

Broadband applications help to improve governance by streamlining the internal functioning of administrative units, facilitating the provision of services to the public and providing access to information. The development of integrated transactional services requires the restructuring of internal management processes, network infrastructure and systems and equipment that support this action. Permanent connectivity makes more sophisticated, one-stop-shop platforms viable for public procurement.

Despite progress in the deployment of telecommunications infrastructure and the adoption of ICTs over the last 20 years, the region faces significant challenges to exploit the benefits from broadband as a platform for social and economic development. These challenges are highlighted by the growing gap in high-speed Internet adoption (Figure 5.6).

Figure 5.5. Bandwidth requirements by type of application

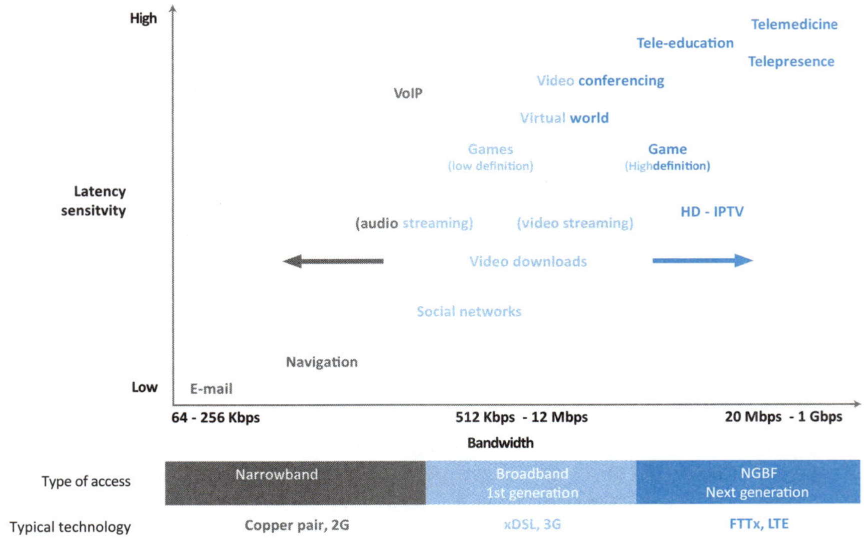

Kbps: *kilobytes* per second.
Mbps: *megabytes* per second.
Gbps: *gigabytes* per second.

Source: Based on OECD (2009), Friedrich *et al.* (2009) and *Athens Information Technology* from Cisco Systems.
http://dx.doi.org/10.1787/888932523025

Figure 5.6. Latin America and the Caribbean and the OECD: fixed and mobile broadband subscribers
(per 100 inhabitants)

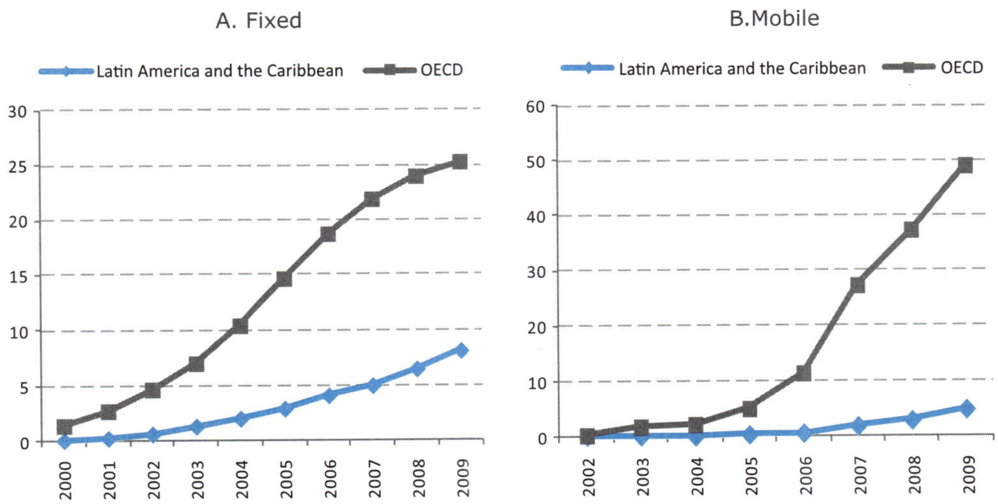

Note: The regional average is a simple average.

Source: Regional Broadband Observatory (ORBA) in the ITU database.
http://dx.doi.org/10.1787/888932523044

5.3.2. Public policies for the massification of Information and Communication Technologies (ICTs)

Given the many demands for public resources in the region, public telecommunications policies, especially policies on broadband Internet, should encourage effective private-sector participation in the development of infrastructure and broadband services. The role of the state in this scheme should focus on regulatory reform geared at increasing technological convergence,[24] guiding investment, and addressing co-ordination failures. It should also make complementary investments to maximise positive externalities, ensure social equity objectives are met and promote competition. In particular, the regulatory sphere must be modernised and adapted to the environment of technological convergence (see Table 5.1).

However, private investment in telecommunications infrastructure is insufficient to maximise the benefits of the broadband system. There are a number of factors that generate investments below what is socially efficient and delay the deployment of high capacity networks, blocking efforts towards social inclusion.[25] These include: *i)* non-linear relationships among providers that require minimal levels of adoption to maximise broadband impact (referred to by economists as a 'big push');[26] *ii)* the existence of externalities in production and consumption of broadband that cannot be captured by the private sector; *iii)* economies of scale and sunk costs in the deployment of fibre-optic networks; and *iv)* problems in the identification and aggregation of demand in marginal zones.[27]

5.3.2.1. Inter-sectoral co-ordination

Broadband development initiatives that do not include a strategic vision weaken the co-ordination of the different sectors involved and make an efficient allocation of resources more difficult. National plans for broadband development require a high level of political commitment, the establishment of mechanisms of checks and balances and accountability, the specification of realistic goals and the clear definition of responsibilities. This ensures funding for the medium- and long-term, so that goals may be met. Similarly, consultation with a wide range of private stakeholders (especially those involved in the provision of infrastructure and service operation), civil society and other government agencies prevents duplication of efforts.

5.3.2.2. Public investment

Public investment in basic telecommunications infrastructure must complement the investments made by the private sector. For instance, public investment in interurban data-transfer networks under an open-access and non-discriminatory model can boost private investment in the last-mile segment.[28] In particular, national, sub-national and metropolitan infrastructure plans must take into consideration fibre-optics deployment.

Public investment must focus on non-competitive segments and areas where potential private profitability is low or non-existent. For example, state investment in alternative data transfer networks is an effective tool for dealing with bottlenecks that appear in certain market segments (especially in backbone networks). Furthermore, public investment can help close social gaps and meet regional development objectives in poor areas or low-density regions, where difficulties in aggregating demand and capturing externalities result in private-investment deficits.[29]

It is possible to identify different financing strategies aimed at minimising the impact of direct public-investment initiatives on fiscal accounts in Latin America. Generally, these initiatives focus on backbone networks and are funded with central government resources, although occasionally local governments take charge. Many of these strategies do not increase direct public spending but rather mobilise existing resources and make use of the government's own connectivity needs.

Table 5.1. Role of the State in the development of broadband systems

Areas	Objectives	Tools
Systemic complementarities	Correct failures in co-ordination for articulation between sectors and the development of synergies.	National broadband strategy. Demand incentives and the promotion of absorption capacity. Promotion of e-government services and local content.
Equity in access and use	Massify access and use to take advantage of positive externalities, including network effects.	Public investment in backbone networks. Redesign and use of resources from universal service funds. Programmes for computer purchase and public access.
Resource management	Efficiently allocate and manage resources, such as the radio spectrum, easements, domain names and numbering.	Liberalisation and flexible use of spectrum. Usage of state infrastructure. Facilitation of access to lamp posts, pipelines and rights of way.
Rules and regulations	Modernise and adapt the regulatory environment to an environment of technological convergence.	Streamlining and flexibilisation of the granting of licenses. Technological neutrality (sole license). Sharing of infrastructure strategy. Definition of the IP interconnection regime.
Spreading technological innovation.	Accelerate learning processes. Increase the capacity for innovation and dissemination of the best technological practices to enable advances in the development process.	Digital literacy programmes and human capital formation. Support for the adoption and training of micro and small enterprises. Promotion of links between academia and the ICT industry.
Public policy	Adapt the public policy approach to a highly dynamic, evolving and innovative environment.	Regional co-ordination of policies and standardisation. Mechanisms for monitoring outcomes. Reduction of the tax burden on the telecommunications sector.

Source: Jordán, Galperin and Peres (2010).

Mobilising existing assets reduces investment needs and makes it possible to take advantage of technologies that increase the transmission capacity of the broadband system without deploying new physical networks. Using fibre-optic networks that have already been deployed at the state level makes use of underused public assets and reduces the need for new investment. Examples of this are recent initiatives in Brazil and Mexico to use fibre-optic networks initially deployed for the control and monitoring of the electricity grid.[30] Similarly, using other existing infrastructure and infrastructure that is currently under construction, such as roads, which could house certain elements of broadband networks, would also reduce investment requirements.

Public investment in the state's own access networks reduces future connection costs and increases trickle down to the rest of society if these networks are also usable by homes and businesses. In all countries, the State is the largest user of connectivity due to its need to connect government departments, libraries, universities, hospitals and schools throughout the country. The development of its own infrastructure is sometimes a necessity in areas that do not attract private investment.

The resources accumulated in universal service funds can be redirected to investments to reduce the risks associated with last-mile connectivity initiatives. Financing local last-mile segment micro-operators would accelerate use of funds, share risks with private stakeholders and optimise the use of resources based on local demand for connectivity.[31] Internationally there is a tendency to expand the funding base of these universal funds with the aim of increasing broadband access.[32]

5.3.2.3. Convergence regulation

Regulatory models that are not adaptable to technological convergence and the limited deployment of fibre-optics largely explain Latin America's lag in broadband access with respect to OECD economies. Latin America's broadband penetration is on average a quarter of that of OECD economies, with prices 50% higher and about one tenth the speed. To favour convergence, regulatory frameworks in Latin America must adapt quickly to the current technological context. Furthermore, a greater deployment of fibre-optics would generate the bandwidth required for the services most valued by society.

Given the dynamics of improvements in technologies associated with the broadband system, it is necessary to permanently revise and adapt regulatory and legal frameworks to accommodate new technological developments. Regulations must be sufficiently flexible to constantly adapt and respond to the speed with which technological changes take place.[33] An appropriate regulatory framework facilitates private investment and directs it towards those segments identified as priorities. It also must be structured in such a way that it guarantees legal security.

The legal systems of most countries in the region remain oriented towards a service-by-service regulation, which does not fully adapt to the needs of technological convergence (see Annex 5.1). Convergence presents a series of challenges, such as the sustainability and scalability of networks and services provided by operators. These challenges can only be addressed by modifying regulations to deal with telecommunications services comprehensively, avoiding segmenting measures that may cause asymmetries and regulatory distortions. This means considering granting broadband Internet access the same regulatory treatment as other services of public interest.

In this respect, regulations should facilitate an efficient, orderly and progressive transition from existing networks to next-generation networks, based on their individual technological and socio-economic characteristics. Investment for fibre-optic deployment in interurban and urban ring connections, which facilitate last-mile service, can be encouraged through a regulation of these access networks following a common carrier model. This would enable them to be used by broadband service providers, fostering competition and avoiding unnecessary duplication of infrastructure investment.

5.3.2.4. Efficient management of State-owned resources

Latin America's geographic and demographic characteristics limit the development of fixed networks. Thus, just as mobile telephones led to the massification of voice services, mobile broadband is expected to have a similar effect in areas with low demand density. Mobile broadband presents several important advantages for the region. These include its lower initial investment requirements, the speed with which networks can be deployed and the scalability and adaptability of its infrastructure investments. In addition, it provides the opportunity to leverage the already massive existence of mobile telephone networks and terminals, which have reached much greater levels of coverage than fixed telecommunications networks.

Resources such as the electromagnetic spectrum are essential to the development of mobile telecommunications. The provision of mobile services depends heavily on spectrum availability and access to it determines the costs of infrastructure deployment and the competitive structure of the market. Therefore, the state must manage the spectrum efficiently to prevent the generation of artificial barriers and to grant concessions that promote competition.

Efficient management of the spectrum is a key policy issue given the scarcity of spectrum available to current and potential operators. This limits network deployment and the quality of mobile broadband services. Given that the majority of the "premium" spectrum[34] is already assigned, it is increasingly difficult to expand existing uses or create new services. However, evidence suggests that this scarcity is partially artificial, as certain segments of the spectrum used by operators in other regions of the world are not utilised or are underutilised in Latin America and the Caribbean. In urban areas a combination of shared, open-access fibre-optic rings with regulated rates and functional segmentation is an option to exploit the capacity of fibre and the versatility and competition of mobile solutions.

5.3.2.5. Adequacy of public policy approaches

The State can act as a catalyst for broadband demand by promoting the use of government e-services. Valuable experiences in tax administration, public procurement and the pension system are particularly relevant for countries in the region and many countries have made significant progress in these areas.

Plans to encourage the purchase of equipment and terminals can boost the adoption of communication technologies for common use. The adoption of broadband requires complementary investments by the users, which includes purchasing terminals. Several countries in the region have taken initiatives in this area, providing tax incentives and improving access to credit for purchasing computers,[35] measures needed in order to expand the existing stock.

In addition to the gap in broadband access, there is also a gap in demand, comprised of households and businesses that have not become users despite having the necessary resources and potential access. Digital literacy initiatives, labour force training and promotion of technical careers seek to reverse this phenomenon by creating the human capital necessary to take advantage of the benefits associated with broadband. The countries in the region have adopted multiple initiatives in this area, which create the possibility of sharing successful experiences and developing joint initiatives on a regional level.

Part of the demand gap is due to a deficit of content and services adapted to the preferences and needs of households and productive units in disadvantaged regions or with a population that is not attractive to private suppliers. Consumers' preference for local contents generates opportunities to develop policies to stimulate its local generation, as well as applications to increase broadband demand. For example, there are interesting experiences of governments stimulating the production of content in indigenous languages and information systems for rural producers.

Shared broadband access will continue to have an important role in the region in the medium term, despite sustained growth in the number of individual subscribers. The guiding role of the state is necessary in order for public access centres, particularly those that receive public funds, to also function as spaces for building skills and for encouraging the adoption of electronic services and the generation of local content. Experiences in the region reveal the potential of these centres to foster broadband demand, while also having positive effects on labour skills and academic performance.[36]

5.4. Towards greater effectiveness of infrastructure policies

Reversing the infrastructure lag in the region requires State intervention through the adoption of new public policies and increased investment. One of the main challenges is to improve co-ordination and coherence among relevant stakeholders in the area of infrastructure. Co-ordination is particularly necessary among agencies at the same level of government, agencies of different government levels, and among public and private stakeholders. For example, better use of existing transport infrastructure would lower the costs of deploying broadband networks. In terms of agencies, better co-ordination of multimodal transport policy should take into account the noticeable differences in external costs of the different modes of transport.

Increased effectiveness of the infrastructure policy cycle permits countries to achieve higher levels of development. In order to identify the bottlenecks that limit the effectiveness of infrastructure policies, it is necessary to evaluate and strengthen the different phases of policy making: prioritising and planning, execution, operation and maintenance. To do this, it is necessary to build a regulatory framework that includes a system of checks and balances and clearly defines transparency and accountability mechanisms.

In the transport sector, the prioritising and planning phase should aim to increase the social benefits from public works through a social evaluation process. Finding a balance between commencing new projects and maintaining existing infrastructure is key to this.

In the telecommunications sector, it is necessary to adapt the regulatory framework to an environment of technological convergence. Regulations should aim to improve the management of state-owned resources such as the electromagnetic spectrum and fibre-optic networks through fixing rates and requiring open access.

The State must apply a strategic vision to private participation in infrastructure, seeking the most suitable partnerships and instruments available to improve the quality of services and goods provided. Adequate project planning and design would indicate when private participation is desirable, without risk transfer being the only criterion. This should be encouraged in an environment that minimises perverse incentives for rent seeking, solves the problems of dynamic inconsistency, mitigates information problems and maximises efficiency and quality in the provision of services.

In the transport sector it is important to follow a strict selection process for private participation (such as "value for money" analysis) and to have well-designed contracts and a fiscal accounting system that does not favour concessions over public projects. This would minimise concession renegotiations, which would considerably reduce hidden fiscal costs.

In the telecommunications sector, especially broadband Internet, it is necessary to set up mechanisms and incentives that foster development of infrastructure where the provision of service is not profitable for the private sector, with the priority being open access to the network.

The institutional framework and civil-service careers in the transport and telecommunications sectors require important reforms. It is necessary to follow hiring schemes that encourage professionalisation, specialisation, and the development of a civil service that is independent from the political cycle and is capable of using sophisticated tools for planning, evaluation and monitoring.[37] Both regulatory bodies and agencies responsible for contracting services and infrastructure must have greater autonomy to ensure better co-ordination among stakeholders.

Annex 5.1. Current situation of convergence legislation in Latin America

Country	Convergence Regulation	Characteristics
Argentina	Decree 764/2000 – Deregulation of telecommunications	Establishes the unified telecommunications license; establishes a 60-day term within which to grant the license; the license has no fixed duration and allows the provision of any kind of service, with or without own infrastructure.
Bolivia (Plurinational State of)	None	
Brazil	Multimedia Communications Services Regulation, Resolution 272, 9 August 2001	Defines Multimedia Communications Service License (SCM); separates network from SCM services; provides rights to numeration and to other resources to SCM.
Chile	None	Law 18.168, 2 October 1982, focuses more on networks than on provision of services, thus favouring "triple-play".
Colombia	Law 1341, 30 July 2009 (ICTs Act)	It incorporates the concept of general enabling for the provision of networks and services; assignment of spectrum usage rights; technological neutrality.
Costa Rica	General Telecommunications Act, Law no. 8642, 4 June 2008	Introduces principals of technological neutrality and convergence; promotes open use of frequency bands; requires only an authorisation to provide telecommunications services; authorisation is processed in a maximum of 2 months; new services can be offered with only a notification to regulators.
Cuba	None	
Ecuador	None	
El Salvador	None	
Guatemala	None	
Haiti	None	
Honduras	None	
Mexico	Convergence Agreement concerning fixed local telephone services and television and/or audio services, 3 October 2006	Determines that provision of voice, data and images in technological convergence is a strategic plan; promotes convergence between wire and wireless networks; permits concessionaires to determine which frequency bands can be used for other services.
Nicaragua	Administrative Agreement 004-2005, 7 January 2005. General Interconnectivity and Access Regulation	Specifically defines access to non-geographic numbers (NGNs), roaming, IP address transfer and other issues related to a next-generation environment.
Panama	None	
Paraguay	None	
Peru	Law 28737, 17 May 2006	Fosters convergence of networks and services; introduces the single concession by means of contracts.
Dominican Republic	None	
Uruguay	None	
Venezuela (Bolivarian Republic of)	Venezuelan Telecommunications Act, 1 June 2000.	Introduces a simplified scheme of general enabling certificate; services are added by modifying the certificate's attributes; regulators have limited time to process requests.

Source: Bustillo (2010).

Notes

1. Perrotti and Sánchez (2011)
2. Calderón and Servén (2010).
3. Gayá and Campos (2009).
4. Perrotti and Sánchez (2011) and Balmaseda *et al.* (2011).
5. This survey, conducted by the OECD Development Centre, is directed at policy makers in the transport and infrastructure planning sectors and attempts to identify the main bottlenecks throughout the policy formulation process hindering effective infrastructure policy. To achieve this, interactions among different stakeholders involved in the infrastructure process are analysed (with an emphasis placed on transport). The survey was carried out in 2011 in Brazil, Chile, Colombia, Costa Rica, Ecuador, El Salvador, Mexico, Paraguay, Peru, the Dominican Republic and Uruguay. See Gutiérrez and Nieto-Parra (2011) for a detailed analysis.
6. In contrast to the perceptions of policy makers, experts think that it is still necessary to considerably weigh public interest considerations. This difference can be attributed to policy makers' perception that public interest considerations should be met by public works that respond to the demands of the public, while the much broader expert index includes perceptions on corruption. (Berkman *et al.*, 2009)
7. Other obstacles, such as the influence of other stakeholders, the overlapping of the same institutions in different stages, the limited participation of citizens and a delayed availability of resources, are not deemed as important by policy makers.
8. Agénor (2009); Rioja (2003); Calderón and Servén (2010).
9. These results were obtained using road-surface deterioration models and vehicle operation costs, using HDM III and IV for Chile (Ministry of Public Works) and Mexico (Ministry of Communications and Transport).
10. For an analysis of the relationship between investments and the political cycle see Nieto-Parra and Santiso (2009).
11. Unsuccessful attempts were made in Chile to create institutions to reduce the bias against infrastructure maintenance. In 2007 legislation was passed creating a Superintendent for Public Works, requiring both public works and private concessions to establish explicit service-level commitments that could be monitored. (Bitrán and Villena, 2011)
12. Cipoletta, Pérez and Sánchez (2011).
13. In this chapter we do not differentiate between concessions and PPPs. See OECD (2008) for the similarities and differences between the two modalities.
14. See Guasch, Laffont and Straub (2007) and Engel, Fischer and Galetovic (2003) for a detailed description.
15. The transfer of financial and market risks to the private sector has costs that depend on the conditions of development of capital markets, which affects financing costs and the level of competition in tendering processes, among other factors.
16. See OECD (2008) for a comparison between OECD economies and Latin America. In Colombia, Congress included some road concessions in the approval of the National Development Plan 2002-06 (see Nieto-Parra, Olivera and Tibocha, 2011). Even in Chile, where the National System of Investment was a regional pioneer, concession projects are exempted by law from entering the national system during the evaluation phase. Furthermore, an adequate value-for-money analysis is not performed.
17. See Donaghue (2002) and Engel, Fischer and Galetovic (2009) for a detailed discussion of the subject.
18. For example, in the UK aspects of "property" as well as "risk transfer to the private sector" are considered when determining whether a project must be incorporated in the public balance sheet, while in New South Wales in Australia it was determined that the assets and liabilities of privately financed bulk-water treatment plants must belong to the public-sector balance sheet (Irwin, 2007).

19. See Economist Intelligence Unit (2010) and Bitrán and Villena (2011) for a recent review on these aspects.
20. For example, in Mercosur the participation of rail, sea and river transport is about a third of the level in the United States and Canada. The normalised Herfindahl-Hirschmann index (IHH) for Argentina is 0.32, while it is 0.20 for Colombia and 0.29 for Mercosur, while for the United States it is only 0.02. This shows the region's higher concentration and low competitiveness.
21. Nieto-Parra, Olivera and Tibocha (2011).
22. In 2005, nearly 60 000 containers coming from or going to Costa Rica travelled by land (on unconditioned roads) to avoid problems of inefficiency and congestion at the port of Limón and to find better port services in Panama. This involved additional costs of between USD 70 and 100 million. (Schwartz, Guasch and Wilmsmeier, 2009)
23. See, for instance, Steffensen and Trollegaard (2000) for a sample of African countries.
24. Technological convergence is understood as the possibility of using multiple networks to provide both traditional communications services as well as innovations in voice, data, sound and image transfer.
25. Rosenstein-Rodan (1944); Murphy, Shleifer and Vishny (1989).
26. Rosston, Savage and Waldman (2010).
27. Berkman Center (2010).
28. Yongsoo, Kelly and Raja (2010).
29. Quiang (2009).
30. See Flores-Roux and Mariscal (2010) for a discussion of Mexico's experience.
31. Galperin and Bar (2007).
32. For example, the national broadband plan in the United States aims to increase the sources of financing for universal service by creating funds for each phase of its implementation. Canada, on the other hand, uses a mechanism which taxes a wide range of telecommunications and other related services, reducing taxes on operators. This mechanism is considered more sustainable in the long term as it causes fewer distortions in the pricing mechanism.
33. For example, mobile telephones and commercial Internet connections reached rates of social adoption of 60% in 15 years, whereas fixed telephony took 75 years to reach that level.
34. "Premium" spectrum or frequencies are those bands which due to their propagation characteristics are able to carry large volumes of information as well as penetrate solid objects such as foliage and walls. This places them in high demand by the industry. They are generally found between frequencies of 600 megahertz (MHz) and 3 gigahertz (GHz). Frequencies below that limit cannot carry high volumes of information while frequencies above cannot travel long distances and penetrate obstacles.
35. Laplane *et al.* (2007).
36. Rojas Mejía (2010).
37. OECD (2010) provides a good example of professionalisation of PPPs.

References

AGENOR P-R. (2009), "Infrastructure Investment and Maintenance Expenditure: Optimal Allocation Rules in a Growing Economy", *Journal of Public Economic Theory*, Vol. 11, No. 2, p.233-250.

BALMASEDA, M., C. DAUDE, A. MELGUIZO AND L. TAFT (FORTHCOMING), "Infrastructure Patterns: An Empirical Analysis with a Focus on Latin America", *Working Paper*, OECD Development Centre, Paris.

BERKMAN CENTER (2010), *Next Generation Connectivity: A review of broadband Internet transitions and policy from around the world*, Berkman Center for Internet & Society, Harvard University.

BERKMAN, H., C. SCARTASCINI, E. STEIN, AND M. TOMMASI (2009), "Political Institutions, State Capabilities, and Public Policy: An International Dataset", Inter-American Development Bank, Washington, DC., www.iadb.org/res/pub_desc.cfm?pub_id=DBA-012, accessed 5 October 2011.

BITRÁN, E., S. NIETO-PARRA AND J.S. ROBLEDO (FORTHCOMING), "Opening the Black Box of Contract Renegotiations: An Analysis of Road Concessions in Chile, Colombia and Peru", *Working Paper*, OECD Development Centre, Paris.

BITRÁN, E. AND M. VILLENA (2011), "Desarrollo institucional para la eficiencia de las concesiones de infraestructura de transportes", mimeo.

BUSTILLO, R. (2010), "Propuesta para la estructura del regulador en convergencia", presentation at the 13th Regulatel-AHCIET (Asociación Iberoamericana de Centros de Investigación y Empresas de Telecomunicaciones) Summit, 14 July 2010, Lima.

CALDERÓN, C. AND L. SERVÉN (2010), "Infrastructure in Latin America", *Policy Research Working Paper Series* 5317, World Bank, Washington, DC.

CARRANZA, L., C. DAUDE AND A. MELGUIZO (2011), "Public Infrastructure Investment and Fiscal Sustainability in Latin America: Incompatible Goals?", *Working Paper*, No. 301, OECD Development Centre, Paris.

DONAGHUE, B. (2002), "Statistical Treatment of 'Build-Own-Operate-Transfer' Schemes", *Working Paper*, No. 02/167, International Monetary Fund, Washington, DC.

ECONOMIST INTELLIGENCE UNIT (2010), *Evaluating the Environment for Public-Private Partnership in Latin America and the Caribbean: Infrascope 2010*. Economist Intelligence Unit.

ENGEL, E., R. FISCHER AND A. GALETOVIC (2003), "Privatizing Highways in Latin America: Fixing What Went Wrong", *Economía*, Vol. 4, No. 1, pp. 129-164.

ENGEL, E., FISCHER, R. AND GALETOVIC, A. (2009). "Public-Private Partnerships: When and How", Documentos de Trabajo, No. 257, Centre for Applied Economics (CEA), University of Chile.

FLORES-ROUX, E. AND J. MARISCAL (2010), "Oportunidades y desafíos de la banda ancha móvil", in V. Jordán, H. Galperin and W. Peres (ed.): *Acelerando la revolución digital: banda ancha para América Latina y Caribe*, ECLAC (CEPAL), Santiago, Chile.

FRIEDRICH, R., K. SABBAGH, B. EL-DARWICHE AND M.SINGH (2009), *Digital Highways: The Role of Government in 21st-Century Infrastructure*. Booz & Company, USA.

GAYÁ, R. AND R. CAMPOS (2009), "La brecha en el crecimiento de la infraestructura de transporte y el comercio de America Latina", Boletín FAL 276, ECLAC (CEPAL), Santiago, Chile.

GALPERIN, H. AND F. BAR (2007). "Diversifying Network Development through Microtelcos", Information Technologies and International Development, Vol. 3, No. 2, pp. 73-86.

GAYÁ, R. AND R. CAMPOS (2009), "La brecha en el crecimiento de la infraestructura de transporte y el comercio de America Latina", Boletín FAL 276, CEPAL, Santiago, Chile.

GUASCH, J.L., J.-J. LAFFONT AND S. STRAUB (2007), "Concessions of Infrastructure in Latin America: Government-Led Renegotiation", *Journal of Applied Econometrics* , Vol. 22, No. 7, pp. 1267-1294.

GUASCH, J.L., J.-J. LAFFONT AND S. STRAUB (2008), "Renegotiation of Concession Contracts in Latin America: Evidence for the Water and Transport Sectors", *International Journal of Industrial Organization* , Vol. 26, No. 2, pp. 421-442.

Gutiérrez, H. and S. Nieto-Parra (forthcoming), "The Policy-Making Process of Transport Infrastructure in Latin America: A Review from Policy Makers" Working Paper, OECD Development Centre, Paris.

Irwin, T. (2007), *Government Guarantees: Allocating and Valuing Risk in Privately Financed Infrastructure Projects*, World Bank, Washington DC.

Jordán, V., H. Galperin and W. Peres (coord.) (2010), *Fast-Tracking the Digital Revolution: Broadband for Latin America and the Caribbean*, ECLAC (CEPAL), Santiago, Chile.

Laplane, M., F. Rodrígues, F. Gutiérrez and F. Rojas (2007), *Asimetrías de información en el mercado de computadoras personales: los casos de financiación de PC para consumidores de bajos ingresos*, ECLAC (CEPAL), Santiago, Chile, http://www.eclac.org/publicaciones/xml/8/28528/Doc123.pdf, accessed 5 October 2011.

Murphy, K.M., A. Shleifer and R. Vishny (1989). "Income Distribution, Market Size, and Industrialization", *Quarterly Journal of Economics*, Vol. 104, No. 3, pp. 537-64.

Nieto-Parra, S., M. Olivera and A. Tibocha (forthcoming) "The Politics of Transport Infrastructure Policies in Colombia", Working Paper, OECD Development Centre, Paris.

Nieto-Parra S. and J. Santiso (2009), "Revisiting Political Budget Cycles in Latin America", Working Paper, No. 281, OECD Development Centre, Paris.

OECD (Organisation for Economic Co-operation and Development) (2008), *Public-Private Partnerships: In Pursuit of Risk Sharing and Value for Money*, OECD, Paris.

OECD (Organisation for Economic Co-operation and Development) (2009), *OECD Information Technology Outlook 2008*, OECD, Paris.

OECD (Organisation for Economic Co-operation and Development) (2010). *Dedicated Public Private Partnerships Units: A Survey of Institutional and Governance Structures*, OECD Paris.

Pérez Salas, G., G. Cipoletta Tomassian and R. Sánchez (2009), "Infraestructura y servicios de transporte y su relación con los Objetivos de Desarrollo del Milenio", working paper, ECLAC (CEPAL), Santiago, Chile.

Perrotti, D. and R. Sánchez (2011), "La brecha de infraestructura en América Latina y el Caribe", Recursos Naturales e Infraestructura, No. 153, ECLAC (CEPAL), Santiago, Chile.

Qiang, C. Z. (2009), "Broadband Infrastructure Investment in Stimulus Packages: Relevance for Developing Countries", *info*, Vol. 12, No. 2, pp. 41-56.Rioja F.K. (2003), "Filling Potholes: Macroeconomic Effects of Maintenance Versus New Investment in Public Infrastructure", *Journal of Public Economics*, Vol. 87, No. 9-10, September, pp. 2281-2304.

Rojas Mejía, F. (2010), *Evolución de los centros de acceso público a las TIC*, ECLAC (CEPAL), Santiago, Chile.

Rosenstein-Rodan, P. (1944). "The International Development of Economically Backward Areas", *International Affairs*, Vol. 20, No. 2, pp. 157-165.

Rosston, G., S. Savage and D. Waldman (2010), *Household Demand for Broadband Internet Service*. Report for the Broadband.gov Task Force, Federal Communications Commission, Washington, DC.

Schwartz, J., J.L. Guasch and G. Wilmsmeier (2009), "Logistics, Transport and Food Prices in LAC: Policy Guidance for Improving Efficiency and Reducing Costs", Sustainable Development Occasional Papers Series, August 2009, No. 2, World Bank, Washington DC, http://idbdocs.iadb.org/wsdocs/getdocument.aspx?docnum=35028412, accessed 5 October 2011.

Serebrisky, T. and L. Trujillo (2005), "An Assessment of Port Reform in Argentina: Outcomes and Challenges Ahead", *Maritime Policy & Management*, Vol. 32, pp. 191-207.

Silva, G. (2007), "¿Por qué las hidrovías y las ferrovías se han relegado en América Latina?", presentation at the 16th Latin American Congress on Ports, Rosario.Steffensen, J. and S. Trollegaard (2000), "Fiscal Decentralisation and Sub-National Government Finance in Relation to Infrastructure and Service Provision", Synthesis Report on 6 Sub-Saharan African Country Studies, World Bank.

Thomson, I. (1999), "Concessions and Road and Rail Transport Optimization", *CEPAL Review*, No. 67, April 1999, ECLAC (CEPAL), Santiago, Chile, pp. 177-189.

Yongsoo, K., T. Kelly and S. Raja (2010), *Building Broadband: Strategies and Policies for the Developing World*, Global Information and Communication Technologies Department, World Bank, Washington DC.

CHAPTER SIX

Better institutions for innovation and productive development

Abstract

Following a period of structural reform oriented towards free trade and exports, Latin America has turned its attention to strategies for innovation and productive development. The region is currently seeking to insert itself in the global knowledge economy. To do this, it will need to achieve better coordination of actions in this field. Governments, firms, scientific agents and civil society act in a context that has been made more complex by changes in the global economy and by new technological paradigms. Despite these difficulties, many countries have made strides thanks to the creation of institutions, methodologies, and instruments that take on the challenge of innovation and technological change. In order to consolidate these advances, the region needs to support the definition of new models of governance, stronger institutions and models of public policy that can mobilise the agents in the national innovation system. These efforts can motivate the commitment of the private sector in innovation, research and development.

6.1. Introduction

Overcoming the challenge of sustainable and inclusive growth will require innovation, i.e. new and "better" products, processes, business models, organisational practices and the creation of new firms. Moving towards this goal will depend on greater co-ordination between policies for innovation and policies for productive development, new forms of public policy governance and a renewed commitment by the private sector to economic growth based on knowledge and innovation.

This chapter is divided into three sections. The first reviews key trends in innovation and productive development in Latin America. The second section analyses the main achievements and challenges in modernising the state to promote innovation. It identifies four main areas in which states have advanced in their capacity to implement more effective policies: the shift towards policy models focusing on innovation systems; the introduction of new modes of governance; the creation of new instruments for financing and technology transfer; and improvements in innovation policy management capacities. The third section proposes some recommendations to consolidate recent gains.

6.2. Main trends in innovation and productive development

In the past decade the agenda for innovation has been given new impetus in Latin America. After the 1990s —when countries in the region prioritised growth models based on macroeconomic stability and inflation control— innovation and productive development have returned as priorities in development strategies.

Innovation is a systemic process that arises from voluntary and involuntary interactions between actors operating within different frameworks and with different incentives. For example, businesses respond to competitive market-oriented strategies, while universities, research centres and laboratories perform based on different criteria, not necessarily directed toward the industrial application of advances in knowledge.[1] The quality and intensity of relationships between the actors in national innovation systems are determined by businesses, institutions, incentive mechanisms, regulations and existing infrastructure.

The region needs to encourage further strengthening of national innovation systems, most of which are at an early stage of development. They are often characterised by the presence of "islands of technological excellence" in contexts of low productivity and little business development. It is fundamental to strengthen domestic scientific and technological capabilities, increase the ability to transform these advances into competitive business opportunities and generate qualified employment opportunities to meet both domestic and international demand.

The advances and challenges in innovation and productive development in Latin America today can be summarised in seven main points:

1) The productivity gap is a persistent problem. The region needs to invest more to close this divide. A comparison of the dynamics of manufacturing industry productivity between Latin America and the United States shows that Latin America has not caught up to the technological frontier, but in fact the divide has widened in recent years.[2] Between 2003 and 2007, labour productivity grew 2% annually in Latin America. Since the mid-1990s it has grown between 3% and 5% annually in the US, primarily due to the modernisation of productive processes resulting from the increasing incorporation of information and communication technologies in business management.[3]

2) The ability to close the productivity gap depends on productive specialisation and the pattern of integration into world markets.[4] The Latin American lag is reflected both in quantity —given the productivity gap— as well as in quality, because of the high sectoral specialisation in natural resource-intensive activities (Figure 6.1). In fact, low productivity growth is associated with the lack of substantive structural change in the region.

Natural resource-intensive sectors still account for 60% of total manufacturing value added, while in the United States, thanks to a strong increase in knowledge-intensive sectors these now represent 60% of total manufacturing value added. This change in the structural composition of its domestic industry almost doubled the country's labour productivity between 1990 and 2007.[5]

Figure 6.1. Production structure specialisation and labour productivity: Latin America and the United States, 1990-2007
(In percentages)

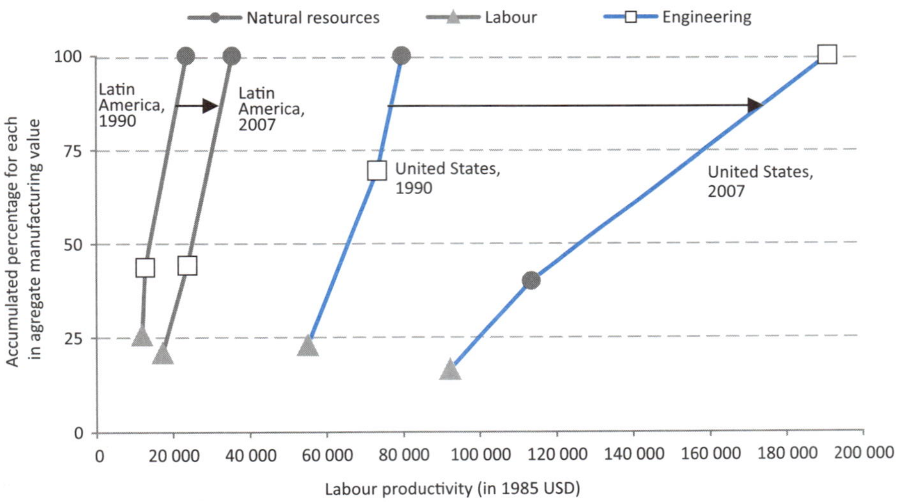

Note: The natural resource, labour and engineering intensive sectors correspond to the activities in divisions 15-17, 20-21, 23-24 and 26-28; 18-19, 22, 25, and 36-37; 29-35 of the International Standard Industrial Classification of All Economic Activities (ISIC Rev. 3), respectively.

Source: ECLAC (2010a).
http://dx.doi.org/10.1787/888932523063

3) Primary products and natural resource-based manufactures account for over 50% of the region's exports,[6] so diversifying exports and, therefore, the production structure is a priority. In recent years there has been a process of "commoditisation" of exports, mainly driven by the increase in demand for primary products and their rising prices. The export structure in Latin America contrasts with that of many OECD economies, which are characterised by product diversification and concentration in medium- and high-tech manufacturing. There are three main groups of countries in Latin America: the Southern Cone countries, concentrating in primary products and natural resource-based manufactures; Central American countries, specialised in low- and medium-tech manufacturing; and a group consisting of Costa Rica, Mexico and Brazil, with the highest degree of diversification of exports in the region, including medium- and high-tech manufactures.

4) There is a mismatch between supply and demand of skilled human resources for innovation. It is necessary to increase both the quality and quantity of human resources for innovation and create incentives for labour absorption. This

challenge is crucial for all countries in Latin America. For example, Argentina and Uruguay are characterised by a high level of education and need to move towards the co-ordination of educational and productive development policies in order to improve the competitiveness of their productive sectors. Brazil, on the other hand, must strengthen the technological intensity of its productive matrix and needs a training policy in line with this effort, while the smaller countries of the region that suffer from intensive "brain drain" need to attract and retain skilled human capital.

5) Latin American investment in research and development (R&D) as a percentage of GDP is less than a quarter of the level found in OECD economies. Investment in R&D as a share of GDP rose from 0.5% in 2004 to 0.6% in 2008; this percentage is much lower than in OECD economies (2.2% and 2.3% for the same years). Heterogeneity with respect to investment in R&D among countries in the region has increased in recent years; for example, Central American investment in R&D does not exceed 0.1% of GDP, while in Brazil it represents 1.2% of GDP.

Figure 6.2. Investment in research and development as a percentage of GDP: Latin America and the Caribbean (selected countries), 2004-08
(In percentages)

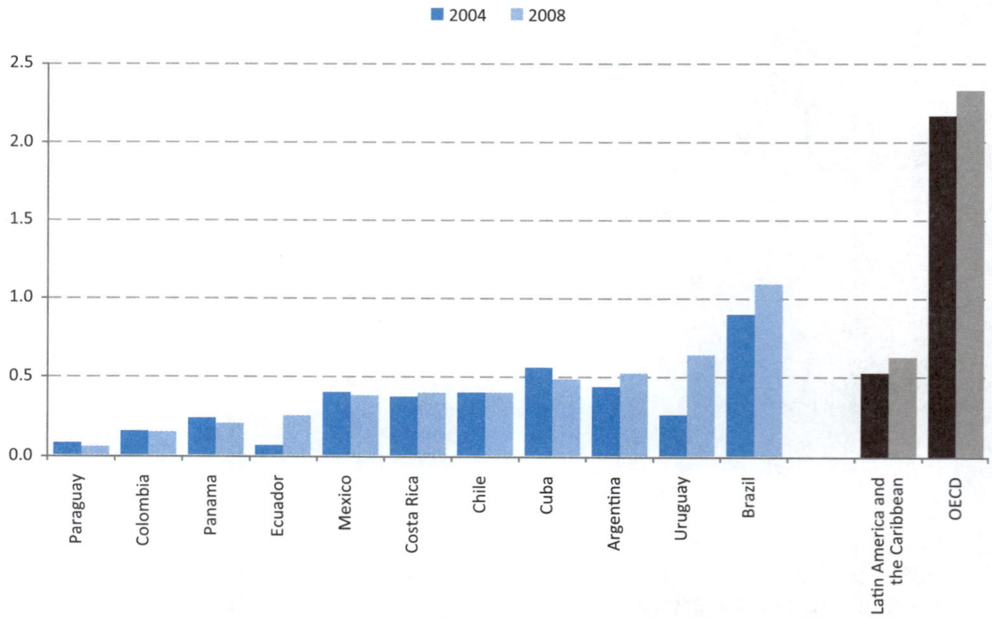

Source: Based on data from the United Nations Educational, Scientific and Cultural Organization (UNESCO), see [http://www.uis.unesco.org/pages/default.aspx] Ibero-American/Inter-American Network of Science and Technology Indicators (RICYT), see [http://ricyt.org] and Main Science and Technology Indicators (MSTI) Database of the Organisation for Economic Co-operation and Development (OECD).
http://dx.doi.org/10.1787/888932523082

6) The private sector invests little in innovation and R&D. Unlike in developed countries, in Latin America the private sector contributes little to innovation (Figure 6.3). The gap in R&D cannot be closed without a substantial increase in private-sector investment, along with greater support from the public sector. Therefore, it is essential to move forward in designing incentives and policies to encourage private-sector investment in innovation activities. This requires co-ordination between policies for technology and innovation and policies for productive development.

Figure 6.3. Latin America and the Caribbean, other emerging countries and the OECD: business investment in R&D as a percentage of GDP, 2007 or the most recent year for which data is available
(In percentages)

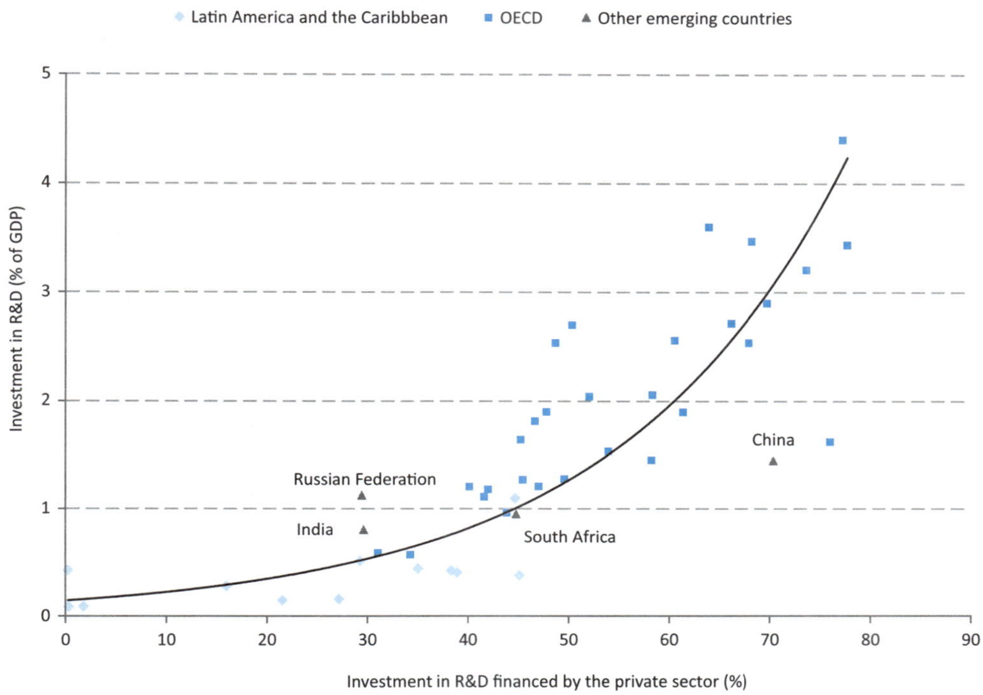

Note: Figures correspond to the year 2002 for Bolivia; 2004 for Switzerland; 2005 for Panama and Paraguay and 2006 for Australia, China, Israel and South Africa.

Source: Based on data from the United Nations Educational, Scientific and Cultural Organization (UNESCO), see [http://www.uis.unesco.org/pages/default.aspx] Ibero-American/Inter-American Network of Science and Technology Indicators (RICYT), see [http://ricyt.org] and Main Science and Technology Indicators (MSTI) Database of the Organisation for Economic Co-operation and Development (OECD).
http://dx.doi.org/10.1787/888932523101

Latin American firms concentrate their scientific and technological activities in the acquisition of machinery and equipment, except for Brazilian firms that invest relatively more in R&D. This contrasts with OECD economies, where the business sector devotes a high percentage of its sales to R&D for expanding the stock of knowledge and developing new applications (see Figure 6.4). This explains the low level of density of linkages in innovation systems in the region. Innovation surveys indicate that there is little co-operation between businesses and scientific and technological research institutes. In Mexico only 4.5% of innovative firms collaborate with institutes on R&D projects, and in countries where this tendency is greater, such as Argentina and Uruguay, the percentage does not exceed 12% of firms.[7] This stems mainly from sectoral specialisation (with most companies in low-knowledge-intensity sectors) and the lack of a culture and incentives for greater collaboration between research institutes and the private sector. Access to markets is also an important factor for innovation. Business development programmes to support the exports of innovative firms are also crucial for creating an environment that encourages private-sector investment in innovation.

Figure 6.4. Latin America and the Caribbean and the OECD: emphasis on innovation activities in manufacturing (% of sales), 2010

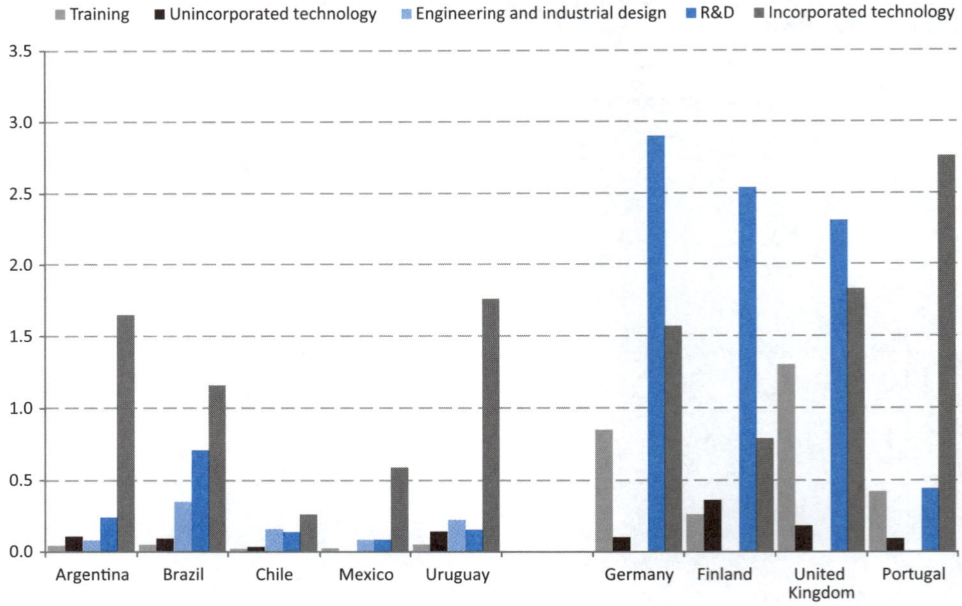

Note: Based on the Bogota Manual (2001), incorporated technology includes capital goods (machinery and equipment) which involve technological change in the firm and which are linked to new products or processes, and hardware. Unincorporated technology refers to the licensing and transfer of technology (patents, trademarks, industrial secrets, etc.), consulting (for production, products, organization of the productive system, organization and management, finances, sales) and software. Engineering and industrial design (EID) include plans and drawings aimed at defining procedures, technical specifications and operative characteristics necessary for the production of new technological goods and the implementation of new processes.

Source: ECLAC/SEGIB (2010), Ibero-American Spaces. Links between Universities and Businesses for Technological Development, ECLAC, LC/G. 2478. Santiago de Chile. Based on National Innovation Surveys in Latin America (Argentina: 1998-2001, Brazil: 2001-03, Chile: 1998-01, Mexico: 1999-00; Uruguay: 2001-03) and Third Survey Innovation of the European Community (CIS3).
http://dx.doi.org/10.1787/888932523120

The innovation profile of firms in the region is mixed. There are important differences in the innovative behaviour of firms depending on size. SMEs in the region face greater barriers to innovation than large firms. According to national innovation surveys, smaller firms face higher obstacles, such as access to credit markets, reduced ability to diversify risks, problems of scale and barriers to exports. These obstacles reduce their ability to invest in innovation activities.[8] Public policies that eliminate or reduce the specific bottlenecks faced by SMEs are key to stimulating innovation in those firms.

7) Patenting in the region is low, but it is on the rise. Still, non-residents patent more than residents in Latin America. However, the countries of the region have increased the number of patent applications in international patent offices, but their performance falls short of the pace of Asian countries. For example, in 1995 Latin American and Caribbean countries registered 196 patents with the United States Patent and Trademark Office (USPTO), while Asian countries (excluding Japan) registered 3 545; in 2009, these numbers were 290 for Latin America and the Caribbean and 20 036 for Asia. At the same time, patent offices in Latin American countries have modernised and advanced in the provision of services and procedures. However, it is non-residents who most often apply for and obtain patents in these offices.[9] If countries in the region are to move forward in designing intellectual-property management systems, they need to support innovation and business development strategies in order to foster innovation.

This brief overview reveals a region that faces major challenges if it is to reach the level of competences and capacities necessary for success in the global knowledge economy. On the other hand, Latin America and the Caribbean is a region on the move, where important progress is being made, even though it is confined to certain sectors, regions or groups of businesses. At the same time, changes in world markets and new technological paradigms (ICTs, biotechnology, nanotechnology, new materials, etc.) are reshaping innovation and are increasing its complexity and forms. These new paradigms require significant investments in R&D as well as complementary activities (business and technology services, training, infrastructure, business development, etc.). Dialogue among businesses, universities, civil society and public-sector agencies is essential for designing better policy instruments and increasing financial resources to strengthen the impact of public action.

The landscape described above poses significant challenges for the state and requires transformations in public policy and institutional capacity to support innovation. Innovation policy is also expected to have short- and medium-term impact on competitiveness in world markets and job creation, creating additional pressure to prioritise innovation in government programmes and in public- and private-sector budgets.

Budget constraints and uncertainty in the dynamics of international markets require more effectively managed public policy, capable of responding to a constantly changing context. Greater transparency, efficiency and effectiveness can only be achieved if support is given to institutional learning in the design and implementation of public policies and investment is made in improved institutional capacities and new forms of governance to facilitate the co-ordination of public policies.

6.3. Modernising the State to promote innovation: what progress has been made in the region?

The countries of the region have made progress in modernising the state to promote innovation in four main areas: *i)* the introduction of public-policy models focused on strengthening national innovation systems; *ii)* new governance models for the design of strategies focused on generating spaces for negotiation and co-ordination between different levels of government (vertical and horizontal co-ordination); *iii)* new policy instruments, in particular the introduction of new financing mechanisms and support for technology transfer; and *iv)* strengthening institutional capacities at both technical and policy-management levels, such as through the creation of strategic intelligence units to define strategies and assess policy impact.

6.3.1. The evolution of policy models: From linear supply to innovation systems

In recent years, Latin American countries have gained experience and made progress in designing and —albeit less frequently— implementing policy. They have also introduced important institutional reforms for the management of innovation policies, although each country has done so at a different pace and with different levels of accomplishment.

The experience of Latin American countries in the design and implementation of innovation policies dates back to the 1950s (see Figure 6.1). In the first period, while there was not an explicit innovation policy, the State laid the foundations for scientific and technological development and for the institutional infrastructure for the management of future science and technology policies. During this period, research institutes and scientific advisory bodies were created to develop the region's domestic scientific capacity in order to support national industrialisation strategies. The aim was to escape the peripheral condition of dependency through technical progress and institutions focused their innovation policies on supply and knowledge generation in sectors identified as strategic for national development.[10]

By the late 1980s, this model had reached its limit, and structural reforms introduced some changes, placing emphasis on trade liberalisation and export-led growth. During this period, public policy played a marginal role, and the main instruments were incentives aimed at demand to boost the private sector. Institutions were modernised and streamlined, and some were closed to avoid duplication of effort. Private-sector approaches to management were introduced, replacing those associated with the scientific world. In addition, some important complementary activities were reduced, such as the provision of rural extension services that facilitated the absorption of technological advances in local agricultural production, thereby reducing the impact of public research institutes and their ability to transfer knowledge to the productive world.[11]

In the most recent period, countries in the region have moved towards more sophisticated innovation policy models focused on the interactions between the scientific and productive sectors and on public-private partnerships for technology development. At first, the spread of the information and communications technologies (ICTs) paradigm absorbed much of the innovation agenda. Issues of access to ICTs and their use in the modernisation of the state, both for management within the public sector and in the provision of services, have been central to the strategies of various countries in the region. This has led to progress in public administration and in creating new and better approaches to public policy management. The institutions responsible for formulating innovation policies, as well as other government institutions, reformed their management in this period, allowing governments to become more open and communicate differently with users. This modernisation has in some cases led to an increase in the cost of managing public institutions because of royalty payments and information technology services. Furthermore, in contexts of high heterogeneity among actors in the system, the transition to e-government has widened the access gap between users based on their skills and location.

Table 6.1. Main innovation policy models

	Linear supply model	**Linear demand model**	**Public-private partnership model**	**Towards a new model?**
Period and national development strategy	Industrialisation by import substitution	Washington Consensus, structural reforms, export-led growth model	Post–Washington Consensus and growth supported by the spread of new technological paradigms and led by export of natural resources	Phase of growing prices for natural resources and post-2008, search for new sources of growth, green economy and growing role of domestic demand
Innovation policy framework	Structuralist	Market failures	National innovation systems	Sectoral innovation systems
Underlying assumption	Public sector is principal provider of scientific knowledge	Private sector is motor for technological change and innovation	Recognition of the complementarity between public and private sector in the generation and dissemination of knowledge	
Sectoral focus	Yes	No	No	Yes
Pattern of knowledge dissemination	From top to bottom	From bottom to top	Two-way	Systemic
Main policy approaches	Centralised and selective policies in support of efforts to create a national manufacturing industry	Horizontal policies and incentive mechanisms aimed at demand (absence of industrial policy)	Support for the generation of consortiums and networks for innovation and focus on technology transfer policies (absence of industrial policy)	Incentives for innovation with involvement of the private sector and sectoral focus (return of industrial policy)
Governance and management criteria for STI institutions	Centralised model oriented towards scientific research The scientific agenda and the academic sector predominate	Minimalist system and prevalence of market mechanisms and efficiency criteria	Modernisation of the management of institutions (rationalisation and modernisation), gradual transition towards systems of open and participatory management, development of mechanisms for collaboration between the public and private sectors	More sophisticated governance models for institutions, emphasis on mechanisms and incentives for dialogue among levels of government (horizontal and vertical) and between the public and private sectors

Source: Primi (2011).

An important breakthrough in the past decade was the concept of a "national innovation system" as the framework for the design and implementation of innovation policies. This approach conceives innovation as a complex, non-linear and non-deterministic phenomenon that requires interaction among the different actors of the system (such as firms, universities and research centres, as well as the public institutions that establish the system of governance for incentives and collaboration among these actors).

This, in turn, requires a public-policy model that includes forms and incentives for collaboration and partnership between the public and private sectors, both at the level of strategy and funding. As a result, institutions responsible for innovation policy need new competences and new spaces for dialogue and consultation. This leads to finding common ground among different interests, such as those of academia, the business world and civil society.

At first, the innovation agenda resulted in a simplified version of the national innovation systems approach, focusing on designing instruments to support collaboration between public and private sectors on innovation. The return of sustained growth in the region, in part due to the rising costs of raw materials and natural resources, has helped to further the development of policy models for innovation, thanks to the existence of potential new sources of funding combined with the need to design policies to support competitive diversification. The use of revenues derived from exports of natural resources for the financing of innovation requires articulated governance models for allowing dialogue with the private sector and the regions where natural resources are found. At the same time, the increased availability of financial resources for innovation increases the pressure on "what to do" and "how to do it", requiring better and more transparent mechanisms for monitoring and evaluation.

Sustained and sustainable growth requires finding effective forms of interaction between the private and public sectors to support the introduction of new processes, new products, new business models and new ways of organising production. Innovation policies need to move towards models that support the generation of scientific and technological capabilities in frontier sectors; at the same time they need to promote the modernisation of production and the adoption of marginal innovations to improve the competitiveness of existing firms. These models require high institutional capacity at different levels of government for their implementation.

6.3.2. New governance models for strategy setting

There is high heterogeneity among countries in Latin America in regard to the institutional framework for innovation and its place in the government power structure. Only five countries have a Ministry of Innovation: Argentina, Brazil, Costa Rica, Cuba and the Bolivarian Republic of Venezuela. In other countries different models prevail: national innovation councils directly under the presidency, as in Chile and Nicaragua, for example; or national councils under different ministries (usually the ministry of industry or education), as in Mexico or Peru.

There are different institutional models, which vary in terms of level of complexity and frequency of contact among different actors. Brazil has the most complex institutional system. The Brazilian Ministry of Science and Technology has an influential and co-ordinating role in defining strategy and execution, together with the Ministry of Development, Industry and Foreign Trade and the Brazilian Development Bank (BNDES). In addition, various agencies are responsible for programme implementation and funding, such as the Brazilian Innovation Agency (FINEP), which offers funds for business innovation programmes, and the National Research Council (CNPq), which funds scientific R&D programmes. Brazil also has a well-articulated governance structure, albeit with significant differences across the country, in which across levels of government each State has its own foundation for R&D support. Other countries in the region have simpler models, some more decentralised (e.g. Mexico) than others (e.g. Chile).

Beyond country differences, a common element is that innovation is a priority of the development agendas of almost all of the countries in the region, although its importance is reflected in the debates that take place than in increased levels of budgetary allocation. The greatest challenge is to design and implement innovation policies that on the one hand support structural change, the diversification of production and the creation of new sectors, and on the other hand promote the modernisation and competitiveness of traditional sectors.

In addition, some structural weaknesses continue to hinder the formulation of innovation policies and to hamper the transition towards more pragmatic and effective policy models. For innovation policy to be effective it needs real financial support. For example, recent advances in Uruguay in terms of institutionalisation and promotion of innovation have taken place thanks to the Ministry of Economy and Finance's support to the country's national innovation strategy.

Weaknesses in the design of policy instruments include: *i)* poor planning capacity and a tendency to allocate resources based on short-term evaluations, *ii)* little capacity to monitor and evaluate implemented programmes, *iii)* insufficient feedback mechanisms between design and implementation; and *iv)* an excessive focus on "inputs" (more R&D, more qualified human resources, etc.) rather than on expected outputs (growing number of export firms, more and better jobs, introduction of new production processes and/or services, etc.).

There has also been little synchronisation between productive development and innovation policy, although this trend has been changing in recent years in some countries, in part thanks to the introduction of sectoral funds in support of innovation.

In recent years, countries in the region have prioritised a series of reforms in the governance and management of innovation policy in order to strengthen the state's capacity to support innovation in the new global economic situation. Most countries have established new institutions and/or new governance models for the formulation of innovation strategies. For example, in Argentina, the establishment of the Ministry of Science, Technology and Productive Innovation in 2008 responded to the desire to promote productive development and innovation and to increase the collaboration between science and business. In Chile, the creation of the National Innovation Council for Competitiveness has been a major advance in enabling institutions, through the Committee of Ministers for Innovation, to make innovation a key issue in the government agenda.

The growing demand for the formulation of innovation strategies has created a need for new spaces for vertical and horizontal co-ordination. In fact, innovation is increasingly a cross-cutting issue in the agendas of different sectoral ministries (such as health, energy, the environment and education), beyond its traditional role for development in agriculture and manufacturing.

There is an increasing need for more co-ordination between different sectoral agendas (of the various ministries) to increase the effectiveness of public action. This also augments the complexity of managing innovation policies, since various visions and conceptualisations of innovation clash, requiring different public-policy tools. Brazil has responded to these challenges by creating co-ordination mechanisms between innovation policy and productive development policy. In this regard, the partnership between the Ministry of Science and Technology, Ministry of Development, Industry and Foreign Trade and the Brazilian Development Bank (BNDES) is a clear advance in institutional design. At the same time, in line with the recent national strategy for growth with social inclusion, the Ministry of Science and Technology has supported the strengthening of institutions in Brazil's federal states in order to promote production structure diversification and to increase the country's scientific, technological and productive strength.

Box 6.1. New governance models for the formulation of strategies in the region: a brief review of the experiences of Argentina, Brazil, Chile and Mexico

Argentina stands out for its long history of public efforts supporting capacities in the field of scienceThese efforts go back to the early 1950s, when the country invested in the establishment of public research institutes, such as the National Commission for Atomic Energy (CNEA), the National Institute for Agricultural Technology (INTA), the National Institute for Industrial Technology (INTI), and the National Council for Scientific and Technological Research (CONICET). Recently, the country has invested in the creation of a new governance model for public policy. The measures taken to facilitate the articulation and vertical and horizontal co-ordination of policy include:

- The creation of the Ministry of Science, Technology and Productive Innovation (2008), which is responsible for formulating policies and programmes and for supervising the bodies responsible for the promotion, regulation and enforcement of policies (the National Agency for the Promotion of Science and Technology [ANPCyT] and CONICET).
- The creation of the Science and Technology Cabinet (GACTEC) and the Inter-Institutional Council for Science and Technology (CICyT) as policy–co-ordination bodies.
- The consolidation of the administration of scientific research grants (CONCYT) and business innovation (FONTAR) under a single agency.

In **Brazil** the National Science and Technology Council (CCT) is the body responsible for strategic formulation and co-ordination in the field of science, technology and innovation and reports directly to the President of the Republic. The CCT has the following tasks: proposing a science and technology policy for the country; developing plans, goals and priorities; conducting assessments; and issuing opinions on specific issues under their purview. The Council is composed of the government ministers responsible for this area, who represent the science and technology community (universities, institutes, regions) and business representatives. It is chaired by the President, and the Minister of Science and Technology is the Executive Secretary.

The Ministry of Science and Technology is in turn responsible for implementing the science and technology policy. The operating arms for the implementation of innovation policies are the National Council for Scientific and Technological Development (CNPq), aimed at developing scientific and technological research, especially through scholarships and grants, and the Financier of Studies and Projects (FINEP), which supports the science, technology and innovation actions of public and private institutions. Additional key players are: the Coordination for the Improvement of Higher-Level Personnel (CAPES), which supports post-graduate studies, and the Brazilian Development Bank (BNDES), linked to the Ministry of Development, Industry and Foreign Trade (MDIC), which provides long-term financing for projects that contribute to national development (including support for seed and venture capital initiatives and direct financing of innovation projects).

There are numerous state foundations and public technology institutes carrying out research and development activities and providing technology services, in addition to public enterprises carrying out research and development in frontier areas (Petrobras, Embrapa, etc.).

In **Chile**, the National Innovation Council for Competitiveness (CNIC), established in 2005, formulates medium-term strategy and counts on academic and business sectors in defining and accomplishing its mission.

Inter-sectoral co-ordination is ensured by the Committee of Ministers (CM), chaired by the Minister of Economy, and comprised of the ministers responsible for areas related to innovation, specialists and representatives of the private sector and academia. The CM administers the National Innovation Fund for Competitiveness (FIC), with royalties from copper mining, and contracts specialised agencies (CONICYT and CORFO, among others) for the implementation of priority programmes.

The system of policy governance that is evolving is based on two pillars: the Ministry of Economy (in charge of business innovation) and the Ministry of Education (in charge of higher education and basic research).

The creation of the CNIC and the CM has made it possible to move forward in the design of strategies and prioritisation mechanisms and create incentives for generating institutional capacities for analysis and evaluation of innovation policy. Progress has also been made in establishing, albeit tentatively, mechanisms for alignment between budget and expenditure on innovation, and in the design of instruments to support targeted rather than horizontal (clusters) innovation. The system still has a number of structural weaknesses that require institutional modernisation, including the CNIC's weak capacity to engage and generate commitments from the private sector and its poor alignment with the Ministry of Finance (Budget Office) in prioritising expenditures.

In **Mexico**, the National Council on Science and Technology (CONACYT) is an advisory body to the federal government specialising in the articulation of public policies by the federal government. It promotes research in science and technology, innovation and development, and the technological modernisation of the country.

CONACYT is the leading body for the strategic management of innovation policy. The Council has introduced sectoral funds to support innovation, highlighting its commitment to increase this support. The Council has a well-developed structure with offices in every state with experience in the mobilisation of local actors to promote business competitiveness. Its tasks include promoting basic and applied research, managing training programmes to develop qualified human resources and fostering productive innovation.

In Mexico, there are also state councils for science and technology, which work in collaboration with the federal level through the National Conference on Science and Technology. Mexico also has a group of research centres co-ordinated by CONACYT to add to the work conducted by public universities. This collaboration is further complemented by a group of providers of science and technology services, which also act as a link between companies and technology institutes (providing information, consulting and training), such as the Information and Documentation Fund for Industry (INFOTEC) and the National Processing Industry Chamber (Canacintra).

Source: OECD (2011).

6.3.3. Introducing new instruments for innovation financing and for technology transfer

A key element in the implementation of innovation and productive development policies is the design of funding mechanisms. This is especially the case in countries where the private sector is largely unfamiliar with the importance of science, technology and innovation for increasing productivity and competitiveness and with rent-seeking traditions linked to the exploitation of natural resources.

A public policy that attempts to boost investment in research, development and innovation (RDI) needs to consider how to involve the private sector in this process, taking into account the major bottlenecks such as high uncertainty associated with investments in R&D; high interest rates; high costs; poor access to credit markets (especially for smaller companies); limited possibilities to develop ties with other companies, universities or research centres; and difficulties in market access and export development, etc.

The incentives for business investment in RDI can be classified based on various criteria (see Diagram 6.1). There are direct incentives (tax credits, non-reimbursable subsidies, subsidised credit, etc.) or indirect incentives (for technical human resources training; investment in public goods; business centres, incubators and parks; technological service centres; etc.). These, in turn, can be horizontal or selective (based on their capacity to distinguish beneficiaries by sector, company size, etc.).

Diagram 6.1 Main features of innovation incentives for companies

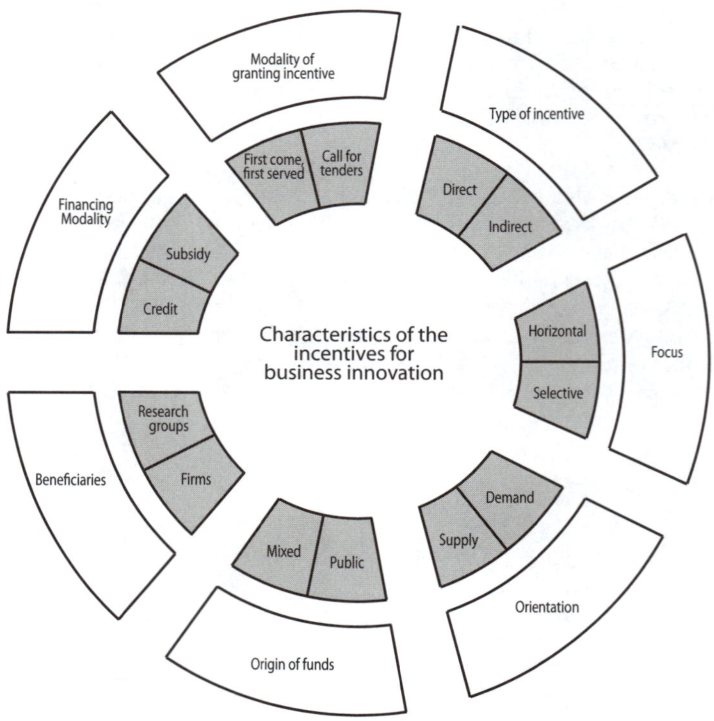

Source: Produced by authors
http://dx.doi.org/10.1787/888932523158

Incentives for innovation can be supply-side, in which case the public sector defines the stimuli designed to boost private-sector investment in research, development and innovation; or demand-side, which occurs when there is a public call for proposals, and the private sector proposes research and innovation projects.

The resources used to finance the innovation activities in firms can come from the public sector – whether through the reallocation of funds or multilateral loans – or from mixed funds generated through financing from the productive sector itself, as in the case of Chile's mining royalties or Brazil's sectoral funds. There are two main financing modalities: through loans or through grants and subsidies. There are many variants of both modalities. For example, loans can take the form of concessional or contingent loans, while grants or subsidies can come in the form of direct grants (such as non-repayable contributions, so-called "matching grants"), or indirect subsidies (such as funding for human resources training). As for how to provide and manage incentives, there are essentially two contrasting ways. One is through a first-come, first-served one-stop shop: if funds are limited, the first projects to be presented are more likely to be approved. The other is through public calls for tenders, in which there is a specific period of time to submit projects for evaluation and funding.

The experience of countries that have progressed in scientific and technological development shows that it is necessary to combine different financing instruments with different forms of credit, as well as with direct and indirect subsidies and tax incentives, to narrow the technology gap. An appropriate combination would provide support for the widespread modernisation of the productive sector and the inclusion of instruments to support firms that have greater financial limitations (such as SMEs), and promote the development of new priority sectors, which requires carrying out technology foresight activities.

There is no single optimal mix of incentives. The most appropriate mix of instruments will depend on the strategic and technological priorities of the country, the characteristics of its tax system,[12] the fiscal situation, its technical capacities, and whether there is an investment bank, among other factors. To increase the effectiveness of support for innovation activities and meet different needs, various instruments must be combined. One option is concessional loans, which finance projects with low technical risk, companies providing counterpart funds. Another option is direct subsidies (which may need to combine support from the state and the private sector), for financing projects for the development of new products and/or processes or the creation of R&D laboratories.[13] There are also fiscal incentives, such as the reduction of import tariffs and domestic taxes for the purchase of R&D laboratory equipment, delayed tax payment, and accelerated depreciation of R&D equipment to facilitate private investment in innovation. It is also important to support the further development of mechanisms for financing such as venture capital, which in general supports the creation of technology-based companies.

Rapid technological progress also involves designing and implementing innovative and flexible instruments to harness new opportunities, such as the BNDES Card introduced in 2003 in Brazil to facilitate investment in projects to improve competitiveness among micro and small enterprises (see Box 6.2).

Box 6.2. The BNDES card, expanding access to credit

The BNDES card (Cartão BNDES) is a product that was created in 2003 by the Brazilian Development Bank. It offers credit to micro, small and medium-sized enterprises with a gross turnover of up to 90 billion Brazilian reais (BRL) (approximately USD 45 million in 2009) and national capital control, and it consists of revolving pre-approved credit.

It is an instrument intended to facilitate access to credit for market sectors that generally face problems with financing and access to credit for the purchase of specific products and services. These products and services must be previously registered with the BNDES (to be registered, products must have a minimum nationalisation index of 60%). This instrument currently provides financing for more than 125 000 registered goods and services, which can be categorised as follows:

- Machinery and equipment
- Medical, dental and hospital equipment
- A range of vehicles
- Heavy transport and cargo equipment and similar equipment
- Vehicle spare parts and tyres
- Inputs for various industry segments (metallurgy, textiles, furniture, leather and footwear, bakery, plastics, etc.)
- Information and telecommunications equipment
- Automation Equipment
- Technology and innovation services
- Software
- Furniture and accessories

The items that are financed include many goods and services to support technological modernisation and facilitate innovation and technical change. Purchase of these good and services also supports and strengthens the sectors producing them and strengthens ties between Brazilian companies.

The interest rate applied is more advantageous than market rates, whether for working capital or for the acquisition of goods. Besides the preferential interest rate, having an approved credit line (so that firms do not need to undergo credit analysis for each operation) reduces the transaction costs of financial transactions for both customers holding the card and financial institutions themselves.

For all the above reasons, the increase in the number and value of operations carried out using the BNDES Card has been significant. The success of the BNDES Card is reflected in the more than 63 000 operations carried out in 2008, an amount equivalent to BRL 934 million (approximately USD 467 million in 2008), representing an 60% increase compared to 2007. The card was thus responsible for the largest number of BNDES operations with micro, small and medium-sized enterprises.

Source: based on information from BNDES.

The return of sectoral innovation agendas has led to the creation of new funding mechanisms for innovation which allocate funds for innovation to specific productive sectors; this is the case of the sectoral funds in Brazil (see Box 6.3), Argentina and Mexico. This requires new institutional capacities for managing the complexity of collaboration between the private sector and public sector and the sectoral selectivity of policies. This also requires increased resources and stable sources of medium- and long-term funding.

Box 6.3. Sectoral funds in Brazil: ten years implementing a new model of financing and governance

The goverance structure and the articulation between different institutions are essential to determine the success of a policy. This is reflected in the scheme of the sectoral funds in Brazil, which focus on innovation and co-operation, with a steering committee formed by members from the Ministry of Science and Technology, sectoral ministries, regulatory agencies, the scientific community and the business sector. Through discussion and negotiation among steering committee members, key decisions regarding the allocation of resources are made. The public are aware of the success of sectoral funds, which support different sectors defined as strategic for the country. This system is considered among the main reasons for Brazil's recent rapid growth in science, technology and innovation (reaching levels of investment in R&D of around 1.2% of GDP in 2009).

The sectoral funds supporting science, technology and innovation activities in Brazil, are built on co-ordination between stakeholders and use sectoral revenue as a source of funding. They guarantee significant returns and promote co-participation among all stakeholders (companies, universities, governments and research institutions) in project planning and the administration of funds.

However, they also have intrinsic weaknesses, which may explain why there is still a low level of disbursement of allocated funds. One particular area of weakness is management and administration, due to the high level of complexity and the number of actors involved in steering committees, as well as the potential overlap of interests that may cause problems in co-ordination.

Figure 6.5. Sectoral funds in Brazil, budget and execution, 1999-2010

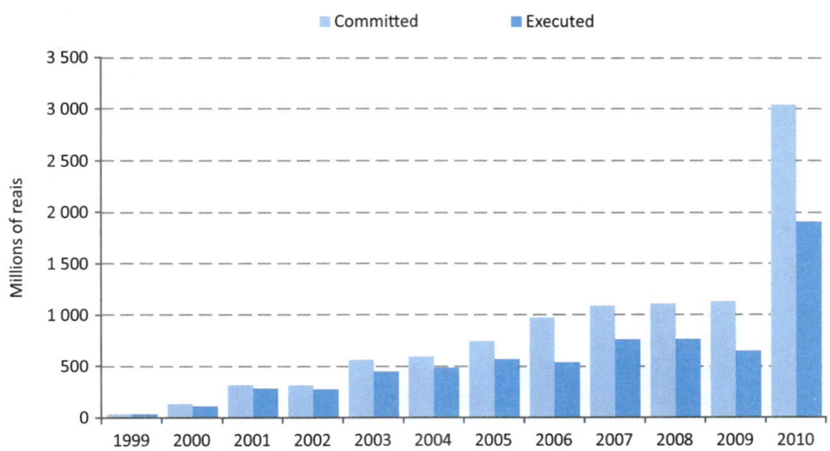

Source: ECLAC/SEGIB (2010), based on information of the Brazilian Ministry of Science, Technology and Innovation (http://www.mct.gov.br).

http://dx.doi.org/10.1787/888932523139

Since 2003, Latin America has been on a path of sustained economic growth with more dynamic trade, primarily due to the rising prices of raw materials (at least in South America). This has resulted in the generation of a surplus. Under the right schemes of governance and with a strong political commitment, this could become a source of substantial funding for policies to promote diversification and innovation. However, this requires a high level of governmental co-ordination to build consensus. The case of Chile's mining royalties is an interesting example of the process of designing an instrument to increase revenue to boost scientific and technological development and of reaching consensus in the area (Figure 6.4).

Box 6.4. Chile's mining royalties: financing innovation through income from natural resources

The law regulating mining royalties was introduced in Chile in 2005 (Law 20 026). This legislation established a specific tax on mining, which was implemented based on the idea that Chile's regions needed extra funds to finance innovation projects to help diversify and boost their economies and to reduce the country's vulnerability to external shocks from rising and falling international copper prices.

The tax is on mining companies with annual sales exceeding 12 000 tonnes of fine copper and is paid in instalments and based on a mine's operating taxable income. For annual sales exceeding the value of 50 000 tonnes of fine copper, a single tax rate of 5% is applied. For annual sales between 12 000 and 50 000 tonnes, a tiered rate is applied, which can range from 0.5% to 4.5%, based on tonnage categories. Mine operators whose sales are 12 000 tonnes or below are exempt from paying the tax.

In parallel with the introduction of the mining royalty, the National Innovation Council for Competitiveness (CNIC) was established. This public-private body acts as a permanent advisor to the President of the Republic on public innovation and competitiveness policies, including scientific and technological development, training of human resources and innovative entrepreneurship. It also acts as a catalyst for important initiatives in these areas. In addition, it defines the country's innovation strategy, identifying the main lines of action to be financed with the funds from mining royalties.

The primary recipient of the royalty funds is the National Innovation Fund for Competitiveness (FIC), whose aim is to finance the promotion of science and technology, human capital formation and innovation in business, culture, institutional structures, infrastructure and regions. The FIC is the financing instrument of the executive branch with budgetary support for the implementation of national and regional innovation policies. These policies aim to strengthen the innovation system at the national and regional levels and provide transparency, flexibility and competitive and strategic direction to state action.

The creation of the FIC has led to a significant increase in the budget for innovation in Chile.[a] However, as is often the case in the early stages of new funds, budget execution has been low. The fact that the legislative process regarding the fund is itself ongoing makes it difficult to turn this resource into a permanent source of funding for innovation. The difficulties of managing these resources include the need to generate a consensus among regional governments, as royalties from the production of natural resources traditionally go to the community where mining takes place as compensation. The generation of adequate mechanisms for dialogue between government levels is critical to advance in the use of these resources as an additional source of funding for competitiveness.

Source: Based on information from the National Innovation Council for Competitiveness in Chile.

a OECD (2010b).

Given the complexity of innovation and technical change, it is not enough to design financial support mechanisms; it is also necessary to foment investment in collaboration and facilitate the flow and application of knowledge in productive systems.

The dynamics of innovation depends not only on the efforts of individual firms, research centres and universities, but also on the interaction among them and on the systemic capacity to create the conditions and incentives for innovation. In this context, public policies play a decisive role in supporting scientific and technological development and innovation, especially when productive specialisation is oriented towards natural resources or labour-intensive sectors with low technology content.[14]

Mechanisms to support technology transfer are essential, making it possible to identify not only the importance of the links among different institutions, but also the channels for the technology transfer and the types of instruments that facilitate the different types of relations among institutions. The forms, intensity and channels of interaction among universities and firms are diverse, and depend largely on the institutional structure of each country. In particular, the use of different channels for knowledge transfer depend on multiple factors, such as: *i)* the specificity of each industrial sector, *ii)* regional location, *iii)* the trajectories of the disciplines involved, *iv)* the duration of contracts, and *v)* the organisational flexibility of the university (i.e. faculty, research group or technology transfer offices) to reach agreements, consider the incentives and channel results towards alternative sources for research. The nature of the collaboration can facilitate the creation of social capital for the different disciplines and organisations, based on trust, interaction and learning for innovation.

Table 6.2 describes interaction channels between universities and firms. Beyond supporting the design of new and better policy instruments it is important to increase the institutional capacity to evaluate incentives and development programmes. Some elements to consider are: low administrative costs; flexibility (the ability to react to changing environmental conditions); impact (incentives should generate externalities, such as associative modes of action to support innovation); transparency (through public tenders, assistance in the formulation of projects, etc.); and additionality (incentives must expand private investment, not replace what companies could finance on their own). At the same time, it is important to take into account the existence of incentives to facilitate collaboration among different agencies and institutions involved in the design, management and administration of funds and incentives. This often determines success or failure in implementing a particular policy instrument.

Table 6.2. Technology transfer: channels, types of relationships and experiences in the region

Type of inter-relationship	Channels for the transfer of knowledge	Policy instruments	Experiences in the region
Human-resource flows	Internships, student training, hiring of graduates	Human resources training Access of firms to skilled human resources who enable them to generate competitive advantages	• Intel and Costa Rican universities (Costa Rica) • Scientific and Technological Development Fund (FONDEF) (Chile) • Funding for Innovation, Science and Technology (FINCyT) (Peru)
Informal contacts among professionals	Professional networks, exchange of information	Technical and professional training Innovation fairs and prizes	• Eaton Trucks Corporation and Unicamp (Brazil) • Innovation fairs (in Brazilian states, Peru, etc.) • Design fairs (São Paulo, Buenos Aires)
Activities for the communication and dissemination of knowledge	Events, seminars, conferences, publications and co-publications	Funding for the spread of scientific-technical knowledge	• Science and Business Meeting on biotechnology with the participation of various institutions (Mexico)
Services	Consultancy services, technical assistance, use of teams	Diversification of sources of university financing Develop and update capacities of researchers and firms in applied science and technology (use of equipment) Solution of firms' specific problems	• Provision of technical services of the University of the Republic (UDELAR) and the Technical Laboratory of Uruguay (LATU) • National Institute of Industrial Technology (INTI) (Argentina) • National Industrial Learning Service (SENAI), Brazilian Support Service for Entrepreneurs' and Small Businesses (SEBRAE) (Brazil)
Joint projects	Co-operation in R&D, research contracts, exchange of researchers, formal work networks, science and technology parks	Financing of innovation consortiums Venture capital Support for research networks	• National Laboratory of Materials and Structural Models of the University of Costa Rica and the Ministry of Public Works and Transport (Costa Rica) • IT district, Buenos Aires (Argentina) • Caren Science and Technology Park of the University of Chile (Chile) • Technology Park Foundation Paraíba (PaqTcPB) (Brasil)
Licensing	Technology transfer offices (TTOs)	Support for licensing and dissemination of technology Business coaching services to update capacities in applied science and technology (use of equipment) of researchers Platforms to co-ordinate specialised demands from firms and university training	• Inova Agency for Innovation of the University of Campinas (Brazil) • Monterrey Technology Institute (Mexico)
Technology-based firms	Transfer of knowledge through the generation of firms from basic or applied research	Spin-offs, incubators, "hybrid" company-university actors	• Ami-tec and the University of Medellín (spin-off in Colombia) • Bio Sidus (Argentina)

Source: Primi and Rovira (2011b).

6.3.4. Strengthening innovation policy management capacities

Latin American countries are making progress in learning how to design and implement innovation policies. One of their main challenges is to strengthen capacities so that the policies work. Experience shows that not only is good policy design necessary, but it is also necessary to invest in building the capacity to manage and implement programmes at all levels of government, especially when introducing new public policy measures.

The challenges faced by Latin American countries include: correcting failures in co-ordination, reducing overlap in policies, strengthening consistency over time and developing a sound decision-making structure for productive development and innovation policies, and strengthening the management and evaluation capabilities of policies. All of this requires highly skilled and experienced policy makers.

In this respect, there are three areas in which the countries of the region have made progress.

1) First of all, the region is investing in new and better management capacities for programme implementation and management of policy instruments.

Building and strengthening institutions and the domestic capabilities needed to design, implement and evaluate policies for productive development and innovation is a process of trial and error, requiring time, resources and a long-term perspective. In particular, the success or failure of policies and instruments implemented to achieve a more productive and innovative system is strongly conditioned by the abilities of those responsible for the design and management of the policies themselves.

Efforts have been made in the region to promote the training and specialisation of technical specialists experienced in developing and implementing science, technology and innovation who can design new instruments and to design new instruments and monitor the implementation of existing ones. One interesting capacity-building experience at the sub-national level is RENAPI (National Network for Industrial Policy Agents), which promotes training in regional industrial policy in Brazil. RENAPI is an initiative of the Brazilian Agency for Industrial Development (ABDI) and consists of a network of experts and officials in charge of industrial policy. Its aim is to promote the regionalisation of productive development policy. The network helps create a common language among participants by supporting the training of officials from around the country who are responsible for industrial policy and R&D.

Another example is the School for Policy Makers in Science, Technology and Innovation inaugurated in 2008 by ECLAC, with support from the German Co-operation Agency and various ministries and agencies responsible for science, technology and innovation in the region. Its main objective is the training of professionals involved in the development, monitoring, evaluation and implementation of science, technology and innovation policies. In this way it will contribute to strengthening the capacities of countries in the region in this field, the transfer of knowledge and experiences and the strengthening of their relations, as well as the identification of joint activities.[15]

2) Countries in the region are advancing in the creation of a regional space for policy discussion to address common challenges and advance in policy learning.

The consolidation of a regional mechanism for policy dialogue responds to the need to advance policy learning and to improve the position of the region in the global economy. It is also a response to the increasing pressure on policy makers to demonstrate the validity and effectiveness of policy measures proposed in a context of major budget constraints and greater transparency in public decision-making. In fact, the exchange and regular evaluation of practices and incentives among peers favours greater accountability in policy-making.

In Latin America there are several experiences in regional scientific collaboration. However, it is necessary to create permanent institutional mechanisms that support co-operation on policy and dialogue and make it viable. The diversity and complementarity among the capabilities and characteristics of the countries in the region represent an advantage for the creation of joint research and training programmes. In addition, the desire to create effective mechanisms for scientific collaboration results from the desire to increase synergies and overcome national boundaries, given the limits of human and financial resources available for scientific research.

A large number of collaborative initiatives and policy dialogues on innovation have taken place in the region, but they lack co-ordination and would benefit synergies were created among them. The panorama of collaborative activities on science, technology and innovation in Latin America is varied. We can identify at least three complementary levels for policy dialogue:

— The ministerial level (or the highest authorities), which defines strategic lines for international collaboration;

— The technical advisory level, which involves meetings with senior advisers of the highest authorities and generally focuses on dialogues related to policy "tactics", such as the design of mechanisms and incentives for science, technology and innovation.

— The policy implementation level, which refers to the dialogue among managers of programmes and policy instruments, aimed at exchanging practices and experiences in the policy implementation phase.

3) Thirdly, the region has advanced in measuring innovation and on strengthening strategic intelligence capacities for policy analysis and monitoring.

There are three major areas in which the countries of the region are advancing and modernising their institutions for decision-making in innovation policy:

— The generation of systems of indicators for decision-making: several countries have invested in establishing units engaged in the collection and dissemination of innovation indicators within national ministries or national secretaries for innovation. This advance is also supported by a vast modernisation of the information systems of ministries and higher bodies in science and technology, which has increased transparency and accessibility to data. This development has taken place in large countries like Argentina and Brazil, as well as in smaller countries such as Costa Rica and Panama.

— Innovation surveys: Latin America is consolidating its experience in the development of innovation surveys.[16] Like in OECD economies, innovation surveys are useful tools to deepen the understanding of innovative behaviour in firms, to assess obstacles to investment in innovation, and to determine the impact of public policies. However, unlike in OECD economies, the comparability of innovation surveys in the region must be improved. This process requires time and investment in institution building and dialogue among policy makers, experts and statistics institutes. Comparability between surveys is not simple and requires serious efforts at harmonisation.[17]

In Latin America, this is even more complex because the surveys follow different models (in Brazil, Chile and Mexico they are based on the Oslo Manual, while in Argentina, Colombia and Uruguay they follow the Bogota Manual). Being a recent phenomenon in the region, only a few countries regularly conduct these surveys and use them for feedback on policies.[18] Comparability between them is still low. Specifically, only Argentina, Brazil, Chile, Colombia and Uruguay carry out surveys regularly, while Mexico does so sporadically, and Costa Rica, Panama, Peru and the Bolivarian Republic of Venezuela are just joining the effort.

— Creating and/or strengthening institutions for data analysis and decision-making: Investing in building data analysis capabilities to aid decision-making is important. It is also necessary to create incentives for the use of data analysis in evaluating and redesigning public policy. Unlike in OECD economies, Latin American countries are still at an early stage in the creation of institutions for policy analysis. The country that has made the most progress in this area is Brazil, where the Institute of Applied Economic Research (IPEA), affiliated to the Strategic Affairs Secretariat of the Presidency of the Republic, and the Centre for Management and Strategic Studies (CGEE), affiliated to the Ministry of Science and Technology, provide analysis and feedback on the implementation and impact of public policy.

6.4. Better governance for better policy

In summary, in the past decade the agenda for productive development and innovation has been given new impetus in the countries of Latin America. Today innovation plays a central role in the development agenda in almost all of the countries in the region, although its importance is more often reflected in debates and speeches rather than in increased levels of budgetary allocation.

The current global and regional economic trends are creating growing expectations regarding the need for medium-term impact of innovation policies on growth and competitiveness in global markets and on the capacity to strengthen domestic markets by generating more and better jobs.

Renewed interest in innovation places new pressure on governments to develop and implement more effective innovation strategies that can mobilise the business sector, especially in a context of high uncertainty regarding the dynamics of global markets. In addition, more effective and transparent management of the public system to support innovation is required for countries facing tight budgetary restrictions, as well as for those currently enjoying a period of high growth based on increasing exports of natural resources at high prices.

Diagnosis of productive development and innovation in Latin America makes it clear that the region needs to move forward in four areas:

1) Invest to close the productivity gap.

2) Raise investment in science and technology and R&D activities.

3) Increase the private sector's commitment to innovation and productive development.

4) Reduce the mismatch between supply and demand of skilled human resources.

This requires new models for public-policy governance capable of articulating actions and fostering agreements for investment in innovation. Institutions need to be stronger and public policy models more sophisticated; they must be capable of mobilising the different stakeholders in national innovation systems and all levels of government. This is particularly true in the Latin American context, with productive specialisation in low-knowledge-intensive sectors, high uncertainty and barriers to access to credit. Public policies therefore play a decisive role in generating incentives for investment in science and technology activities and for competitiveness based on added value and innovation.

In recent years, the countries of Latin America have made great strides in policy learning and have introduced significant reforms in innovation policies. Although there is still great heterogeneity in institutions and in governance models in the region, we can identify some common trends.

Among the advances are: strengthening the institutional framework for innovation (Argentina, Chile, Uruguay); creating and consolidating new funding models for innovation (Brazil, Chile, Colombia, Mexico); greater synchronisation between supporting innovation and developing strategic productive sectors (Argentina, Brazil, Chile, Mexico, Panama, Uruguay); growing attention to the territorial impact of innovation strategies, especially in relatively larger countries (Argentina, Brazil, Colombia) and improved institutional capacity to measure and assess the dynamics of innovation and the impact of public policies (Argentina, Brazil).

To overcome its structural weaknesses in innovation and in its capacity to support the development of production and technology, governments need to develop better governance models, which should be able to align actions and create synergies between different programmes and levels of government. To do this, the region must:

- Consolidate the synchronisation between innovation strategies and productive development by increasing the capacity to articulate programmes for sectoral and value-chain development. This requires governance mechanisms that promote dialogue among the ministries of economy and finance, trade and industry and innovation. It also requires financing mechanisms with a sectoral approach and the participation of all the stakeholders in the national innovation system (universities, businesses and civil society) in defining priorities. Innovation policy must also be synchronised with policies to support productive development to ensure more effective action and greater impact.
- Strengthen the capacity to develop innovation strategies. States must improve vertical co-ordination (between different levels of government) and horizontal co-ordination (between the different ministries responsible for different areas of innovation such as industry, agriculture, health, education, infrastructure, etc.) for defining priorities. There must also be greater private-sector participation in innovation.
- Increase resource-allocation capacity through multi-year plans to facilitate investment in medium- and long-term projects, and in parallel, increase the financial and business sectors' commitment to innovation. This requires investing in strategic intelligence in public administration and creating spaces for dialogue to establish trust mechanisms while increasing the state's regulatory capacity in the area.
- Evolve towards outcome-oriented policy models, designing policies that target outputs (more and better jobs and greater competitiveness) and consider inputs (such as R&D spending and human resources training) to be the means to achieving the strategic objectives.
- Strengthen the capacity to measure innovation. Investment is needed to create institutional spaces and feedback mechanisms between policy design and implementation in order to improve the capacity of policy makers to define and implement new, more sophisticated instruments. It is important to invest in the generation of innovation indicators and to create incentives for the use of information in policy assessment.
- Invest in the training of human resources responsible for managing policy on innovation and productive development and promote regional dialogue to exchange experiences and develop greater knowledge on innovation policy design and implementation. The innovation challenge for Latin America needs each country to have its own development agenda based on its specific production, historical and cultural characteristics. But it also requires a regional agenda in order to achieve the critical mass required in certain areas of knowledge and production for its successful integration into an increasingly competitive and dynamic global economy.

Notes

1. OECD (1997); ECLAC (2004).
2. ECLAC (2010a).
3. ECLAC (2010a).
4. ECLAC (2008).
5. ECLAC (2010a).
6. The figures refer to 2008, the last year for which data is available from the source used, the United Nations Commodity Trade Statistics Database (COMTRADE) [http://comtrade.un.org].
7. Primi and Rovira (2011a).
8. López and Orliki (2006).
9. According to data from the national patent offices, in the countries of Latin America and the Caribbean approximately 90% of patent applications are filed by foreigners, while in more developed countries, it is national actors who are most active in terms of patenting (ECLAC, 2010b).
10. ECLAC (2004).
11. The case of Brazil and the impact of the closure of agricultural extension centres on the performance of Embrapa illustrates the adverse affects of some rationalisation measures.
12. For example, direct subsidies can be an option in a context where fiscal pressure is low and tax breaks are not foreseen for R&D activities.
13. Another distinctive characteristic of this type of incentive is that it can be used for horizontal as well as targeted policies, and it encourages collaboration between firms and public R&D organisations.
14. ECLAC (2004); Cimoli, Ferraz and Primi (2005).
15. In particular, the atmosphere of exchange in the School has fostered the development of proposals and projects for bilateral or multilateral technical co-operation, which have involved various institutions.
16. Cimoli, Primi and Rovira (2011).
17. OECD (2009b).
18. Primi and Rovira (2011a).

References

CIMOLI, M., J.C. FERRAZ AND A. PRIMI (2005), *Science and Technology Policy in Open Economies: The Case of Latin America and the Caribbean*, Production Development, No. 165 (LC/L.2404), ECLAC (CEPAL), Santiago, Chile.

CIMOLI, M., A. PRIMI AND S. ROVIRA (FORTHCOMING), "National Innovation Surveys in Latin America: Empirical Evidence and Policy Implications on Cooperation and Innovation", in *R&D Cooperation in Latin American Innovation Strategies: Empirical Evidence and Policy Implications from National Innovation Surveys*, ECLAC (CEPAL)-IDRC.

ECLAC (ECONOMIC COMMISSION FOR LATIN AMERICA AND THE CARIBBEAN) (ECLAC) (CEPAL) (2004), *Production Development in Open Economies*, ECLAC, Santiago, Chile.

ECLAC (CEPAL) (2008), *Productive Transformation 20 Years after*, ECLAC, Santiago, Chile.

ECLAC (CEPAL) (2010a), *Time for Equality: Closing Gaps, Opening Trails*, ECLAC, Santiago, Chile.

ECLAC (CEPAL) (2010b), Science and Technology in the Latin American Pacific Basin: *Opportunity for Innovation and Competition*, ECLAC, Santiago, Chile.

ECLAC (CEPAL)/SEGIB (SECRETARÍA GENERAL IBEROAMERICANA) (2010), *Espacios iberoamericanos. Universidad y empresa: vínculos entre universidad y empresas para el desarrollo tecnológico*, ECLAC, Santiago, Chile.

LÓPEZ, A. AND E. ORLIKI (2006), *Innovación y mecanismos de apropiabilidad en el sector privado en América Latina*, ECLAC (CEPAL)-WIPO.

OECD (ORGANISATION FOR ECONOMIC CO-OPERATION AND DEVELOPMENT) (1997), *National Innovation Systems*, OECD, Paris.

OECD (2007), *OECD Reviews of Innovation Policy: Chile*, OECD, Paris.

OECD (2009a), *OECD Reviews of Innovation Policy: Mexico*, OECD, Paris.

OECD (2009b), *Innovation in Firms: A Microeconomic Perspective*, OECD, Paris.

OECD (2010a), *The OECD Innovation Strategy: Getting a Head Start on Tomorrow*, OECD, Paris.

OECD (2010b), *Measuring Innovation: A New Perspective*, OECD, Paris.

OECD (2011), *Hacia un mecanismo para el diálogo de políticas de innovación: oportunidades y desafíos para América Latina y el Caribe*, OECD Development Centre, Paris.

PRIMI, A. AND S. ROVIRA (FORTHCOMING, a), "Innovation and Cooperation in Latin America: Evidence from National Innovation Surveys in a Comparative Perspective", in id. *R&D Cooperation in Latin American Innovation Strategies: Empirical Evidence and Policy Implications from National Innovation Surveys*.

PRIMI, A. AND S. ROVIRA, (FORTHCOMING, b), *Nuevos mecanismos de financiamiento y de apoyo a la transferencia tecnológica en América Latina: una revisión crítica*.

PRIMI, A. (FORTHCOMING), *Science, Technology and Innovation Policies and Development: The Case of Latin America*, UNU-Merit

ORGANISATION FOR ECONOMIC CO-OPERATION AND DEVELOPMENT (OECD)

The OECD is a unique forum where governments work together to address the economic, social and environmental challenges of globalisation. The OECD is also at the forefront of efforts to understand and to help governments respond to new developments and concerns, such as corporate governance, the information economy and the challenges of an ageing population. The Organisation provides a setting where governments can compare policy experiences, seek answers to common problems, identify good practice and work to co-ordinate domestic and international policies.

The OECD member countries are: Australia, Austria, Belgium, Canada, Chile, the Czech Republic, Denmark, Estonia, Finland, France, Germany, Greece, Hungary, Iceland, Ireland, Israel, Italy, Japan, Korea, Luxembourg, Mexico, the Netherlands, New Zealand, Norway, Poland, Portugal, the Slovak Republic, Slovenia, Spain, Sweden, Switzerland, Turkey, the United Kingdom and the United States. The European Union takes part in the work of the OECD.

OECD Publishing disseminates widely the results of the Organisation's statistics gathering and research on economic, social and environmental issues, as well as the conventions, guidelines and standards agreed by its members.

OECD DEVELOPMENT CENTRE

The OECD Development Centre was established in 1962 as an independent platform for knowledge sharing and policy dialogue between OECD member countries and developing economies, allowing these countries to interact on an equal footing. As of March 2011, 17 non-OECD countries are full members of the Centre's Governing Board. The Centre draws attention to emerging systemic issues likely to have an impact on global development and more specific development challenges faced by today's emerging and developing countries. It uses evidence-based analysis and strategic partnerships to help countries formulate innovative policy solutions to the global challenges of development.

For more information on the Centre and its members, please see www.oecd.org/dev

ECONOMIC COMMISSION FOR LATIN AMERICA AND THE CARIBBEAN (ECLAC)

ECLAC is one of the five regional commissions of the United Nations. ECLAC was founded in 1948 for the purpose of contributing to the economic development of Latin America and the Caribbean, co-ordinating actions to promote that development and reinforcing economic ties among the region's countries and with other nations of the world.

Over the years, the institution's in-depth analysis of the region has taken the form of two main lines of action: economic and social research and the provision of technical co-operation to governments. The Commission's ongoing concern for growth, technical progress, social justice and democracy has characterised the integral approach towards development that now forms part of the legacy of its rich intellectual tradition.

The 33 countries of Latin America and the Caribbean are member States of ECLAC, together with the United States, Canada, and several European and Asian countries that have historical, economic or cultural ties with the region. The Commission thus has a total of 44 member States. In addition, nine non-independent Caribbean territories hold the status of associate members.

OECD PUBLISHING, 2, rue André-Pascal, 75775 PARIS CEDEX 16
(41 2011 05 1 P) ISBN 978-92-64-12170-6 – No. 59683 2011